THE POEMS OF
ROBERT SOUTHWELL, S.J.

'Peeter Playnt' in Southwell's hand
(Stonyhurst College MS. A. v. 4, fol. 50)
See Appendix I

THE POEMS OF
ROBERT SOUTHWELL, S.J.

EDITED BY

JAMES H. McDONALD
Priest of the Congregation of Holy Cross

AND

NANCY POLLARD BROWN

OXFORD
AT THE CLARENDON PRESS
1967

Oxford University Press, Ely House, London W. 1

GLASGOW NEW YORK TORONTO MELBOURNE WELLINGTON
CAPE TOWN SALISBURY IBADAN NAIROBI LUSAKA ADDIS ABABA
BOMBAY CALCUTTA MADRAS KARACHI LAHORE DACCA
KUALA LUMPUR HONG KONG TOKYO

© *Oxford University Press 1967*

PREFACE

THE task of recovering the text of the poems of Robert Southwell, S.J., has been greatly helped by the labours of the late Revd. James H. McDonald, C.S.C. His diligent survey of manuscripts and early printed editions of Southwell's work was issued for presentation to members of the Roxburghe Club in 1937 as *The Poems and Prose Writings of Robert Southwell, S.J.: A Bibliographical Study.* In the preparation of this work, and in its subsequent printing by the Oxford University Press, Father McDonald expressed his indebtedness to Sir Leicester Harmsworth, who permitted him to examine and record his collection of early editions, together with a manuscript previously unknown, now at the Folger Shakespeare Library, Washington, D.C. In the course of his work on the *Bibliographical Study*, and in the years following, Father McDonald made considerable progress towards a new edition of the poems. In due time he prepared a draft typescript. Unfortunately, plans for a revision of the typescript and the publication of the poems had to be postponed on account of his increasing ill health, which in 1954 forced his retirement from his teaching duties at the University of Notre Dame, and he sought better health in the kinder climate of Los Angeles. In the following year, when it was clear that he would never again have the strength to undertake sustained editorial work, he asked me to carry out the revision of his typescript and to see the work through the press.

My own studies in the work of Robert Southwell previously had been limited to various critical problems; like all those who have entered this tortuous way I was extremely handicapped by the condition of the printed texts, and by the lack of any modern edition, and I was most eager that a reliable text should be made available. But when I undertook the work of the revision of Father McDonald's manuscript, it was immediately apparent that very substantial changes had to be made. In the light of more recent bibliographical studies many of the decisions made by Father McDonald were no longer defensible. Collation of the texts according to modern standards revealed many significant variants previously unrecorded, and further investigation of the conditions controlling the publication of the earliest printed editions indicated relationships between printed text and surviving manuscripts which had not been interpreted. In my gradual exploration of these editorial problems I continually referred to Father McDonald's work. In the copy of his typescript which he made available to me I recorded the mass of collation variants on which my evaluation of the manuscripts and of the numerous editions was finally based; on the foundation of his initial attempt I learned to erect the fabric of the text. Although in his failing health he was no longer able to take any part in the editorial work, the course of the preparation of the text was one of his chief interests until his death in 1959. My debt to his work can never be sufficiently expressed.

I am alone responsible, however, for the decisions represented in the text, including those which have determined order and copy-texts. The grouping of the poems in the earliest printed volumes now appears to me to distort Southwell's intentions for his poetry, and I have therefore adopted the order in the manuscript collections, which, although almost certainly unauthoritative in its entirety, may well incorporate groups of lyrics arranged as Southwell wished them to be presented to his readers. The textual authority of the printed texts, on the other hand, is not to be set aside for that of manuscript copies of uncertain date whose spelling and accidentals represent the personal habits of successive copyists. After full collation the following copy-texts were selected: the first edition of *Saint Peters Complaint, With other Poemes*, printed by John Windet for John Wolfe in 1595, from the copy at the Henry E. Huntington Library, for the poem 'Saint Peters Complaint' and the group of twelve lyrics with which it was first printed; Wolfe's second edition, from the copy in Trinity College, Cambridge, for the eight lyrics added to the earlier group; Gabriel Cawood's edition of 1602, from the copy in the British Museum (as selected originally by Father McDonald), for the group of seven additional lyrics it contains; and the first edition of *Mœoniœ*, from the copy in Trinity College, Cambridge, which on examination I was able to identify as an edition earlier than those known to Father McDonald. For the poems not printed in these earliest printed volumes I accepted the text of the manuscript at Stonyhurst College, A. v. 27, as most reliable, and probably earliest of those surviving. Poems in the Harmsworth manuscript, now at the Folger Shakespeare Library, which I consider of doubtful authenticity, although they were

accepted as Southwell's by Father McDonald, have been relegated
to an appendix.

The greatest difficulty in preparing a new text of the poems lies
in the absence of any clear authority. All relevant evidence support-
ing textual decisions has been presented in the Textual Introduction, in the critical apparatus, and in the Commentary. It is hoped
that the lyrics are not overweighted by this editorial accumulation,
but without this information the text would be considerably less
useful. Those who are concerned with textual problems may share
the burden of weighing evidence in the work of retrieving what
Southwell wrote at all those points where the process of transmission has introduced variant readings and verbal corruptions.
Those who are interested in critical evaluation may estimate the
achievement of the poet on the basis of the whole body of English
poems set out in an order in which they have never before been
presented in print.

Throughout all my work I have attempted to follow Father
McDonald's intention: to make Southwell's poetry available to
students in a text based on a study of all known manuscript and
printed materials. I am deeply grateful to all those scholars who
have helped me with their counsel and encouragement. Professor
Louis L. Martz, of Yale University, first suggested that I should
make a study of Southwell's poetry when I arrived in the United
States as a Commonwealth Fund Fellow in 1950. Since that
time I have benefited many times from his scholarly wisdom. The
Revd. Philip S. Moore, C.S.C., has continued to give me his support
during the long years in which I have attempted to carry out the
wishes of his friend. My textual studies could not have been completed without the co-operation of those who have the manuscripts
and early editions in their care. I gratefully acknowledge the assistance given by the late Most Revd. J. H. King, Archbishop-Bishop
of Portsmouth (R.C.), who allowed me to examine in his house
in Winchester the manuscript and early editions in the Virtue and
Cahill Library; the Rector of Stonyhurst College, who gave me
permission to use the manuscripts at Stonyhurst; the Rector of
Oscott College, who allowed me to examine the Peter Mowle
Commonplace Book when it was deposited at the Bodleian Library;
Professor Ralph M. Sargent, for permission to reproduce two poems
of Sir Edward Dyer from his edition; and the Trustees of the British
Museum, for permission to use the two manuscripts there. I am

also most grateful for the help I have received from the librarians of Trinity College, Cambridge; of the University Library, Cambridge; of the British Museum; of the Bodleian Library; of the Henry E. Huntington Library, San Marino, California; of the University of Notre Dame, Indiana; and of Wellesley College, Wellesley, Massachusetts. I remember especially the personal interest shown by Mr. H. M. Adams, of Trinity College, Cambridge; the Revd. H. Chadwick, S.J., of Stonyhurst College; Mr. David Rogers, of the Bodleian Library; and the late Revd. Christopher Devlin, S.J. Most of all, I am indebted to Dr. Louis B. Wright, director of the Folger Shakespeare Library, Washington, D.C. Dr. Wright assisted me with fellowships in 1954 and 1955, and since my return to the United States in 1957 to live in Washington he has offered me every facility for work in the Library. Members of his staff have been unfailing in their help. On many occasions I have called upon the invaluable bibliographical knowledge of Dr. James G. McManaway and Dr. Giles E. Dawson. Miss Dorothy E. Mason, reference librarian, has been a dear friend through troubles and adversities. In the later stages of my work, as in the first, I have been most fortunate in obtaining helpful critical comment, not least from the adviser to the Clarendon Press, who has given me much guidance in preparing the manuscript for publication. I would also like to record my debt to Sister Margaret, S.N.D., President of Trinity College, Washington, D.C., and to my colleagues there. To all these, and many more whose kindness gave me the incentive to carry on the task, I would like to record my sincerest thanks. I am sorry if I have not made the best use of their advice; it was a most rewarding experience to recognize in their patience and generosity the signal marks of the finest traditions of the scholarly world.   N. P. B.

Trinity College,
Washington, D.C.

CONTENTS

REFERENCES AND ABBREVIATIONS

I. SOUTHWELL'S WORKS

EC   *An Epistle of Comfort.* Secretly printed in England, 1587-8 (Allison and Rogers, no. 781)

MMFT   *Mary Magdalens Funerall Teares.* Cawood, London, 1592 (edition unrecorded *S.T.C.*; copy in Folger Shakespeare Library)

TD   *The Triumphs over Death.* Busby, London, 1596 (*S.T.C.* 22972)

Modern editions of the poetry:

Walter   Walter, W. Joseph. *St. Peter's Complaint, and other Poems; by the Rev. Robert Southwell.* London, 1817

Turnbull   Turnbull, William B. *The Poetical Works of the Rev. Robert Southwell.* London, 1856

Grosart   Grosart, The Revd. Alexander B. *The Complete Poems of Robert Southwell, S.J.* The Fuller Worthies Library. Privately printed, 1872

Other works are cited in short-title forms. References to the Letter to his Father and the Letter to his Brother are made to the text edited by J. W. Trotman, who included the letters with his edition of *The Triumphs over Death*, London, 1914. Quotations from *An Humble Supplication to her Majestie* are made from the edition of R. C. Bald, Cambridge U.P., 1953. References to *A Short Rule of Good Life* are to the edition secretly printed in England, 1596-7 (Allison and Rogers, no. 787).

II. OTHER WORKS

Allison and Rogers   Allison, A. F., and Rogers, D. M. *A Catalogue of Catholic Books in English Printed Abroad or Secretly in England, 1558-1640. Biographical Studies*, vol. 3, nos. 3 (January 1956) and 4 (April 1956)

Briquet   Briquet, Charles M. *Les Filigranes: Dictionnaire historique des marques du papier dès leur apparition vers 1282 jusqu'en 1600.* 2e édition. Leipzig, 1923

C.R.S.   *Publications of the Catholic Record Society*

Devlin   Devlin, Christopher, S.J. *The Life of Robert Southwell, Poet and Martyr.* London, 1956

Janelle   Janelle, Pierre. *Robert Southwell the Writer.* London, 1935

McDonald   McDonald, James H., C.S.C. *The Poems and Prose Writings of Robert Southwell, S.J.: A Bibliographical Study.* Oxford, for the Roxburghe Club, 1937

Martz   Martz, Louis L. *The Poetry of Meditation: a Study in English Religious Literature of the Seventeenth Century.* Yale U.P., New Haven, 1954

O.E.D.   *The Oxford English Dictionary*

Stationers'   Arber, Edward, ed. *A Transcript of the Registers of the Company*
Register   *of Stationers of London; 1554–1640 A.D.*, 5 vols. Privately
       printed, London and Birmingham, 1875–94
S.T.C.   Pollard, A. F., and Redgrave, G. R. *A Short-title Catalogue*
       of Books Printed in England, Scotland, and Ireland, and of
       English Books Printed Abroad, 1475–1640. Bibliographical
       Society, London, 1926

Biblical references are made to the Authorized Version. Quotations are also cited from the A.V. unless there is some significant variation between the English text and that of the Vulgate with which Southwell was familiar. At such points the version of the Douay Bible may be cited if it is closer to the Latin, and therefore to passages in the poems, although there is no evidence to show that Southwell knew the version of the New Testament it contains (Rheims, 1582).

GENERAL INTRODUCTION

THE death of Robert Southwell at Tyburn on 21 February (O.S.) 1595 was at once the end of his work as Mission priest and the beginning of a wider public interest in his literary achievement. His life in the Society of Jesus had been dedicated to the Roman Catholic cause in England; the prose and poetry he wrote in English had been undertaken in order to further his work as priest. During the last years of the sixteenth century and the first decades of the seventeenth his reputation was based on his work as a lyric poet whose songs expressed a depth of religious love attested to by his death as a martyr for his faith.

Southwell's original intention for his poetry is no longer to be clearly distinguished. The order of the lyrics was distorted in the first attempts to make up popular volumes of religious verse, issued anonymously so that it should not betray its Jesuit origin, and the text of the poems at many points was corrupted as a result of faulty or ignorant copying, or over-assiduous editing. In the task of restoration the part played by the poems in his missionary endeavour must constantly be kept in mind. Beneath the musical cadences of the lyrics lies an undeviating didactic intention; the conventional diction is given a new relevance, and traditional motifs a deeper significance. It is necessary to read them with knowledge of the years of preparation for his work on the Mission, and with some understanding of the pressure under which he lived in the short period he served, from the landing at the beginning of July 1586 to his arrest in June 1592.

Southwell's recent biographers have acknowledged the close relationship between the poems and his work on the Mission. Professor Pierre Janelle speaks of Southwell's 'apostolate of letters', and the phrase is echoed in the work of his latest biographer, Father Christopher Devlin, S.J. What is now known of the details of Southwell's life has been carefully assembled from autobiographical documents and letters, and from less trustworthy materials supplied by his earliest biographers. Among this material documents from his early life abroad contain indications of experience formative in his growth as a poet, and the records of the years of missionary activity tell of conditions of living which had a shaping influence on the poems as they were written.

I

Father Devlin's account of Southwell's earliest years shows his upbringing conforming outwardly to that of many Catholic youths whose autobiographies are found in the records of English schools and colleges overseas. His English boyhood war spent in his father's house at Horsham St. Faith's, Norfolk, the house of a prosperous family of important local standing. It had been built by his grandfather, Sir Richard Southwell, in the grounds of the old Benedictine priory which had come to him as a prize at the period of the Dissolution. From him it devolved upon Richard, his eldest son, though of illegitimate birth, who had married Bridget, daughter of Sir Roger Copley, of Roughway, Sussex. Robert was their third son, born towards the end of 1561, according to rather vague references to his age made when he entered the Society of Jesus, and at the time of his trial. Like many young Catholics of the time he was sent abroad for his later education. In 1576, when he was about fifteen years old, he was entered at the Jesuit school at Douai, and given lodging in the English College there. For a short time he was sent for greater safety to the Jesuit College of Clermont in Paris. He returned to Douai when the political situation quietened in 1577 and shortly afterwards applied to enter the Jesuit novitiate at Tournai. After an initial repulse he was accepted into the novitiate in Rome in the following year. As student at the Roman College (later named the Pontifical Gregorian University), as tutor and prefect of studies at the English College, as an ordained priest, as prefect of the Sodality of the Blessed Virgin, as unofficial news correspondent regarding the progress of the Mission in England—all his experience was directed to a single end, towards which he strove with a youthful eagerness that had sometimes to be subdued by his superiors, but which developed before he left for England into the clarity of purpose that sustained him throughout all the frustrations and sufferings that led to martyrdom.

His zeal inevitably led to a series of spiritual crises, growing pains of importance only because they are part of the experience that shaped him as a poet. The earliest record, a prose passage known as the *Querimonia*, has been preserved only in a Latin translation by

Henry More, whose study of Southwell was included in his seven-teenth-century history of the Jesuits on the English Mission.[1] Al-though it is clear from his treatment of other records that More had little interest in preserving the original character of the docu-ments he translated, nevertheless there is no reason to doubt the authenticity of these sentences of passionate dedication to the service of God. The *Querimonia* is attributed to the time after Southwell's early attempt to enter the Society of Jesus had been rebuffed. Another time of unhappiness and self-tormenting im-patience is recalled in a holograph draft of a letter addressed to John Deckers about the end of 1580. Southwell writes of his experience at Douai when he was seeking guidance concerning his vocation. He relates an anecdote of his first meeting with Deckers, and the formation of a friendship which proved the means by which he gained greater equilibrium of spirit.[2]

The most important record of his spiritual history, however, is contained in the *Exercitia et Devotiones*.[3] This compilation includes the account of his early life he was required to write as a novice in the Society, together with notes on his spiritual training and private meditations. Although the passages of self-revelation can seldom be accurately dated, Father de Buck and the later biographers are probably right in ascribing them in order to the various crises of the years in Rome, from his entry into the Society in 1578 to his de-parture for England in 1586.[4] These comparatively brief sections reveal his struggle to subdue his natural inclinations to the moral discipline he sought to impose, and to subject his personal longings to the obedience required by his superiors. He rebuked himself most vehemently when he was inclined to forget how his work as a Jesuit priest would enable him to be of most use to his family and

[1] *Historia Missionis Anglicanæ Societatis Jesu* (St. Omer, 1660), p. 173.

[2] Latin text and English translation printed in *C.R.S.* v. 294–300, with reproduction of the first page of the autograph letter, preserved at Stonyhurst College.

[3] A manuscript copy dated 11 February 1607, preserved at the Bibliothèque royale de Belgique, and a slightly later copy at the Jesuit Résidence at Ghent, have been collated and edited by J. M. de Buck, S.J., and printed as *The Spiritual Exercises and Devotions of Blessed Robert Southwell, S.J.* (London, 1931), with English translation by P. E. Hallett. A third manuscript copy made in Louvain, formerly in the Phillipps collection, is now in the Folger Shakespeare Library.

[4] The dates of Southwell's entry to the novitiate, and of his first vows exactly two years later, are based on evidence in the *Exercitia*; the Brussels MS. gives the date of his vows as *in die S. Lucæ* (18 Oct.) [1580], which accords with his arrival at the Roman College on 17 October 1578 (see Devlin, p. 40). The Ghent and Folger MSS. give the date as *in die S. Luciæ* (13 Dec.).

countrymen.[1] His biographers have analysed the progress of the spiritual training recorded in the *Exercitia*, and Janelle has pointed to its precepts echoed in Southwell's later writings.[2] Here, in effect, is the history of the formation of the poet. Chafing at the constrictions and dismays that were part of his life in Rome, Southwell recorded in the *Exercitia* his inner suffering, breaking into imaginary dialogue, posing fiercely probing questions to which he himself gave the answers his training and beliefs supplied. Step by step in these revealing passages the sensitive and rebellious spirit is brought to obedience, the subjective concern grows towards understanding of the service demanded even in the life of the imagination, and gradually an objectivity not usually associated with the lyric writer is developed.

This process is the reversal of the experience of the love poet whose poetic method Southwell adopted. The individual praying for the favour of the one lady whose beauty and virtue excel in his eyes—at least for the purpose of his protestations—expresses in his verse the particular qualities that make his situation unlike any other. The poet strives to persuade his lady to change, to show more sympathy for the suppliant who desires that she become more like himself, and so grant his wishes. The religious poet is the poet of a Lover who cannot change. The suppliant must change, must grow in love to a greater awareness of the love offered him. And in this growth of understanding, of self-knowledge, he moves away from particularity, towards his essential being. In his own life this attainment of spiritual maturity prepared Southwell for his death as a martyr; it also gave him the imaginative objectivity to teach others the way to the love of God. Because his writing was part of his apostolate, his personal experience of the religious life of which he spoke was further removed than the involvement assumed by the love poet. His purpose in writing was one of service, not of self-expression. Interior problems are resolved; the confidence of faith reaches out to common humanity seeking the way to God in common suffering.

This spiritual growth is signified by a change in the language Southwell employed. The records of personal experience in the *Exercitia* are written in Latin, the language of his spiritual training.

---

[1] De Buck, no. 56: 'Petes: "Quid ergo me Deus ad Societatem . . . hoc tantummodo argumento et ratione perduxerit, quod nempe patria, proximi, parentes, etc., mea opera videbantur egere, quibus in Societate tantum, et non in aliis dictis ordinibus, adesse possem?"' English translation in de Buck, and in Devlin, p. 40.

[2] Janelle, ch. iv.

There survive also a few Latin poems and a group of meditations and prayers which probably date from this period.[1] English was for him the language of his apostolate. When he used English he sought to interpret and to teach. Although he was never cut off entirely from the use of English, there is some evidence that during his years of training abroad he was no longer fluent, and that before his return as a missionary priest he had to work hard to recover native ability in the language.

At Douai, as a schoolboy boarder at the English College, he would have found himself in a group of young men determined to preserve their sense of their English heritage, and he would have heard sermons in English given by the students on Sundays and feast days. At Paris, however, he would have been immersed in a student society quite apart from the current of English Catholic life on the Continent. In the university the students were forbidden to speak any language except Latin. Father Devlin has seen some significance in the fact that the *Querimonia*, an account of the spiritual perplexities which harassed Southwell before his acceptance into the Society, was first written in English, as if the use of the language was an expression of his temporary alienation from his Flemish friend, John Deckers, who was accepted before him.[2] Later, in the novitiate in Rome, Southwell was further removed from his compatriots and from the free use of English. In the *Exercitia* there are no words of English. Even at the English College, where the seminarians hoped that they would eventually return on the Mission, the use of English was restricted; the occasional English visitor, such as young William Cecil in 1586, for whom Southwell acted as guide to the sights of the city,[3] could not provide sufficient opportunity to maintain natural fluency.

It would appear that at this period of his life Southwell was more fluent in Italian than in English,[4] and there can be no doubt that he

---

[1] Latin poems and prose are preserved in the holograph manuscript at Stonyhurst College, A. v. 4. A volume of Latin meditations, *Meditationes de attributis divinis ad amorem dei excitantes*, attributed to Southwell, is bound with the copy of the *Exercitia* at the Folger Shakespeare Library.   [2] Devlin, p. 32.

[3] A reference to this visit occurs in Southwell's letter to Sir Robert Cecil, William Cecil's uncle, which has recently been acquired by the Folger Shakespeare Library (MS. V. a. 421).

[4] The only vernacular phrase in the *Exercitia* is in Italian, a joke inaccurately told that recalls a conversation in Italian during recreation in 1582 (Ghent and Folger MSS. only), in de Buck, pp. 194, 197. Three of Southwell's letters are in Italian: one written to Persons assuming the disguising phraseology of merchant correspondence; one a

was interested in the language as a literary vehicle. His reading of Italian verse and prose had greater influence upon his literary taste than his explorations in any other vernacular; through translation of Italian texts into English he strove to regain fluency in his native tongue. His most substantial piece of translation is from an Italian version of *A Hundred Meditations on the Love of God* of Diego de Estella, whose work he presumably did not know in the original Spanish. He undertook this considerable task at some time later than the publication of the Italian version in 1584 or 1585, probably completing it when he was in England.[1]

Southwell's need to study English before his return on the Mission is stated by his earliest biographer, Diego de Yepez, whose report was largely the work of Father Joseph Creswell, S.J. It is recorded that Southwell 'applied himself with much diligence to the study of his native tongue, which he had already nearly forgotten, because he had left England very young'.[2] Later Southwell's concern that the priests in training for the Mission at the English College should have adequate practice in their own language is expressed in a letter to Father Alphonsus Agazzari, S.J., Rector of the College, written on the experience of the first few months of pastoral work in England. In it Southwell speaks of the great demand for those who can preach: 'It is of the greatest necessity that they are sufficiently practised that they acquire facility in speech and can draw on a repertory of subjects.'[3]

newsletter addressed to the Jesuit provincial in Naples; and the third a note to Father Agazzari, Rector of the English College, Rome, reporting progress on the journey to England. (Letters in *C.R.S.* v. 301, 303, 306.)

[1] Southwell's translation exists in two independent manuscript copies, one in a seventeenth-century hand, preserved in the Jesuit library in Farm Street, and a later copy at Stonyhurst College. In a dedication transcribed in the Farm Street MS. the original copyist states that he has made his copy from Southwell's autograph in his possession, and he speaks of Southwell's intention of presenting the translation to Lady Beauchamp's mother. This Lady Beauchamp was Anne, daughter of Sir Robert Sackville, later Lord Buckhurst and second Earl of Dorset, and Margaret, daughter of Thomas Howard, third Duke of Norfolk. Anne married Edward Seymour, who succeeded to the title of Lord Beauchamp in 1612. John Morris, S.J., edited the work in 1873 in the belief that it was Southwell's original composition. For a discussion of the date of the publication of the Italian translation of the *Meditations* by Gianbattista Peruschi, S.J., see Janelle, pp. 144–5.

[2] *Historia particular de la persecución en Inglaterra* (Madrid, 1599), quoted in Janelle, p. 32. Father Creswell's part in the *Historia* has been shown by A. J. Loomie, S.J., in *The Spanish Elizabethans* (Fordham University Press, 1963), p. 206.

[3] 'Concionatores hic magnopere desiderantur, ideoque pernecessarium est ut ibi assuefaciant se, ut et facilitatem in dicendo et rerum copiam usu acquirant.' Letter of 22 December 1586, in *C.R.S.* v. 316.

The autograph papers preserved at Stonyhurst College (A. v. 4) provide some evidence of Southwell's efforts to gain fluency in English. Among them is the 'Peeter Playnt', identified by Professor Mario Praz as a draft of a translation of part of Luigi Tansillo's *Le Lagrime di San Pietro*,[1] and an incomplete draft of a sermon on Mary Magdalen (fols. 56–60, 62), which Professor Janelle has shown to be based on an Italian text of a Latin devotional treatise attributed to Saint Bonaventure.[2] From the condition of the manuscript of the sermon on Mary Magdalen it is possible to see what difficulties Southwell found in writing. The first section, for instance, illustrates his struggle to express his thoughts in a language which was still awkwardly recalcitrant. The passage is studded with words crossed out and interlineations, phrases are rearranged within the sentence, and at a few points, apparently at a loss for suitable words or synonyms in English, Southwell has written Latin equivalents between the lines (⌐. . .⌐):

Her griefe was renewed in that first ⌐she had⌐ bewayled his takynge away ⌐defūctū⌐ out of lyfe and ⌐now⌐ she bewayled his takyng away ⌐out⌐ of the graue . . . his ded bodye ⌐corpus defūcti⌐ she fyndeth not . . . (fol. 56)

She is become breathless ⌐exanimis⌐ she is waxed senselesse feelyng she feeleth not seyng she seeth not . . . (fol. 56ᵛ)

In view of his ingrained tendency to draw upon Latin for the expression of religious thought, his vocabulary in the sermon as in his later work is surprisingly free from words of Latin origin. The Latin influence is strongest in structural inversions, which are at times quite unacceptable in English syntax, as, for example, in the description of Mary Magdalen's 'notorious griefes', 'which wᵗʰ teares haue temped fayne she would but she could not '(fol. 56ᵛ). His natural inclination to musical balance in rhythm and sound, highly developed in his later writing in both verse and prose, leads him in this early fragment to use elaborate and contrived phrases, echoing the artificiality of his Italian original.

Similar rhetorical graces are imposed upon a third passage of English prose in the manuscript, a single page (fol. 37) which, like the *Querimonia*, is apparently the record of another time of inner questioning and searching self-examination. Here he asks whether

---

[1] See Appendix I. The place of the 'Peeter Playnt' in the history of the long poem 'Saint Peters Complaint' is discussed in the Textual Introduction IV. iv, p. lxxxvi.

[2] Janelle, p. 184.

the attraction he feels for a handsome youth is one of sexual instinct alone, or whether it is by the guidance of God that he should be particularly concerned for the spiritual welfare of one so blessed with physical beauty:

Why should I not rather iudge that god would bend by his fauoure good mennes inclination vnto him and marke him with this amiable collisance [cognizance] that who so vewed his pson myght desyre the lyke comelynesse in his soule and thynck it there dutye to pcure that he should bee most lyke vnto god in goodnesse whome god hath made so lyke vnto him in goodlynesse

As may be expected, Southwell's English spelling in these manuscript pages, written before he regained complete facility in the language, shows a tendency to phonetic reproduction. The preponderance of simplified forms of so many words is unusual even in this period, when phonetic spelling was not uncommon. The holographs supply examples of the use of single consonants and vowels in words where they are regularly doubled, and of single vowels replacing diphthongs, the elision of letters not pronounced, the occasional loss of a final *e*, the alternation of *i* and *e* and sometimes of *o* and *u*.

In the preparation of this edition the spelling in these holograph pages has been carefully examined for its importance in determining the textual authority of the manuscripts and printed editions of the poems, in which unusual spelling forms have been weighed as evidence of remnants of Southwell's original spelling. Occasionally textual variants can be explained by the possibility of ambiguous spelling forms in the holograph. Unfortunately Southwell's inconsistency in spelling makes any decision regarding a text's precise relationship with the holograph impossible; it is likely also that in later years, when he gained complete fluency in English, his spelling habits would have been considerably modified. The most that can be done with any sense of security is to relate an unexpected spelling occurring in the work of copyist or compositor to Southwell's spelling as revealed in this manuscript, and in the consideration of textual cruces to suspect an original error based on a spelling peculiarity.

These English holograph pages are in fact a rare record of a poet's training in his language. The vocabulary, drawn largely from everyday speech, which is characteristic of his lyric verse, is seen evolving in the work of translation; his instinctive feeling for the musical and rhythmic phrase threatens to overload his prose style with excessive decoration. Above all, there is evidence of the effort expended in regaining the facility he needed, and of the pleasure of the young writer as the words are allowed to flow unchecked in sudden rhetorical abundance.

II

Southwell's poetry in English was written during the six years of his work as a priest on the English Mission, from the time of his return in July 1586 to his arrest in June 1592. The record of his life in these years is necessarily a compilation of scraps of evidence. Part of the fragmentary picture may be pieced together from references in the prose writings, each one of which is related to some event, personal or public, which occurred during this period; part is provided by his letters; and part by comments made by those who knew him and by those who wanted to know more about him, whether fellow-priest or priest-hunter, Catholic or schismatic, friend or foe. In recent years the materials have been augmented by two important discoveries: the group of letters written by Southwell and Father Henry Garnet, his superior on the Mission, to Father Claudius Aquaviva, General of the Society of Jesus, and a copy of the letter Southwell wrote to Sir Robert Cecil during his imprisonment.[1] The letters to Aquaviva were used extensively in Father Devlin's biography, and although he found them disappointingly business-like and matter-of-fact, the information he has culled from them confirms many details in the previously hazy picture.

Southwell's letters to Aquaviva, dated from 7 January 1587 to 29 December 1588, augmented by four letters already known and published by J. H. Pollen, S.J., and a few sketchy abstracts of letters now lost, supply truly rich documentation for the first two and a half years of his missionary work.[2] In this time also Southwell wrote *An Epistle of Comfort*, his longest prose work.[3]

[1] The letters to Aquaviva were found by Father Philip Caraman, S.J., in the Jesuit archives in Rome, *Fondo Gesuitico* 651. Father Caraman speaks of a group of thirteen letters in his biography of Henry Garnet (London, 1964), p. xi. The letter to Cecil is in the Folger Shakespeare Library, MS. V. a. 421.

[2] Letters previously known are listed in McDonald, pp. 63–65. The letter to Deckers (McDonald, no. 24) was written not from England, but directly before the Channel crossing ('ex portu'); the letter intercepted with that addressed to Aquaviva, 25 July 1586 (McDonald, no. 24a), was not the letter to Deckers, but a letter to Agazzari, known in abstract only (*Calendar, State Papers, Dom., 1581–90*, vol. 195, no. 119, p. 377). The letters from England for this period are in *C.R.S.* v. 307–28.

[3] *An Epistle of Comfort* was printed by a secret Catholic press in England, 1587–8. (See Allison and Rogers, no. 781.)

The latter part of his work in England is, in contrast, barely documented. In the period January 1589 to June 1592 two letters of those sent to Aquaviva are known, dated 16 January and 8 March 1590; a fragment of a third letter of July or August 1591, known only in an Italian version, was probably originally another report to Aquaviva.[1] The year 1589 is marked only by a Latin translation of a letter sent to Philip Howard, Earl of Arundel, after his arraignment in April,[2] and the letter to his father, dated 22 October, later published with *A Short Rule of Good Life*.[3] In September 1591 Southwell completed *The Triumphs over Death*, also in epistolary form, addressed to Arundel after the death of his half-sister, Lady Margaret Sackville.[4] His translation of Diego de Estella's *A Hundred Meditations on the Love of God* was either unfinished or not yet copied out at the time of Lady Margaret's death in August. The prose poem, *Marie Magdalens Funerall Teares*, was completed and ready for publication in the same year.[5] According to the writer of the Preface to Southwell's *A Short Rule of Good Life*, printed by Garnet's secret press after his death, the revision of this rule for the Catholic layman was 'amongst the last of his fruitefull labours for the good of soules';[6] it may therefore also be assigned to this period. There are some undated letters which belong to the time of his active life as a priest, including the letter 'to a wandering priest'—*de vitando vago vivendi genere*—which is known only in the Latin translation in More's account, and two letters to relatives, one a draft of a letter to his father and the other a short note from 'P.B. to his coosyn W.R.'[7]

---

[1] *C.R.S.* v. 328–33.

[2] More's Latin redaction of the letter to Arundel (*Historia*, p. 186) was re-translated by Henry Foley, S.J. (*Records of the English Province of the Society of Jesus*, i [London, 1877], pp. 335, 336); the second part of the letter is printed in *C.R.S.* xxi. 320.

[3] Manuscript copies of Southwell's letter to his father are in *S*, *VC*, and *A*, described in Textual Introduction (I), and in other collections (see McDonald, pp. 11–12, 30). The earliest edition of the *Rule* and the letter has been dated 1596–7. (See Allison and Rogers, no. 787.)

[4] *The Triumphs over Death* was edited by John Trussel and printed by Valentine Sims for John Busby in 1595. (See McDonald, p. 111.) Manuscript copies are in *S*, *VC*, and *A*.

[5] John Wolfe printed the *Funerall Teares* for Gabriel Cawood in 1591; it was entered in the Stationers' Register, 8 November 1591. (See McDonald, p. 109.)

[6] Preface to the Reader, sig. a5. (Allison and Rogers, no. 787.)

[7] The priest whom Southwell chides for his manner of performing his duties may be James Younger, who arrived from the seminary in Valladolid in the spring of 1591, and who was captured in 1592. (See Devlin, pp. 226, 274.) Records of Younger's examinations are in the State Papers, where he is called Young, alias Thomas Christopher, alias George Dingley. (*Calendar, S.P., Dom., 1591–4*, pp. 261, 263, 267, &c.)

Two items of a different tenor may be assigned to the last months before Southwell's imprisonment: one is a series of notes on the treatment of Catholics in England, compiled during the latter part of 1591 and sent to Richard Verstegan in Antwerp for propaganda use abroad; the other is Southwell's own contribution to political controversy, *An Humble Supplication to her Majestie*, which at several points draws upon the material sent to Verstegan.[1] The *Supplication* bears every indication of having been written at great speed between the issue of the Proclamation dated 18 October 1591—probably published late in November—and the end of the year.

These personal documents through which Southwell's activities may be traced can be augmented by Garnet's letters for the period July 1586 to May 1595. All these materials are of importance here only as they contradict or confirm earlier assumptions concerning the conditions under which the poems were written. The evidence is still sparse, and confirmation of many statements is not to be found, but the outline of an administrative structure within which the priests undertook vigorous pastoral work in their allotted areas is now clear, and supersedes the earlier notion that they were forced to spend much of their time in isolation, shut away from the sight of all but those who might be most trusted. The establishment of this administration was Garnet's work; he describes its formation in a letter to Aquaviva dated 9 June 1588.[2] Southwell was stationed in London, leaving his superior free to travel further afield. In this central position Southwell met incoming priests, provided lodgings for those whose journeys brought them through the capital, and corresponded with Aquaviva on a wide range of topics affecting their lives, giving accounts of the persecution as observed in London and as reported to him from elsewhere, and occasionally commenting on rumours flying in the air of foreign invasion and treachery at home.

Southwell's letter is printed in More's *Historia*, p. 188, and translated in part in Devlin, p. 222. Manuscript copies of the letters to his relatives are in *VC* and *A*, where the first is said to be addressed to a brother. The letter 'to his brother' is printed in Foley, i, p. 347; J. W. Trotman printed both letters from *A* in his edition of *The Triumphs over Death* (London, 1914), pp. 65, 68.

[1] The letter to Verstegan is attributed to Southwell by Anthony G. Petti in his edition of *The Letters and Despatches of Richard Verstegan*, C.R.S. lii. 1. R. C. Bald has reconstructed the conditions under which the *Supplication* was written in his edition (Cambridge, 1953), Introduction, pp. ix–xi.

[2] Devlin, p. 161.

Southwell's occupation of a house in London gave him an independence that was invaluable to his work on the Mission. When Thomas Pormort, a priest who had known Southwell at the English College in Rome, arrived in England in 1590, he was welcomed, fed and clothed, and brought with honour into Southwell's own house, 'which is a mark of singular esteem in times of persecution'.[1] Southwell's success in London depended to a great degree on help offered by the Countess of Arundel.[2] Father Devlin believed that he occupied a house she owned at Acton, Middlesex,[3] but the distance of Acton from London counts against such an identification. She had another house near Billingsgate, and perhaps it was here, close to the Tower and close to the houses of Catholic friends and relatives, that he set up headquarters. Father John Gerard, who met Southwell for the first time on his arrival in England at the end of 1588, speaks with approval of Southwell's 'domus privata' in London, where he received Garnet on his visits to the city, and where he had even been able to arrange for the printing of his books.[4] This press may have produced *An Epistle of Comfort*, with the misleading assertion 'Imprinted at Paris' on its title-page. In its first form the *Epistle* had been a personal letter to the Earl of Arundel, imprisoned in the Tower. A surprisingly detailed account of a secret press operating from a house where the Earl had formerly lived was given towards the end of 1588 in the first of the Martin Marprelate tracts, *An Epistle to the Terrible Priests of the Convocation House*, in which the writer asserted that the Archbishop of Canterbury, informed of the work of the illicit press, had declined to take any action, although it had been reported that the press was in the Charterhouse, and that the printing was being done by employees of 'J.C. the Earle of Arundels man'. The writer's anger was particularly violent because of this apparent leniency towards Catholic printing, when the Puritan printer, Waldegrave, suffered the loss of all his equipment: 'Why set you not that printing presse and letters out of Charterhouse,

---

[1] Statement of Father James Standish, *C.R.S.* v. 189, and Devlin, p. 220.

[2] An account of his life in her household is contained in *The Lives of Philip Howard, Earl of Arundel, and of Anne Dacres, his wife*, compiled by a family priest some years after Southwell's death. The *Lives* was published in 1857 from manuscripts at Arundel Castle, but a manuscript account 'Of Father Southwell's coming to live with her', transcribed by M. A. Tierney, was not published until March 1931, when it appeared in *The Month*, pp. 246–54, edited by C. A. Newdigate, S.J.

[3] Devlin, p. 141.

[4] *John Gerard: The Autobiography of an Elizabethan*, trans. Philip Caraman, S.J. (London, 1951), p. 26.

and destroye them as you did Walde-graves? Why did you not apprehend the parties, why? Because it was poperie at the least, that was printed in Charterhouse'.[1] The Puritan controversialist may not have been accurate in his facts. He implied that the printer was John Charlewood, who until the Earl's disgrace in 1585 had proudly called himself 'printer to the Rt. Hon. the Earle of Arundel', and whose books had occasionally been issued 'From Howard House', the new name of the Charterhouse. It would have been a rash undertaking to issue Catholic books from a place where the printer had worked openly in the days before unlicensed operations were curtailed. It would seem more likely that Southwell was able to use a more secluded place.

The generosity of the Countess of Arundel in the midst of her personal tribulations enabled Southwell to move freely about his business; at times of greatest peril she hid him in her own house, attended by her most trustworthy servants. These periods of confinement are described with some imaginative detail by one of Southwell's earliest biographers, Father Daniello Bartoli.[2] There is no reason to believe that such a state of affairs lasted for long at any one time. On the contrary, the letters to Aquaviva are a record of a most active pastoral and administrative career.

Garnet's plans for the Mission included a regular meeting every six months at which the priests themselves found spiritual refreshment. The occasions of Garnet's return to London at roughly six-monthly intervals in 1586, 1587, and 1588 mark the times when the two Jesuits heard each other's confessions and renewed their vows. At such times they were joined by aspirants to the Society, and by some of the secular priests. Southwell describes the value of their meetings in a letter to Aquaviva of 21 December 1588, when the short period of recuperation was the more precious after months of persecution following the Armada.[3]

---

[1] *An Epistle (Oh read over D. John Bridges, for it is a worthy worke: Or an epitome of the fyrste Booke . . . The Epitome is not yet published . . . In the meane time, let them be content with this learned Epistle.)* (reprinted London, 1843), p. 31. An account of Howard House (the Charterhouse) is given by J. H. Pollen in his collection of documents concerning the Earl of Arundel (*C.R.S.* xxi. 350–1).

[2] Janelle, p. 42, quoting from the Latin version of Bartoli's history of the Jesuits in England (*Europeæ historiæ Societatis Jesu pars prior, Anglia, ex edito Romæ Italico . . .* Interprete R. P. Ludovico Janino. Paris, 1671).

[3] Caraman, *Henry Garnet*, pp. 57, 127–8. References to Garnet's presence in London occur in letters: *C.R.S.* v. 313 (21 December 1586); Devlin, pp. 151–2, 160, 167, 189. For Southwell's letter of 21 December 1588 see Devlin, pp. 179–80.

When other Jesuits arrived in England it became necessary to meet in houses offering secure hiding-places outside London. Most fully documented is the meeting at Baddesley Clinton in October 1591, when the house was raided and the priests barely escaped by hiding in a flooded tunnel underneath a wing of the house.[1]

The achievement of the Mission priests during these years is the more impressive in view of the continued persecution. The difficulties they encountered were most acute at times of political crisis, but even at the worst times the pastoral work went on. The suffering of the Catholics during the summer of the Armada was particularly severe, and Southwell's letters show his concern for the effect of the government's policy of branding as treasonable Catholic landowners to whom the country people had formerly turned at times of national danger.[2] At the end of August he sent eyewitness accounts of the executions of Father Gunter and Father Leigh and of the laymen who suffered with them. His experience during these months enabled him to see clearly the insidious effect of religious strife, which revealed the finest and the worst in the national character:

At this time, my Father, I beg you to give some thought to the loyal faith of the Catholics, of that very same faith that has been long admired in this people naturally inclined to religious sensibility; and to consider that the crazed bestiality of their enemies is truly not inherent in the whole nation, but a disease brought by heresy, viciously attacking not only faith itself, but the laws and discipline that govern human nature; and thus you may come to look upon Catholic constancy as a revelation of spiritual strength all the more lovely, and the heretics' error the more deserving of our pity.[3]

Towards the end of the year, when the persecution had eased, Garnet sent Southwell on an extended missionary tour which took him, as he says, 'round a great part of England'. His report in December gives some detail of the way he carried out his work: 'I have sometimes been to call on the Protestant Sheriffs to look after secret Catholics in their households; and they, seeing my fine clothes and my bevy of aristocratic youths, and suspecting nothing

---

[1] Gerard, *Autobiography*, pp. 41–43; Devlin, pp. 235–8; Caraman, *Henry Garnet*, pp. 128–36.

[2] Letters of 10 and 11 July 1588; Devlin, pp. 163, 167.

[3] Letter of 31 August 1588; *C.R.S.* v. 321–5 (Latin text).

so little as the reality, have received me with imposing ceremony and truly sumptuous banquets.'[1]

Against such a background of bitter ordeal and the sweet success of youthful adventure Southwell wrote his poetry. In it he summons his countrymen to live lives of moral integrity, to seek spiritual strength in humility and religious love. Above all, he speaks of the necessity of repentance and the cleansing properties of suffering undertaken in the name of faith.

Although he had only six years on the Mission, it is remarkable that in his post in London he escaped arrest for so long. His presence in England was known from the beginning. Thomas Morgan, Paris agent of the Queen of Scots, reported Southwell's departure for England with Garnet in a letter of 3 July 1586 to Gilbert Gifford, who passed it for deciphering to Thomas Phelippes; from his hands it would have reached Walsingham about the same time that Southwell arrived in London on 8 July. Further details reached Walsingham in August.[2] He became a particularly desirable prey. He was in the first place a Jesuit, and he held an integral position in the organization of the English Mission. In his pastoral work the qualities of character by which he drew others to him made him outstanding, even among his richly gifted fellow-priests. Father Gerard wrote of him: 'He was so wise and good, gentle and lovable.'[3] Besides his work as priest and administrator his achievement as a writer was already making his influence widespread amongst Catholic families of great distinction. In the last months of his freedom the hunting of the priests grew more intense, and, had Southwell known it, the authorities had gained an essential piece of information to help them in their arrest: a description of his physical appearance. The information had come from John Cecil, a priest sent on the Mission from the seminary at Valladolid. He had been arrested soon after his arrival in England in the spring of 1591, and his unfitness for the task to which he had been assigned is all too clearly revealed in the long, meandering depositions by which he tried to gain official favour by telling all he knew of plans made abroad, and of the work of the priests in England. He told of a commission Father Persons had given him to sound out Catholic

---

[1] Letter of 28 December 1588; Devlin, p. 182.
[2] *Calendar, S.P., Scotland VIII, 1585–6,* vol. 18, no. 551, p. 499; vol. 19, no. 685, p. 598; see also Devlin, pp. 98, 109.
[3] *Autobiography,* p. 17.

feeling with regard to Lord Strange as a possible candidate to succeed Elizabeth on the throne, if Strange would initiate correspondence on the subject with Cardinal Allen and the exiles in the Low Countries—'but this was to be revealed to none but Southwell or Garnet'. In a deposition taken a few days later, on 25 May, Cecil gave a detailed description of Southwell, whom he had known in Rome.[1]

Not much time remained. In February 1592 Garnet, who had taken over Southwell's post in London and sent him into the country for a respite, wrote to Aquaviva of their desperate state: 'There is simply nowhere left to hide.'[2] A report on activities of priests in London given by Chomley—a mysterious creature of the London underworld who was apparently willing to give information on any cause, and who was later to accuse Marlowe of atheism—includes a reference to 'Mr. Cuthwell, a Jesuit' who had been at the houses of Dr. Smythe and Mr. Cotton in Fleet Street.[3] But Southwell was not to be taken without the most elaborate scheming on the part of Topcliffe.

Details of the story of Southwell's arrest at the house of the Bellamys at Uxenden, near Harrow, were given in evidence taken from Robert Barnes in 1598, when, after five years of imprisonment incurred for his assistance to priests, he gave a damning indictment of the methods used by Topcliffe in his work as priest-hunter.[4] His account is confirmed by Garnet's letter of 16 July 1592 to Aquaviva, from which Southwell's visit to Uxenden is seen as the first stage in his journey to Warwickshire.[5] On 25 June he had met Thomas Bellamy by appointment in Fleet Street, and had travelled with him to Uxenden. There, in the house which, as Garnet wrote, 'had long lacked a consoler', Southwell preached and gave Holy Communion to the congregation of local Catholics who had gathered to meet him. That night, on information given by Anne Bellamy, Thomas's sister, who had become the tool of Topcliffe, the house was raided and Southwell seized. In the letter to the Queen announcing his

---

[1] *Calendar, S.P., Dom., 1591-4*, vol. 238, no. 160 (21 May), p. 39, and no. 179 (25 May), p. 45. Cecil is called by his alias, John Snowden.

[2] Devlin, pp. 255-6.

[3] *Calendar, S.P., Dom., 1591-4*, vol. 241, no. 35 (? Jan. 1592), p. 176.

[4] Barnes's account is printed in M. A. Tierney's edition of Charles Dodd's *Church History of England* (1739), iii (London, 1840), Appendix 37, p. cxci; see also Devlin, pp. 275-7.

[5] Devlin, p. 277.

success Topcliffe congratulated himself: 'I never did take so weighty a man.'[1]

The years that remained were years of solitary imprisonment. Southwell was taken first to the cell in Topcliffe's own house, the 'stronge chamber in Westminster churche yearde', where, as he explained in his letter to the Queen, 'if your highness pleasur bee to knowe any thinge in his hartte', he planned to torture him immediately by hanging him against the wall, which, 'lyke a Tryck at Trenshemoare, will inforce hym to tell all'. The next day he was taken to the Gatehouse, and on 28 July committed to the Tower, where he began the long ordeal that Garnet described as 'that blessed solitude'.[2]

At the time of Southwell's arrest Garnet came directly to London, sending a brief word to Verstegan of the crisis that had come upon them all. A few days later he was able to amplify his first message with more details, and in the usual guarded language of merchant activities revealed what administrative changes had been made: 'I wrote how my marchant was arrested, but his elder brother hathe undertaken his busynesse, who with all other freindes are well.'[3] Although he was then finding the capital too 'whot' for him, Garnet, as 'elder brother', took over the key post in London; his letters at this time, and later at the time of Southwell's execution, give the most reliable accounts of what happened. Further details of Southwell's imprisonment are given by the 'yonger brother to your partner', John Falkner—possibly an alias for John Gerard, since the name is suitable for one with such love of hawking. He was able to add that 'the marchant that was arrested continued still in his distress, till, of late, that his father by his freindes hath laboured that he is not now used in the extremest manner as he was'.[4] The intervention of Southwell's father to obtain some relaxation of the terrible conditions under which he was first held is related also in Yepez's *Historia*.[5] Garnet was able to send him a breviary, which Southwell took with him when he was transferred to Newgate directly before

---

[1] B.M. Lansdowne MS. vol. 72, no. 39, in J. Strype, *Annals of the Reformation* (Oxford, 1824), iv, p. 185, and in part in Devlin, p. 283; the first page of the letter is reproduced in Philip Hughes, *The Reformation in England*, iii (London, 1954), 'Torture II' inserted between pp. 384 and 385. (Topcliffe's frequent abbreviations have been expanded in quotations.)

[2] Letter of 7 March 1595; Devlin, p. 293.   [3] *C.R.S.* lii. 68.

[4] Ibid., p. 69. See also later reports of 15 and 18 October 1592, based on a letter of 14 September received by Verstegan from England.

[5] Quoted in Janelle, p. 68, and Devlin, p. 289.

his trial and execution. While Garnet was writing his letter of
7 March 1595 the breviary was returned to him. He scrutinized it
carefully, and found pin-scratches only, including the name *Jesus*,
and various other signs which might have been used in the examination of conscience.[1] Garnet concluded that the absence of any ink
mark indicated that Southwell was never permitted to write. He was,
however, allowed writing materials on one occasion, in order to
make an appeal to Sir Robert Cecil that he should be brought to
trial. The letter is dated 6 April 1593,[2] and in it Southwell states
specifically that he had not been previously permitted to write, and
that it was as a favour from the Lieutenant of the Tower, Sir Michael
Blount, that he was then being allowed the privilege of his appeal.
There is no reason to doubt his statement, nor is there any evidence
to suggest that the restrictions placed upon his imprisonment were
in any way mitigated during the twenty-three months that remained.

The conditions of Southwell's arrest and imprisonment bear
directly upon the problem of reclaiming an accurate text for his
poetry. In the months before his arrest it would indeed have been
difficult to keep personal papers in good order; his poems may have
had scant attention when he was busy with the preparation of the
prose works of immediate topical concern in the last months of
1591, although there is some internal evidence, which will be presented in the Textual Introduction (IV. iv), that suggests he was
working on his long poem, 'Saint Peters Complaint'. From the time
of his arrest the dissemination of his literary work lay in other hands.

During his long imprisonment there was some hope that he
might be ransomed, although Aquaviva warned Garnet in a letter
of 10 October 1592 that the ransoming of Jesuits might make the
Society open to criticism and scandal.[3] When he was finally brought
to trial he was taken first to the fearful cell called Limbo, in Newgate,
and from there, in great haste and secrecy, he was brought before the
Queen's Bench on 20 February 1595. His actions and his words
at the end of his life are reported by Garnet in his two letters of
22 February, his report to his Italian friends of 7 March, and the
long letter of 1 May.[4] Two eyewitness accounts also survive. He was
tried before Sir John Popham, Chief Justice of the Queen's Bench,
indicted under the Statute of 1585 for the treason of returning

---

[1] Quoted in Janelle, p. 69.   [2] Folger Shakespeare Library, MS. V. a. 421.
[3] Letter in *General Archives, S.J.: Flandro-Belgæ*, i. 507; Janelle, p. 70.
[4] Caraman, *Henry Garnet*, pp. 194-9.

as an ordained priest of the Church of Rome and of administering the sacraments of the Church. The prosecution conducted by Edward Coke, the Attorney-General, attacked him most bitterly on the question of his advocacy of equivocation. Southwell's attempt to answer his accusers was made more pitiful by his physical weakness; Garnet wrote that he had so little strength that he asked a Newgate jailer to stay near at hand to help him at need, since '(as a result of his bitter tortures) his sides were not strong enough to shout'.[1] One of the eyewitness accounts, that of Thomas Leake, a Catholic priest, reports that he excused his inability to speak more effectively, saying: 'I am decayed in memorie with long and close imprisonment, and I have bene tortured ten times. I had rather have indured ten executions. I speak not this for my self, but for others; that they may not be handled so inhumanelie, to drive men to desperation, if it weir possible.'[2] Found guilty by a jury that did not delay to discuss his case, he was condemned and led back as a prisoner to Newgate. The following day he was taken to execution.

Southwell's last hours are recorded by close friends and co-religionists. In their natural desire to welcome another martyr in this man whom they had so long admired they emphasize the spirit of joyful contentment which they saw in him, sustaining him from the time he left the court until he died on the scaffold. The practice of prayer and meditation in which he had been trained did not desert him as he was dragged on the hurdle through the muddy streets of wintry London. His gentleness of spirit was seen for the last time in the manner of his recognition of friends in the crowd—a warning spoken quietly to a woman who approached the hurdle, a handkerchief and a rosary thrown into the mass of faces below the triangular structure of Tyburn Tree. His actions were not dramatic nor his words scornful. He refused to enter the dialectical ambiguities of religious controversy, although the Chaplain of the Tower was prepared to argue with him; he professed himself to be a Catholic priest and a Jesuit; he prayed for the Queen, and the country, and for his own soul. His last words showed once more his clearsighted recognition of suffering as the common experience of human life, to be welcomed as the way to spiritual regeneration:

And this I humbly desire almightie God that it would please his goodnes, to take and excepte this my death, the laste farewell to this miserable

---

[1] Letter of 1 May 1595; Devlin, p. 294.
[2] Leake's *Relation, C.R.S.* v. 335.

and infortunate lyfe (althoughe in this moste happy and fortunate) in full satisfaction for all my sinnes and offences, and for the Comfort of many others; which albeit that it seeme here disgracefull, yet I hope that in tyme to come it will be to my eternall glory.[1]

Together with other English martyrs, Southwell was beatified by Pope Pius XI in 1929.

[1] From the account preserved at Stonyhurst College entitled *A Brefe Discourse of the condemnation and execution of Mr Robert Southwell*, as given in Janelle, p. 89.

TEXTUAL INTRODUCTION

SOUTHWELL'S poems have been preserved in five manuscript copies of a compilation of the short lyrics, and two manuscript copies of the long poem, 'Saint Peters Complaint', none of which bears any precise indication of the date it was copied, and in two printed collections, *Saint Peters Complaint, With other Poemes*, and *Mœoniæ*, both appearing first in 1595, the year of his execution. Later editions make some additions to the original printed groups of lyrics. In the absence of authoritative texts his intentions for the presentation of his poetry can never be known with certainty, and his text must be recovered from these sources at some remove from his holograph or an authorized copy. The modern editor is faced with the problem of selecting copy-texts from manuscripts which, though copied with considerable respect for the text in transmission, are nevertheless marred by scribal errors and misplaced editorial zeal, and from printed books where the original intention of the Catholic missionary priest is overlaid by the commercial caution of the London printing houses. But after collation of the manuscripts and all known copies of the earliest printed editions, when all the evidence is collected and sifted, it is possible at many points to recognize what is most consistent with Southwell's habit of thought and his manner and tone of expression. Besides the problem of the text other problems arising from the nature of the materials have to be solved: the canon, the dates of composition, and the order of the lyrics.

The only collection of poems which Southwell is known to have prepared for circulation was a group of short lyrics to which he refers in a prose dedicatory letter addressed to his 'loving Cosen', a letter now preserved in two manuscripts and in the editions of *Saint Peters Complaint*. No copy of the collection Southwell made now exists, and its contents can only be surmised. After his arrest in June 1592 it is assumed that one of those closest to him—we cannot tell whether he was priest or layman—undertaking the burden of literary executorship, compiled the collection of fifty-two short lyrics which have survived in five copies; it is likely that his work was accomplished very shortly after Southwell's imprisonment.

Southwell's own collection was incorporated in this larger compilation, and the two introductory items which he had prepared, the prose letter to his 'loving Cosen' and a poem 'To the Reader', giving an account of his intentions in writing his poetry and sending it into the world, were set in front to preface this larger group. What was saved at this time became a matrix for later copyists. In view of the conditions under which the poems were written, and of the months of acute apprehension before the crisis of Southwell's arrest, followed by the need of immediate changes in the missionary organization, we must indeed be grateful for the preservation of so many lyrics.

It is possible that this editor was also responsible for the preservation of the single long poem attributed to Southwell, 'Saint Peters Complaint'. It is not part of the compilation of short lyrics, but it is known in two early manuscript copies. A copy came into the hands of the first publisher of the poetry, and the poem holds pride of place in the earliest printed collection, *Saint Peters Complaint, With other Poemes*, 1595 (*Ca*). The problems attaching to the textual history of this poem have to be considered separately.

The printed editions of the poems are of particular importance because of their early date, and in spite of changes in the presentation of the lyrics made by the publishers, and carelessness in printing, it is necessary to consider these texts in some detail.

A full account of the manuscripts and printed books is contained in Father McDonald's *Bibliographical Study*. Only a summary description of those items he included will be given here, although additional bibliographical materials will be described in greater detail, together with some indication of the contribution each has made to the establishment of the text of this edition.

I. MANUSCRIPTS OF THE SHORT LYRICS

The five copies of the manuscript compilation can be identified by the collections in which they now are:

Stonyhurst College Library, MS. A. v. 27—*S*
Virtue and Cahill Library, See of Portsmouth (R.C.), MS. 8635—*VC*
British Museum, Additional MS. 10422—*A*
British Museum, MS. Harleian 6921—*H*
Folger Shakespeare Library, Harmsworth MS.—*F*

The first four of these manuscripts reproduce the same fifty-two short lyrics, which occur in the same order in all four; the fifth, *F*, following generally the order of the same group, omits those poems published in the earliest printed edition, *Saint Peters Complaint, With other Poemes*, 1595 (*Ca*), and adds a group of poems of doubtful authenticity.

None of the manuscripts can be closely related to the compilation made by the first editor, which may have retained typical features of Southwell's holographs. Each copyist has given his work a distinctive character which is not found again in any of the other manuscripts or in the printed texts; nevertheless some textual relationships are discernible.

I

STONYHURST COLLEGE, MS. A. v. 27 (*S*): 18·3 × 13·9 cm.; 80 leaves ([a]+1–79; only a fragment remains of the first leaf), in contemporary vellum binding with a central gilt medallion containing the letters I H S.

The volume was probably originally a volume of blank paper, sheets normally folded in quarto and sewn as gatherings of four leaves, but with some irregularities. The watermark throughout the volume may be identified with Briquet no. 5096, assigned to the 1580's, manufactured in Troyes by the Denise family.

The manuscript contains:

i. *Fols. 4–18*. Southwell's letter to his father, dated 22 October 1589. The title contains the name *Rob: Sou:*, and the letter is signed *R.S.*

ii. *Fols. 20–36*. Dedicatory letter, text, and eulogistic poems in Latin and English, published as *The Triumphs over Death*. It was originally written for Philip Howard, Earl of Arundel, after the death of his sister, Lady Margaret Sackville, and dated 'The last of September, 1591'.

iii. *Fols. 38–74*. Prose dedication and introductory stanzas, 'To the Reader' (beginning 'Deare eye that doest peruse . . .'), and the group of fifty-two short lyrics, in the order in which they are printed in this edition.

The other leaves in the volume are blank, except for a line in a child's hand on fol. 2: 'iereneme walDegrave is a gooD garle

BVt that noBoDi cer for her.' Jeronima's unhappy cry leads to one possibility in tracing the provenance and approximate date of the manuscript. The obituary notices of the English nuns of the Benedictine Abbey in Ghent record the death of Dame Hieronima Waldegrave, daughter of Nicholas Waldegrave, Esquire, on 22 July 1635.[1] She had entered religion twelve years previously, when she was about 20. Her father Nicholas was the second son of Sir Edward Waldegrave of Borley, Essex;[2] her mother was Catherine, daughter of Weston or Winstan Browne of Rookwood Hall, Roding-Abbess, Essex. On the basis of this identification the child Jeronima, born about 1603, scribbled in her irregular childish hand on the blank page of her father's manuscript perhaps in 1608 or 1609, and in this way she furnished a very plausible *terminus ad quem* in determining the approximate date of the manuscript. But Jeronima also had a cousin of the same name, daughter of Charles Waldegrave, her father's elder brother. Perhaps it was this little girl, and not the future Dame Hieronima, who recorded her misery at finding herself so unjustly unloved.[3]

This manuscript is the most reliable of the five copies now known. It is written in a single hand, except for one poem and occasional corrections by another. Both are secretary hands typical of the late sixteenth century, of scribal regularity. The principal copyist worked carefully, making few errors. He used few punctuation marks, confining these mainly to full stops—often at the foot of pages— and rarer commas. Letters elongated with a flourish obscure any punctuation at the end of lines. Although the manuscript has fewer marks of punctuation than the other manuscripts, in this it probably resembles Southwell's holograph more closely. The omission of such marks is most noticeable in passages such as 'Of the Blessed Sacrament', ll. 31–36, a stanza in which S has no punctuation marks, VC has five mid-line commas and a final full stop, A has two mid-line commas in the last line, and H has four mid-line commas.

---

[1] *C.R.S.* xix. 20. Father McDonald first suggested this identification of Jeronima; his note on the Waldegraves (p. 20) is rather confused.

[2] Nicholas Waldegrave's mother, Frances Neville, married Lord Chidiock Paulet after Sir Edward's death, and dedications made to her, and a poem on her name, were copied into Peter Mowle's Commonplace Book (*O*), pp. 94, 339, 340, and 342–3.

[3] Pedigree of the Waldegrave family, in Henry Foley's *Records of the English Province of the Society of Jesus*, v (London, 1879), opp. p. 382; Thomas Wright, *History of the Topography of the County of Essex* (London, 1831), i, p. 556, and ii, p. 343; Sir Egerton Brydges's edition of *Collins's Peerage of England* (London, 1812), ii, p. 373, and iv, p. 237.

None of the copyists of these manuscripts, however, were consistent in punctuation habits.

The original transcription of the poems was made from a manuscript resembling A,[1] but corrections have been made by a second hand after reference to another manuscript copy which was textually more accurate. This second scribe inexplicably took over the task of copying for the length of one complete poem, 'The prodigall childs soule wracke' (fols. 60^v–61). In making his corrections he improved readings where obvious errors had been introduced by the first copyist, and occasionally changed a spelling, but his most important work involves textual changes which could not have been made without consulting a textually superior copy.

In his edition of Southwell's poems in 1872, A. B. Grosart announced his discovery of this manuscript at Stonyhurst and used it as the source for his text, believing that the second hand was Southwell's autograph.[2] Although, as Janelle pointed out,[3] Grosart attributed far greater authority to the manuscript than can possibly be warranted, nevertheless it remains the most responsible of the five manuscript copies now in existence. In this edition S has been used as copy-text for those poems which do not appear in the early English editions: 'The death of our Ladie', 'The Assumption of our Lady', the last two stanzas of 'Christs bloody sweat', 'Of the Blessed Sacrament of the Aulter', the short twelve-stanza form of 'Saint Peters Complaynte', 'Decease release', and 'I dye without desert'.

Nothing is known of the history of the manuscript from the time it was in the hands of Jeronima Waldegrave until Grosart's record of it at Stonyhurst College. It seems most likely, however, that it is the manuscript described by Dr. George Oliver at Bury St. Edmunds, Suffolk, in 1832, a manuscript reported lost at the time of Grosart's preparation of his edition of the poems, and untraced by Father McDonald.[4]

---

[1] Corrections where S originally agreed with A may be seen at the following points: 'The Visitation', l. 5 (where A agrees with *Mœoniæ* [*Ma*]); 'Josephs Amazement', l. 12 (? original word in S is obliterated); 'Of the Blessed Sacrament', l. 32; 'Saint Peters Complaynte', ll. 8 and 69 (where A agrees with H in both places); 'A Phansie turned', l. 97; 'Seeke flowers of heaven', l. 20 (where A agrees with *Ma*, *VC*, and H); 'I die alive', l. 9; 'What joy to live?', ll. 9, 13 (where *VC* agrees with A), and 23; 'Losse in delaies', l. 12; 'Loves servile lot', ll. 22 and 45 (where *VC* and *Saint Peters Complaint, With other Poemes*, 1595 [*Ca*], agree with A); 'Lewd Love', l. 10 (where H agrees with A); 'Fortunes Falsehoode', l. 38; 'Content and rich', l. 21 (where *Ca* agrees); 'Scorne not the least', l. 11 (where *Ca* and H agree).

[2] Grosart, pp. xi, xxvi ff.   [3] Janelle, p. 305.   [4] Grosart, p. xxvi; McDonald, p. 25.

Dr. Oliver examined the manuscript in the library of the Catholic Chapel at Bury St. Edmunds, and published his account first in *The Catholic Magazine and Review* (Birmingham) in 1832, and later in his *Collections towards illustrating the Biography of the Scotch, English and Irish members, of the Society of Jesus* (London: Charles Dolman, 1845).[1] Between the time of Dr. Oliver's first reference to the manuscript and the publication of his book in 1845, however, the Jesuit priests who had staffed the Chapel handed their charge over to secular priests. It seems most reasonable to assume that when they moved from Bury the Jesuits would have sought the safest possible depository for their treasures in the great Jesuit library at Stonyhurst College.

II

VIRTUE AND CAHILL LIBRARY, MS. 8635 (*VC*): 76 leaves, of which the first is missing. The manuscript is bound with sigs. A–E of a copy of John Wolfe's first edition of *Saint Peters Complaint, With other Poemes*, 1595; this section of Wolfe's volume contains the text of 'Saint Peters Complaint'. The binding is of contemporary vellum, with a gilt device and the letters I H S, closely resembling that of *S*. The margins of the manuscript were cropped in binding, as may be seen by the partial cutting away of the gloss in the poem 'Christs returne out of Egypt', opposite l. 9. The leaves have been made to correspond in size with those of the printed text, 18 × 13·8 cm.

The manuscript is made up of gatherings of eight leaves, each consisting of two sheets of paper (with the exception of a single gathering of one sheet only). The paper has an elaborate watermark of a heraldic shield, quartered with spread eagle, castle, and two lions rampant, facing each other, with a crown above and a pendent fleece below. (Similar watermarks containing these elements, but with the arms of Austria set in the middle of the shield, may be seen in Briquet nos. 2291 and 2292. These are watermarks of 1587 and 1588, occurring, with variants, in books printed in the eastern German States and in the Low Countries.)

---

[1] In Dr. Oliver's description of the manuscript he cites the title of each poem, a record of the number of stanzas and of lines, and, in most instances, the first few words. Unfortunately he does not reproduce the original spelling consistently and he has occasional difficulty with the earlier hand, which would appear to have been a secretary hand, as is the hand of the copyist of *S*. His account includes the items in *S* except the prose introduction to the lyrics.

The manuscript contains:

i. *Fol. 1 (missing)*. This leaf may have held the prose dedication; there cannot be much doubt that it contained the introductory stanzas, 'To the Reader'. The earlier existence of the dedicatory poem is indicated by the numbering of the poems in the manuscript, which now begins with '2' (fol. 2). The missing leaf may have been deliberately removed when the manuscript was bound with the segment of the printed volume, which includes the dedication and the introductory poem (sigs. A2–3).
Fols. 2–51ᵛ. The poems are in the order of *S*, except that the order of 'Mary Magdalens blush' and 'S. Peters remorse' (fols. 22ᵛ, 24) has been reversed.
Fol. 52. Blank.
This part of the manuscript, fols. 1–52, was apparently planned as an entity. The final gathering is made up of one sheet only (fols. 49–52).

ii. *Fols. 53–62*. Southwell's letter to his father, the first item in *S*, and included also in *A*. It is signed *R. S.*

iii. *Fols. 62ᵛ–63*. 'An other letter perswasory to the same', beginning 'Understanding that you were resolved . . .' and signed *R. S.* This letter is headed 'A letter written to his brother' in *A*, where it is unsigned.

iv. *Fol. 63ᵛ*. 'An other letter written to one of his kinsmen', beginning 'I knowe not how to write . . .' and signed *R. S.* This letter is also in *A*, where it has the superscription 'A letter writen by P. B. to his coosyn. W. R.'.

v. *Fols. 64–75ᵛ*. Dedicatory letter, text, and appended poems of *The Triumphs over Death*, as in *S* and *A*.
Fol. 76. Blank.

The manuscript is of considerable value as a textual source. It was transcribed by a single hand, a regular and clear secretary hand, probably of the early seventeenth century. A *terminus a quo* for the date of its transcription is provided by an error in the title of the Epitaph concluding *The Triumphs over Death*, which commemorates 'Lady Buckehurst' in mistake for Lady Margaret Sackville. Sir Robert Sackville, Lady Margaret's husband, held the title of Lord Buckhurst from 1603 to 1612, when he succeeded his father as second Earl of Dorset. Although this error would indicate that the manuscript was transcribed at some time within these years, it is possible that it occurred first not in *VC* but in a copy from which *VC* descended.

The scribe was seldom careless in copying his text (although he made an unusual number of errors in copying 'A vale of teares'); there are few signs of erasure or emendation. He did not use abbreviations. In punctuation he inserted commas medially in the lines as the sense required, seldom at the end of lines; full stops occur at the end of stanzas, and occasionally in the middle of stanzas. Other marks of punctuation are rare.

VC agrees with *S* at thirteen points in the text of the poems,[1] and there are also two distinctive features found in both manuscripts independent of verbal analogies. The first of these features which both have in common affects the order of stanzas in the text of 'Lewd Love is Losse': in *VC* ll. 23–30, 31–36 are reversed; in *S* the original scribe, who followed the order of the poem as it was printed in Wolfe's second edition of *Saint Peters Complaint* (*Cb*) and as it appears in the other manuscripts, marked the stanzas for reversal. (The correct order of the lines is doubtful, since both stanzas contain a series of illustrations of the theme of the poem, and the sense is unaffected by a change in order.) The second, a marginal gloss on *Nazareth* in 'Christs returne out of Egypt', l. 9, occurs only in *S* and *VC* (where it has been cropped in the later binding of the manuscript).

But in spite of these points of agreement, the link between the manuscripts is not simple to establish. At a number of other points obvious similarities between *VC* and the printed text of *Mœoniæ* (*Ma*) indicate that there is a link with the copy available to John Busby.[2] The text of *VC*, however, is much more accurate than the printed text.

[1] *S* and *VC* offer identical readings at the following points where other textual sources differ: 'Her Nativity', l. 14 (a doubtful reading); 'A childe my Choyce', l. 3; 'New Prince, new pompe', ll. 9 and 27; 'Sinnes heavie loade', ll. 12, 14, and 39; 'Christs sleeping friends', l. 17; 'Marie Magdalens complaint', l. 39; 'At home in Heaven', l. 30; 'Fortunes Falsehoode', l. 10 (a rare word of doubtful connotation); 'Content and rich', l. 40; 'Scorne not the least', l. 11 (change in *S* by second hand to agree with *VC*).

[2] The text of *VC* agrees with that of *Ma* at the following points: 'Her Spousals', l. 15; 'The Virgins salutation', ll. 7 and 15 (where *A* also agrees at both points); 'His circumcision', l. 2; 'The flight into Egypt', l. 4; 'Christs sleeping friends', l. 37; 'A holy Hymme', l. 23; 'A vale of teares', ll. 5 and 65 (where *A* and *F* also agree with *Ma*); 'The prodigall childs soule wracke', ll. 11, 26 (with slight variation), and 27; 'Seeke flowers of heaven', l. 20 (where *A* and *H* also agree).

A brief report by Dr. L. F. Powell on this manuscript, which had then only recently come to light, was inserted into Father Mc-Donald's *Bibliographical Study*,[1] but no extensive account has been published. Nothing is known of its early history, although, as Dr. Powell noted, various signatures appear in the volume, two dated 1677 and 1678.

III

BRITISH MUSEUM ADDITIONAL MS. 10422 (*A*): 19·6×14·4 cm.; 110 leaves, damaged at the inner margins as a result of earlier binding. The volume has now a B.M. binding of dark-blue leather (nineteenth or twentieth century), lettered *Robert Southwell's Poems and Letters*.

The volume was originally made up of gatherings of eight leaves—two sheets folded in quarto. Each leaf has now been remounted in binding. The watermark is a pot watermark resembling Briquet nos. 12731 (French, mid-sixteenth century) and 12772 (French, late sixteenth century), with the letters *L D* in a central band, and the initial *I* below.

The manuscript contains:

  i. (A preliminary leaf, now lost, almost certainly contained the prose dedication, as in *S* and *H*, and probably originally in *VC* also.)
  Fol. 1(defective). The verse address 'To the Reader'; the verso is blank. This leaf is numbered in a modern hand '1'; that this was originally the second leaf is clear from the evidence of an earlier numbering, probably by the scribe himself, now frequently lacking as a result of cropping in binding.
  Fols. 2(defective)–47. The group of fifty-two lyrics in the same order as in *S* and *H*, and (with a single variation) in *VC*.
 ii. *Fol. 47–47ᵛ*. 'The Author to the reader', the dedicatory poem introducing the long 'Saint Peters Complaint'. The poem is transcribed immediately following the last lines of the last

---

[1] McDonald, p. 22. The manuscript was examined by Father Herbert Thurston, whose sheet of notes is still loose in the volume. Before the Second World War it was in the Virtue and Cahill Library in Portsmouth, Hants, and it was saved from destruction when the library was bombed by the foresight of the late Most Revd. J. H. King, Archbishop-Bishop of Portsmouth (R.C.), who took it with other library treasures for greater safety to his own house in Winchester.

poem in the group of lyrics, 'Scorne not the least', the last four lines of which are carried over on this leaf. The last stanza of the introductory poem is transcribed on the verso of the leaf, with a blank space following.

Fols. 48–64ᵛ. 'Saint Peters Complaint', the long form of the poem, 132 stanzas.

iii. *Fols. 65–82.* Southwell's letter to his father, as in *S* and *VC*.

iv. *Fols. 83–84.* 'A letter written to his brother', as in *VC*.

v. *Fols. 84ᵛ–85.* 'A letter writen by P. B. to his coosyn, W. R.' This letter is also in *VC*.

vi. *Fols. 86–109.* Dedication, text of *The Triumphs over Death*, and the Latin and English eulogistic poems, as in *S* and *VC*.

Blank pages at fols. 82ᵛ, 85ᵛ, 108ᵛ, and 109ᵛ–10 mark divisions in the manuscript.

The manuscript is in one hand throughout. Unfortunately, as Father McDonald wrote, 'the copyist sometimes solved his own difficulties with the text, and to all appearances he had more regard for the elegance of his written page than care for his readings'.[1] The copyist transcribed the body of the prose and verse in a secretary hand, varied with titles in an Italian hand. Letters in both secretary and Italian forms are ornamented with flourishes. In the transcription of the poems punctuation is rare at the end of lines, although medial commas are frequent.[2] He also used a number of conventional abbreviations, and throughout the part of the manuscript containing the poems he indicated the link between the gatherings of eight leaves with catchwords. Some of the numerous errors have been corrected—some apparently at the time of transcription, some later, though in the same hand—but many have escaped revision. A great number of spelling errors have been caused by the omission of essential letters, making nonsense of the text, and the omission of whole words also indicates both careless copying and inadequate revision.[3]

---

[1] McDonald, p. 25.

[2] In 'A childe my Choyce', for instance, the copyist has used twenty-one commas to indicate sense divisions in mid-line—one completely misplaced—and only one full stop, at the end of l. 9, where the rhythm of parallel phrases requires no great pause.

[3] Errors and revisions in 'Of the Blessed Sacrament', ll. 69–70, illustrate the haphazard work of the copyist. In l. 69 he omitted the word *be* in the phrase (here transcribed from *S*) 'or be Tenn thowsand fedd'; in the next line ('All to ech one, to all but one doth cumme') the copyist wrote first *All to each one or bee*, then changed *or* to *to*, crossed out *bee*, and proceeded *all but one.* . . . In spite of the eyeslip which caused trouble in the second line, he apparently never detected the omission in l. 69.

In spite of the general unreliability of the text, the manuscript is of interest because of the number of points of agreement with the printed texts, particularly with the first edition of *Mœoniæ* (*Ma*).[1] The addition of the long poem 'Saint Peters Complaint', with its introductory poem, is of particular importance, as will be shown in the discussion of the textual problems connected with this section of the manuscript.

A probably dates from the beginning of the seventeenth century. The attribution of Sir Edward Dyer's 'A Fancy' to 'Maister dier' in the title of the parody ('A Phansie turned to a sinners complaint') suggests that the transcription was made before Dyer's knighthood in April 1596, but it is more likely to be a copyist's slip.

The manuscript was formerly in the Heber library, where it was used by W. Joseph Walter in the preparation of his edition of 'Saint Peters Complaint' and a group of sixteen lyrics (London, 1817). He printed from it three poems which had been omitted in English editions, 'Of the Blessed Sacrament', 'Decease release' (which he incorrectly entitled 'Decease is release'), and 'I dye without desert'. The manuscript was acquired by the British Museum in April 1836, and it was later used as a textual source by William B. Turnbull in his edition, which he called 'the first complete collection', published in London in 1856. He included all the poems printed in the early volumes, together with the three first published by Walter, and three items previously unpublished, 'The death of our Ladie' and 'The Assumption of our Lady', and the two concluding stanzas of 'Christs bloody sweat'. He omitted the short form of 'Saint Peters Complaynte', which he would have found in the manuscript. It was also known to Grosart, who had a poor opinion of the copyist's work, but he nevertheless recognized its importance where it confirmed superior readings in *S*.[2] *A* was also used as copy-text in the edition of *The Triumphs over Death* published by John William Trotman in 1914.

[1] See, for instance, 'The Virgine Maries conception', l. 6; 'Her Spousals', l. 16; 'The Virgins salutation', ll. 7 and 15 (where *VC* agrees at both points), and 12 (two readings); 'The Visitation', l. 5; 'His circumcision', l. 14; 'S. Peters remorse', ll. 40 and 42; 'A vale of teares', l. 65 (where *VC* and *F* agree); 'Seeke flowers of heaven', ll. 4 and 20 (where *VC* and *H* agree). In 'Her Nativity', l. 14, 'The Epiphanie', l. 15, and 'A vale of teares', l. 42, the reading of *A*, originally agreeing with the other manuscripts, has been changed, so that it now agrees with *Ma*. It is not possible that *A* was a direct ancestor of *Ma*, since many of its errors do not recur, but the copyist of *A* may have referred occasionally to another manuscript closer to *Ma*.

[2] Grosart, p. xxiv.

IV

BRITISH MUSEUM MS. HARLEIAN 6921 (*H*): 20·3×14·1 cm.; 44 leaves, with an insertion of 14 blank leaves of paper bearing the same watermark, making a total of 58 leaves. The bottom of each leaf has been much damaged by water at some time before the present binding, which was carried out by the Museum during the nineteenth century, with the title *Southwell. Poems on Religion*.

The watermark is a variant of Briquet nos. 3453 and 3454, both more elaborate designs, developed from the simpler design of a cardinal's hat, with a five-petalled flower as counter-mark. The marks indicate Italian manufacture, typically Venetian, during the sixteenth century.

The manuscript contains:

i. *The first leaf*, unnumbered, pasted to the fly-leaf of the volume. The verso contains a table of Contents, in the same hand as the manuscript.

ii. *Fols. 1–42*. Prose dedication, introductory stanzas, and the group of fifty-two short lyrics, as in the other manuscripts already described.

iii. An insertion of *14 blank leaves*.[1]

iv. *The final leaf* of the manuscript, also blank, except for a name and a date: *Charles Cavendish 1620 Anno Dm̄i 1620*. These inscriptions, in apparently the same ink and in the same hand as the rest of the manuscript, are upside down in the volume.

This manuscript is clearly later than the three already described. It may have been compiled about 1620, as suggested by the date on the final leaf. It is written in an Italian hand in which the letters are not joined. There are a number of errors, and some unusual spellings. Mid-line punctuation occurs frequently, but there is no punctuation at the end of lines.

The name of Charles Cavendish associates *H* with the family whose later connexion with the Earls of Oxford would account for its presence in the Harleian collection. The most promising identification is with that Sir Charles who was a young man of about 25 in 1620, a younger brother of William Cavendish, who became

---

[1] These inserted leaves may have been intended for the transcription of 'Saint Peters Complaint', which with its introductory poem took 13½ leaves of letterpress in its first printing (*Ca*).

first Duke of Newcastle. Sir Charles may not, however, have been the copyist, although he may well have had the copy made.[1] He was a scholar and a gentleman, who was remarkable for his nobility of mind and of conduct in a strenuous age. He was unfortunately deformed from birth, but he drew great affection from those who knew him well. Clarendon said of him that he was 'one of the most extraordinary persons of that age, in all the noble endowments of the mind'.[2] His talents led him to scientific, and particularly to mathematical, investigation, and he moved freely in the world of scholarship during years of exile on the Continent. Tributes to his character are made in the writings of his sister-in-law Margaret, Duchess of Newcastle.[3] He died on 4 February 1654.

Readings link the manuscript with A and with that used as copy-text for the edition of the poems published by Cawood in 1602, *Saint Peters Complaint Newlie augmented With other Poems*.[4] A curious reversal of riming words in 'Josephs Amazement', ll. 8 and 10, is found in H and S (before correction), but this error is possibly coincidental, since the changes do not greatly affect the sense of the stanza.

H was examined by Grosart, but he believed it to be so full of copyist's errors that he rejected it as a serious source for textual evaluation, except where it agreed with the other British Museum manuscript, A, in confirming the readings of S.[5]

V

FOLGER SHAKESPEARE LIBRARY, HARMSWORTH MS. (F): 17.8×13.1 cm.; 88 leaves. The manuscript is bound with a made-up copy of John Wolfe's first edition of *Saint Peters Complaint, With other Poemes*, 1595. The original seventeenth-century calf binding

[1] A business letter written by Sir Charles in 1633, now in the Cavendish–Talbot MSS. (X. d. 428 [172]) in the Folger Shakespeare Library, is in a much less regular hand, and the signature bears only superficial resemblance to that in H.

[2] *Life of Edward, Earl of Clarendon* (3 vols., Oxford, 1827), i, p. 292; quoted in A. S. Turberville's *A History of Welbeck Abbey and its Owners* (London, 1938), i, p. 132, n. 2.

[3] *Nature's Pictures drawn by Fancies Pencil*, in Turberville, i, p. 132. Turberville reproduces a portrait of Sir Charles. See also *The Lives of William Cavendishe, Duke of Newcastle, and of his wife, Margaret Duchess of Newcastle* . . . ed. M. A. Lower (London, 1872), p. 89.

[4] Points of agreement in H, A, and *1602*, offering alternative readings, occur in 'New Prince, new pompe', ll. 9 and 27; 'Sinnes heavie loade', ll. 12 and 14. Identical errors in H and *1602* occur in 'New Prince', l. 27; 'Josephs Amazement', ll. 7 and 65; 'Davids Peccavi', ll. 7 and 28; and 'A Phansie turned', l. 68.

[5] Grosart, pp. xxiv, xxvi.

d

of the volume was replaced by a modern binding in 1959. The manuscript was foliated and repaired when the volume was rebound.

The manuscript is made up of paper of varying thickness, each sheet folded to make leaves roughly corresponding in size to a quarto volume. Fols. 3–50 (section iii, below) bear manuscript signatures as in a printed book in quarto, a–m⁴, the fourth leaf remaining blank. Each gathering of four leaves is normally made from a single sheet of paper; the six sheets comprising fols. 19–42 are so folded that chain-lines run vertically.[1] The paper is drawn from a number of different sources; the most distinctive watermark, occurring in three sheets in the later part of the manuscript, resembles closely the watermark listed in W. A. Churchill's *Watermarks in Paper in the 17th and 18th Centuries* (Amsterdam, 1935), no. 574, a paper of Nicholas Le Be of 1619 (cf. Briquet no. 8077).

The manuscript contains:

i. *Fol. 1* (sig. H4 of the printed book). 'Saint Peters Complaynte', of which the title and the first four lines of the twelve-stanza version are lacking. The poem was originally complete, written on the blank space at the end of the letterpress of the Wolfe edition, sigs. H3ᵛ and H4. (Sigs. H1–3 of this copy of the printed book are now missing and have been replaced with leaves from another copy.)

ii. *Fol. 2*. A single leaf on which are written two poems, '*Conceptio B. Virginis sub porta aurea*', and '*Præsentatio B. Virginis*', not found in any of the other manuscripts.

iii. *Fols. 3–50ᵛ*. The first part of this section, fols. 3–41ᵛ, contains (fols. 3–10) the fourteen poems of the Sequence on the Virgin Mary and Christ, including the two poems already in the printed volume to which this manuscript is appended, and (fols. 10–41ᵛ) twenty-seven poems roughly in the order of the other manuscripts, with the omission of all those in the printed volume and of the twelve-stanza version of 'Saint Peters Complaynte'. Three of the poems—'Decease release', 'I dye without desert', and 'Loves Garden grief'—are transposed from normal places to the end of the group. At this

---

[1] Two gatherings are not cognate: fols. 11 and 14 are on paper different from that of fols. 12 and 13; in fols. 55 and 58 chain-lines are vertical, while in fols. 56 and 57 they are horizontal.

point the manuscript, with the addition of the poems printed
in Wolfe's edition, accounts for the whole group of fifty-two
lyrics found in the other manuscripts.

The remainder of the section (fols. 41ᵛ–50ᵛ) contains twelve
poems not found in the other manuscripts. These include
another short version of the 'Complaint'; three poems published in *Mœoniæ*, 1595, entitled here 'Our Ladie to Christ
upon the Crosse' (with great textual variation), 'To the wound
in Christes side', and 'Upon the image of death'; and another
version of 'The Virgins salutation', entitled 'The Annuntiation altered from that before'.

  iv. *Fols. 51–68ᵛ.* The poem known as 'A Fourfold Meditation',
      attributed here to Philip, Earl of Arundel.

   v. *Fols. 69–86ᵛ.* Fourteen poems, in English and Latin, attri-
      buted to Henry Vaux, son of Lord Vaux.[1]

  vi. *Fols. 86ᵛ–88ᵛ.* An incomplete poem in an irregular childish
      hand, beginning 'Up drowsie Muse pule downe thy harpe
      from pinne'.

The incomplete state of the last poem suggests that other leaves
were rejected when the manuscript was first prepared for binding
with the printed sheets. What was retained was otherwise the work
of a single hand, an undistinguished Italian script. The detailed
punctuation, indicating the logical pattern of thought in each stanza,
points to a date perhaps as late as 1650. The signature of 'I. Phillips'
and the date 1774 appear on the title-page of the printed book;
the volume passed to the Folger Library from the Harmsworth
collection.

The unusual features of the compilation provide some information,
necessarily rather negative, about the nature of the materials with
which the compiler was working. First, he already had in his
possession the copy of Wolfe's first edition (*Ca*) which now makes up
the main portion of the printed sheets comprising the first part of the
volume. (It now lacks the original title-page, sig. A1, and sigs. H1,
2, and 3.) Not only did he make a considerable number of corrections and other changes in the letterpress, but as he worked on his
manuscript copy he omitted all those poems in the printed text,
with the exception of the two poems which Wolfe had so arbitrarily

---

[1] Seven of the poems attributed to Henry Vaux are published in Godfrey Anstruther,
O.P., *Vaux of Harrowden* (Newport, Mon., 1953), Appendix C, p. 502.

removed from their proper places in the Sequence, 'The Nativitie of Christ' and 'Christs Childhoode'; these two he copied with the rest of the poems of the Sequence, in the places where they correctly belong. Second, the order in which he copied the poems indicates his use of a manuscript closely resembling those that have survived. It was apparently a late copy, containing some textual points of likeness with *H*, and the manuscript used for the printing of the additional poems in 1602. The slight variations made in the order of the poems in *F* do not appear to have much significance. The compiler omitted the twelve-stanza version of 'Saint Peters Complaynte' because he had already copied it in the blank space at the end of the letterpress. Three other poems were transferred to the end of the group of lyrics. It is a strange coincidence that two of them, 'Decease release' and 'I dye without desert', were poems excluded from all early printed editions; they are found together in the other manuscripts, and it may be that in the manuscript used by this copyist the leaf on which they were written had become detached. Perhaps it was also merely accidental omission that transposed the third poem, 'Loves Garden grief', to the end of the group.

A third point, and the most perplexing, concerns the additions made by the compiler. It is apparent that he had, together with the printed book and the manuscript, a number of other sources, presumably manuscripts of single poems, or perhaps of groups of poems; the passage of twelve lines inserted in the text of 'Christs bloody sweat' may have originated in such an independent source. From the materials available he selected twelve poems to add to that section of the manuscript which already contained the bulk of Southwell's lyrics; two other poems, connected in style and subject-matter to the Sequence, are inscribed on a single leaf, now bound in the front of this section. The authenticity of these fourteen poems will be examined in the discussion of the canon of the poems.

The numerous changes made by the compiler both in the pages of the printed text and in his own manuscript show him to be not only copyist but assiduous editor. In most cases his method of revision was to erase the offending letters—whether printed or from his own pen—and to make the changes he desired by writing in ink upon the roughened surface, leaving blurred letters and ink-stains through the thickness of the paper. At other points he deliberately obscured the original reading by writing directly over it; sometimes he added letters or marks of punctuation, scarcely distinguishable in the manuscript except by slight differences in the colour of the ink. His perseverance is, however, a very doubtful virtue. He removed obvious misprints or scribal errors—his own or those in his copy. He was at pains to clarify corrupt passages, but very often his changes are fanciful and weak elucidations of a text he failed to understand. His changes in 'Saint Peters Complaint' do not at any point prove that he had access to a manuscript copy of that poem; changes in the lyrics where the text is not in agreement with either the printed editions or the other manuscripts clearly do not represent authoritative revision. Although his irresponsibility is to be regretted when every scrap of textual evidence must be considered in the problem of securing both canon and text of Southwell's work, nevertheless it must be remembered that this compiler was engaged not so much in copying as in assembling a volume of poems gathered for his own taste and pleasure, and including work clearly attributed to other hands than Southwell's, more in the tradition of the commonplace book than in the tradition of the manuscript transmission of texts.

VI

Besides these five manuscript copies containing the short lyrics the poems are preserved in commonplace books of the seventeenth century. Of those that have been examined the only one to draw directly upon manuscript sources is the compilation of Thomas Fairfax, preserved in the Bodleian Library (MS. Eng. Poet. b. 5; *B*), dating mainly from 1651 and 1652, with a few later entries dated 1654 and 1657. He copied, among other verse, thirty-one poems of Southwell's, including some which would only have been available in manuscript, and four of those doubtfully attributed to him. The poems are scattered throughout the compilation, and the order in which they appear is independent either of the order in the manuscripts or of that in the printed editions. Other commonplace books in which a number of the lyrics are transcribed from early printed sources include the compilation made by Thomas Read, student of Magdalen College, Oxford, in 1624, now in the Arendts collection, and the volume in the Harleian collection (B.M. MS. Harleian 6910). Manuscripts of this nature, marked by the personal taste of the scribe, or of the adult who guided a child's writing task, are of interest only as they shed light upon the manner of the transmission of texts; none shows any textual authority.

VII

Although the common tradition of the five manuscripts of the short lyrics is unquestionable, the precise relationship of one to any of the others, or to the ancestor from which they all derive, can no longer be discerned. But in spite of the loss of so many intermediary links, and the absence of any clear line of descent, particular family features suggest relationships between the manuscripts, and reveal also links with the manuscripts—now lost— which provided the copy-texts of the printed volumes.

Unfortunately few of the numerous points of agreement which might be held to indicate relationship are significant; most are typical scribal variants. But where more noteworthy substitutions have been made, if they are added to the body of less significant evidence it is possible to make some evaluation of the manuscripts in the transmission of the text. *S*, carefully written by an original copyist whose work was later corrected after reference to a more authoritative manuscript source, is undoubtedly the most reliable. *VC*, which has many points of agreement with *S*, must also be considered an important textual source. The text represented by *A*, however, is one in which numerous corruptions have already appeared; a number of these are also to be found in the earlier state of *S*, and yet others are perpetuated in the inaccurate texts of *Mœoniæ* and of the additional poems printed in *Saint Peters Complaint*, 1602, and in *H*. *F*, in which the typical features of the copy-text have been overlaid with much editorial activity, also provides many points of agreement with *A* and *H*, and with the printed text of the poems in the edition of 1602. The value of all these manuscripts in the recovery of the text of the short lyrics can be better estimated after more particular examination of the printed editions.

II. MANUSCRIPTS OF 'SAINT PETERS COMPLAINT'

Southwell's longest poem, 'Saint Peters Complaint', was chosen by John Wolfe to stand first in the earliest printing of the poems, a volume which incorporated the name of the poem in its title, as if to persuade the purchasers that they were getting solid return for their outlay. His choice is the more interesting because the poem had no place in the manuscript compilation of lyrics. In the five existing copies it is included only in *A*, where it is added as a separate item at the end of the lyric compilation, preceding the prose letters and the text of *The Triumphs over Death*. A second manuscript copy is contained in the Commonplace Book of Peter Mowle of Attleborough (*O*). Little textual authority can be claimed either for the manuscript copies of the poem or for the printed version.

The copyist of *A*, as has been said in the discussion of the earlier part of his manuscript, was extremely careless, seldom revising his work, which is marred by the omission of words and letters, and by the substitution of words. The same errors are to be found throughout his transcription of the 'Complaint'; again some are clearly the result of reading manuscript copy.

O, described in detail by Father McDonald, is a volume of both prose and verse on religious subjects, copied diligently from various sources, including both printed books and manuscripts. The volume was originally acquired by Peter Mowle as a book of blank paper, bound in leather with the initials *P M*—one on each side of a central design—on each cover. The paper was folded into quarto size, bound in gatherings of 8's. Its watermark, a pot with the letters *P D* in a central band, with *B* below, identifies it with Briquet no. 12793, a paper found in Bayonne in 1583. Peter Mowle bought it at some time before his first dated entry in 1589; as he proceeded to copy out the various items he would occasionally tear away a leaf, presumably a method of deleting serious copying errors. Shorter items were sometimes compressed on to a blank page between longer items.[1] On the verso of the first leaf of the quire on which the beginning of the 'Complaint' is transcribed (p. 137, according to the early pagination), Mowle has recorded a gift sent to the Viscountess Hereford of Parham at the New Year 1592, an entry interpreted by Father McDonald as a reference to the copying of the poem; but his argument that the copy was made at this early date is inconclusive. It is likely that the gift consisted simply of those items on the same page as the record of the name and date—a Christmas poem

---

[1] McDonald, p. 29. Various dates relating to the transcriptions are haphazardly scattered: 28 April 1595 (p. 1), 1597 (p. 90), 1592 (p. 137), 26 December 1601 (p. 161), 1602 (p. 162), 1589 (p. 164), 1590 (p. 266), 1595 (p. 339), 1595 and 1606 (p. 340), 1605 and 31 January 1605 (pp. 355–6).

of five stanzas, and a stanza of greetings by Mowle himself, sent 'With a Picture of the Nativitie of our Lord'. The transcription of the 'Complaint' on other leaves of the same gathering suggests that it was not copied about the time of the New Year's celebrations of 1592 (probably January 1593), but after that date. The top section of p. 138 has been cut away. Below it a line is drawn, and the title of the poem follows: 'SAINT PETERS Complainte after his relapse in the denyall of our Savyour, with a Lyvelye and sweet discorse of his sorowe for the same, set forth into most seemlye (Inglysh) meeter, the rather for the delight of the Devout Reader.' Well-known lines entitled here 'Doctor Heath uppon the Blessed Sacrament of the Aulter', beginning 'As Christ willed yt and spake yt', are transcribed on the same page, with a pen drawing of an acorn, and a design of flowers and acorns. The verso, p. 139, contains lines entitled 'Mr. Moore his verses' in the hand of 'Peter Mowld Junior' (as on pp. 355-6, where the date of *31 Januarii 1605* is found). 'The Author to the Reader', the introductory poem to the 'Complaint', follows on p. 140, and the poem begins on the verso of the leaf, p. 141, numbered '1' in Peter Mowle's hand.

Little confidence may be placed in the work of Peter Mowle. He was, it is true, a more accurate copyist than the compiler of *A*, but his text bears the signs of thoroughgoing textual emendation. At many points it is clear that the meaning has not been fully understood; at others an unusual word has been replaced by one in common use, sometimes when such a change seriously weakens the meaning or reduces it to nonsense. At a few points extensive changes have been made, as at ll. 19-20, where Mowle's text runs:

> Yee mourning plaintes, ye ecchoes of my ruthe
> whose lowdest skrikes, in frighted conscience ringe.

Mowle's responsibility for these editorial changes cannot be assessed, nor, since he was compiling his volume for his personal use, can he be censured for his lack of literary judgement. He was undoubtedly a devout Catholic, neither artistically sensitive nor with more learning than might become a provincial gentleman, but entirely well-meaning, and confident of the merit in his labour.

Although their textual relationship has been partly obliterated by the careless copying in *A* and the editorial changes in *O*, both manuscripts show numerous points of agreement. In at least thirty-one instances they provide readings superior to those of the earliest printed text (*Ca*),[1] and at fourteen other points they are in agreement where the text of *Ca* provides a better reading or a reading where changes to accord with the manuscripts are not justified.[2] In both sixteen stanzas (ll. 235–330) are erroneously transferred to a place later in the poem, after l. 714. *A* provides Biblical references as sidenotes to the text of the poem. Not all are accurate, and there is no reason to suppose that they are Southwell's notes. They were provided, however, early in the textual history of the poem, appearing also in the second edition of the 'Complaint' (*Cb*) and thereafter in the English editions to 1615.

As will be shown in an attempt to reconstruct the circumstances of the composition of the poem, these two manuscript sources and the manuscript which was used in the printing of the two earliest editions were closely related to a common ancestor, itself probably not far removed from Southwell's holograph.

III. THE EDITIONS

The first editions of the poems in 1595 followed immediately upon the execution of Southwell in February. The popular demand for the poetry reflects the extraordinary response of the London crowd to Southwell himself. The first edition of *Saint Peters Complaint, With other Poemes*, appearing probably in March, was followed by a second edition before some of the type for the first edition had been distributed. When Gabriel Cawood secured the copyright in April and started his series of editions, he may have been confident that he had obtained the rights to a commercial success. The other compilation of poems, *Mœoniæ*, was issued by John Busby in three editions all dated 1595, and even if the date does not accurately indicate the time of the appearance of the later editions, it points to the enthusiasm for the poetry in that year.

The manuscript copies from which the printed texts were set up were transcriptions of the poems made by Catholic copyists for dissemination of the work among those of the Old Faith. The publishers were responsible for the selection of poems, changes in their order, and variant textual readings. In their handling of the materials they had available they showed much greater freedom than the

---

[1] Ll. 33, 107, 171, 193, 205, 239 (punctuation), 258, 273, 288, 391, 399, 425, 439, 484 (2), 501, 517, 551, 606, 615, 628, 638, 640, 659, 671, 674, 700, 709, 748, 788, 789.
[2] Ll. 37, 69, 108, 166, 215, 235, 289, 513, 546, 580, 583, 630, 698, 735.

Catholic copyists, and they were careful to select poems that did not express specifically Catholic doctrine. The initials *R. S.* on the title-page of *Mœoniæ* and the references to the earlier volume, *Saint Peters Complaint*, in John Busby's prefatory letter 'To the Gentlemen Readers', indicate that the identity of the writer of the poems in both volumes was no secret to the publishers or to their London customers.

I

John Windet was commissioned by John Wolfe to print the first edition of the poems, *Saint Peters Complaint, With other Poemes* (*Ca*; *S.T.C.* 22957 [*ii*]). It was followed immediately by a second enlarged edition from the same printing-house (*Cb*; *S.T.C.* 22957 [*i*]), and then by a third, formally entered in the Stationers' Register by Gabriel Cawood on 5 April, 1595, and printed by James Roberts for Cawood during the same year (*Cc*; *S.T.C.* 22956).

The first volume from the press is a slim one, comprising the prose letter of dedication and the poem addressed to the reader (used as introductory material to the whole compilation of lyrics in the manuscripts), the introductory poem to 'Saint Peters Complaint' followed by the long form of the poem, and twelve short lyrics. The collation of the volume is as follows:

4°: A–E⁴ [each leaf signed; misprinting D3 as D5] F–G⁴ [regularly signed] H⁴ [signed to H2; H4 blank]; 32 leaves.

The variation in the method of signing gatherings corresponds to the main division of the contents of the volume. The first part, sigs. A–E, contains the title-page, introductory material, and the text of 'Saint Peters Complaint'; the second part, sigs. F–H, contains the twelve lyrics, in the following order:

'Mary Magdalens blush'
'Marie Magdalens complaint at Christs death'
'Times goe by turnes'
'Looke home'
'Fortunes Falsehoode'
'Scorne not the least'
'The Nativitie of Christ'
'Christs Childhoode'
'A childe my Choyce'
'Content and rich'
'Losse in delaies'
'Loves servile lot'.

Seven of these poems are to be found among the final ten lyrics in the manuscript compilation. Three are poems on the child-hood of Christ, two of them drawn from their proper places in the Sequence on the Virgin Mary and Christ. The last poem in the volume, 'Loves servile lot', has been oddly mistreated: ll. 49–76 of the poem are omitted, and in their place the last four stanzas of 'Seeke flowers of heaven', ll. 9–24, are substituted. This error was corrected in Wolfe's second edition, *Cb*, when the full text of 'Loves servile lot' was published and the lines from 'Seeke flowers' silently omitted. In this second edition Wolfe also included a further eight lyrics, all drawn from the last group of poems in the manuscript compilation.

The contents of these two editions indicate Wolfe's possession of manuscript copies of the 'Complaint' and of the group of lyrics. The selection, remaining unchanged until Cawood's additions in 1602, suggests that Wolfe did not have available a manuscript of the same type as those now surviving, but one less complete, made up largely of the Sequence and the group of poems to be found at the end of the manuscript compilation. The only other collection of the lyrics known to have been made is that gathered by Southwell himself and sent to his relative with the dedicatory letter and the verse address 'To the Reader', used by Wolfe in his edition. Copies of the collection were probably in circulation, and Wolfe may have come into possession of one of them as long ago as 1591, when he printed *Marie Magdalens Funerall Teares* for Cawood. But whether or not Wolfe's copy was indeed a manuscript of the poems Southwell assembled, it was either a less extensive manuscript collection or an incomplete manuscript of the full compilation; it is most im-probable that he deliberately held back from publication lyrics he had bought for printing, allowing John Busby, with his publication of *Mœoniæ*, to seize the opportunity he missed. If he is not to be held guilty of such commercial misjudgement, it must be concluded that Wolfe had no complete copy of the full manuscript compilation, and that Busby came into possession of one after Wolfe's second edition appeared.

The three copies of *Ca* now known to exist have been collated in preparing this edition. Only one, *Ca* (*HEH*), in the Henry E. Huntington Library, is complete as it was first issued. The copy *Ca* (*F*), formerly in the library of Sir Leicester Harmsworth, now in the Folger Shakespeare Library, is made up from two and perhaps three separate copies, and bound with F; sigs. H1–3, and probably also the title-page, sig. A1, were added to an original copy in the possession of the compiler of F, who made revisions in the printed text, including slight changes in ink in the three leaves substituted for the original leaves of sig. H. The original leaf H3 contained the title and first four lines of 'Saint Peters Complaynte', the poem the compiler transcribed in the blank space at the end of his original volume, and which survives on the remaining leaf H4. The third copy, Ca (VC), from the Virtue and Cahill Library, now at Winchester, is imperfect, consisting only of sigs. A–E, and bound with VC. Because of the accidental printing of sig. D on two sheets— evidently picked up together from the pile supplying the press, their contiguous sides remaining blank as they were machined— this copy may never have been complete. Alternatively, although it would appear to be a strange action to discard a printed text in favour of manuscript materials, it is possible that the leaves containing the short lyrics (sigs. F–H) were removed when the copy was bound with the manuscript, and that at the same time the first leaf of the manuscript, containing the introductory items included in the printed book, was similarly torn away.

The small volume is freely decorated, and a study of the recurrence of the title-page device and ornaments used in the letterpress, based on an examination of books in the Folger Shakespeare Library, points to John Windet as the printer responsible for both editions of the *Complaint*, although his name does not appear. The most noteworthy feature of the printing of the volume is the amount of type that was undistributed before work was started on the second edition, Cb. Pages of type which were corrected and used again in printing Cb include outer and inner F, inner G, and outer and inner H. The speed with which the editions followed each other is also indicated by the obvious error in the confusion of the text of the poem 'Loves servile lot' with that of 'Seeke flowers of heaven', which would perhaps not have remained undetected if this last sheet, sig. H, had not immediately been added to the rest and the volume put on sale. While the type was still standing, the error was recognized, and the pages revised for the second edition.

Although this blunder was missed in Ca there is some evidence in the three copies now remaining that in the course of printing the earlier sheets some press-correction was undertaken. The evidence relates only to the forme of outer D, which in the copies *HEH* and *VC* has been printed from an 'uncorrected' state, while in *F* some attempt to correct has been made, with the result that two textual errors are introduced ('Complaint', ll. 631 and 712). The casual correction of the forme ignored at least six other errors in the text which it contains. It is clear that no collation of the printed text and the manuscript copy was undertaken, but only occasional reference was made to the copy.

Many of the errors occurring in the text of *Ca* are those customarily found in work printed or transcribed from manuscript copy. Probably as a result of hasty setting, when the compositors' normal spelling habits tended to be replaced by those in the manuscript copy, the text retains some of the 'abbreviated' phonetic spelling forms that Southwell habitually used. A greater number of forms of this distinctive kind is to be found in *Ca* and *Cb* than in any of the manuscripts or in later editions of the poems, and their presence strengthens the suggestion that Wolfe had in his possession manuscripts not far removed from the holographs both of the 'Complaint' and of the short lyrics. An error which occurred early in the transmission of the text of the 'Complaint'—the transposition of sixteen stanzas (ll. 235–330) to a place after l. 714—is found also in the Wolfe editions.

Although the text of *Ca* shows many signs of hasty preparation, with numerous careless errors left uncorrected, nevertheless at nine points in the 'Complaint', at l. 26 in 'Marie Magdalens complaint', and at ll. 15 and 27 of 'Loves servile lot', the readings are superior to those of later editions.[1] The changes made in the edition immediately following, *Cb*, probably necessitated only incidental reference to the same manuscript copy deposited at the printing-house when *Ca* was set in type. The correction of the text could have been carried out in most cases by careful reading, with attention to metrical regularity and grammatical structure, by an editor with the advantages of a wider vocabulary and more accurate scriptural knowledge than was possessed by the earliest compositors. Subsequent revision of the text at times of later publication on no occasion took the form of consistent collation with an earlier manuscript source. In spite of its shortcomings, therefore, *Ca* must be regarded as a substantive text, which in the absence of any authoritative textual

---

[1] In the 'Complaint' superior readings are found at ll. 5, 319, 420, 429, 611, 628, 661, 665, and 698.

source deserves serious study as the earliest dated compilation and printing of Southwell's poetry.

II

The second edition of *Saint Peters Complaint* (*Cb*) adds twenty-eight lines to 'Loves servile lot' and a further eight lyrics to the compilation. For these poems it must be treated as a substantive text. It has already been shown in the account of *Ca* that this second edition from Windet's press followed hard upon the first, so that standing type was corrected and used again. In page layout it follows *Ca* to sig. H3, the point at which the earlier edition appended stanzas of 'Seeke flowers of heaven' to the first part of 'Loves servile lot'. In *Cb* these transposed lines are removed, and the text of 'Loves servile lot' is completed, followed by the additional eight lyrics:

> 'Life is but losse'
> 'I die alive'
> 'What joy to live?'
> 'Lifes death loves life'
> 'At home in Heaven'
> 'Lewd Love is Losse'
> 'Loves Garden grief'
> 'From Fortunes reach'.

These lyrics, all drawn from the latter part of the manuscript compilation, were printed in the order in which they occur in the surviving manuscripts, omitting only those poems already printed in the earlier edition.

The collational formula of the volume is as follows:

4°: A–E⁴ [each leaf signed] F–H⁴ [regularly signed] I⁴ [each leaf signed] K²; 38 leaves.

Only two copies of this edition are known. One, *Cb* (*TC*), is in the Capell collection at Trinity College, Cambridge, and the other, *Cb* (*HEH*), at the Henry E. Huntington Library. Some press-correction, confined to the correction of misprints—in one case, the substitution of a preferred spelling—was carried out in the formes for outer C, inner F, and inner I in these copies; other slight variations appear to be accidents in impressing the type.

In the examination of the two editions issued by Wolfe the close relationship between them becomes increasingly clear. Not only is *Cb* a page-by-page reprint of a 'corrected' copy of the earlier edition,

to the last poem it included, but *Ca* is followed also in the reproduction of the same ornaments on corresponding pages—with an
inexplicable transposition of ornaments on F4 and G3—and in the
copying of catchwords and signatures.

The reason why a second edition was undertaken so soon after
the printing of the first can now only be surmised. Unlike most
publishers, who normally advertise the addition of material in successive editions, Wolfe made no reference to the enlarged group of
poems in *Cb*. It is possible he was disappointed with the condition of
the text so hastily put out, insisting on revisions and additions to
maintain his sales. The text of *Cb* shows in fact considerable revision
both in the sheets that were completely reset and in those where
standing type was corrected. Sidenotes giving Biblical references
were set in the margins of the 'Complaint', not always accurately.
These sidenotes, which are in *A* also, must have been present in the
manuscript copy, although ignored in the earlier edition. Apart from
the correction of obvious misprints, at nineteen points in the text
of the 'Complaint' the reading of *Ca* is improved in *Cb*; in twelve
of these the later reading is confirmed by *A* and *O*, in two by *A*
alone, and in two by *O*. The number of corrections suggests that
reference was made to the manuscript copy, although most changes
could have been improvised by a careful reader.[1] Textual corruptions recurring in later editions are introduced in nine instances
where *Ca* is seen to be superior; these changes have support from
both manuscripts in one instance, from *A* alone in two, and from
O alone in three instances. In the shorter poems nine superior readings are supplied in *Cb*; only one, in 'Loves servile lot', l. 10, is a
change that presupposes reference to a textual source.[2] Although
many of the obvious misprints and textual errors in the earlier
edition are removed, presumably with some reference to the same
manuscript sources used in the preparation of *Ca*, there is no evidence of systematic collation and, except for its additions, the volume
cannot be considered a truly substantive text.

[1] The text of the 'Complaint' is improved at ll. 101, 171, 201, 235, 273, 278, 351,
391, 399, 501, 548, 551, 606, 628, 669, 671, 674, 709, and 788.
[2] 'Times goe by turnes', l. 3; 'Fortunes Falsehoode', l. 37; 'Scorne not the least',
ll. 11 and 18; 'Content and rich', l. 21; 'Losse in delaies', ll. 20 and 41; 'Loves servile
lot', ll. 10 and 45. These changes in 'Loves servile lot', together with the addition of the
final twenty-eight lines of the poem, are offset by deterioration in the text at ll. 15 and
27, the retention of corruptions at ll. 31 and 36, and the introduction of a faulty reading
in the newly supplied final lines at l. 65.

III

Cawood's edition of 1595 (*Cc*) shows careful textual revision, but there is no evidence that it is of substantive authority. Cawood was the first to make a record in the Stationers' Register.[1] His entry is dated 5 April 1595:

> Master Cawood / Entred for his Copie a booke entituled *Saincte PETERs Complainte with MARY MAGDALENs blusshe and her Complaint at CHRISTes deathe*[,] *with other poemes* / Master Binges hande beinge at it. Master HARTWELLes hande was likewise at the Copie. / . . vi^d

Isaac Bing, who approved the entry, was Under Warden, serving with Cawood, who was himself Senior Warden of the Company in this year. Although entry was technically required before publication, under penalty of fines, in contemporary practice publishers frequently disregarded the rule, and Wolfe's neglect is not an unusual occurrence. Nevertheless, it seems very likely that it was he, and not Cawood, who obtained the necessary ecclesiastical licence, granted by Abraham Hartwell, secretary to Archbishop Whitgift, and one of the official licensers of books. The 'booke' submitted for examination to the Wardens of the Stationers' Company was either the manuscript copy of the poems as it had been prepared for the printing of *Ca*, and enlarged with additional lyrics for *Cb*, or a copy of one of the two editions already printed. In either case, it was the same that had been submitted for the earlier ecclesiastical licence, and which therefore already bore Hartwell's signature.

The work of printing was carried out by James Roberts,[2] who was responsible also for the three successive editions of *Saint Peters Complaint* (*1597*, *1599*, and *1602*). He later printed an edition of *Marie Magdalens Funerall Teares* for William Leake, to whom Cawood's privileges were assigned.

The collational formula of *Cc* is as follows:

4°: A–B⁴ [all leaves signed] C⁴ [regularly signed] D–E⁴ [all leaves signed] F⁴ [regularly signed] G–H⁴ [all leaves signed] I⁴ [regularly signed]; 36 leaves.[3]

---

[1] *Stationers' Register*, ii, p. 295.

[2] A single compositor prepared the pages of type. On the evidence of his spelling habits he may be identified with Compositor Y, whose work in the quarto editions of *Hamlet* (*Q2*, 1604/5) and of *The Merchant of Venice* (1600) has been examined by J. R. Brown (*Studies in Bibliography*, vii. 17).

[3] Examination of quartos issued from Roberts's printing-house during the period 1594–1601 has not brought to light any other example of a book containing more than

In the same way that *Cb* was set up from a 'corrected' copy of *Ca*
to the last poem included in the earlier edition, so Roberts used a
copy of *Cb* as copy-text in the work of printing this third edition.
The contents of *Cb* and *Cc* are identical but, as may be seen from
the collational formulas, Roberts compressed the same material into
thirty-six leaves, and thus avoided the necessity of printing the half-
sheet K which completed the earlier volume.

Although the entry in the Stationers' Register and points of
textual superiority led Father McDonald to suppose that Cawood's
edition was the first legitimate printing, based on Wolfe's earlier
'pirated' edition (*Ca*) and an independent source which Cawood had
procured,[1] an examination of the editions shows clearly that *Cc* is in
fact a third edition, and that no new materials were available in its
preparation. Printing irregularities and textual variants confirm the
relationship. In the printing, changes in catchwords illustrate the
sequence of the editions: on sig. E4^v, for instance, at the end of
the 'Complaint', *Ca* has 'Mary' as catchword for the title of the first
of the short poems, which actually is repeated on F1 as '*Mary*'; *Cb*
also has 'Mary' as catchword, following *Ca*, but in the title it appears
as '*Marie*'; *Cc* takes the catchword '*Marie*' from the title in *Cb*, but
later sets the title itself in roman capitals: 'MARY'.[2] Textual changes
provide incontrovertible evidence of the order of the printing. In
the text of the 'Complaint' *Cc* assigns the sixteen stanzas incorrectly
transposed in the earlier editions to their proper place in the poem.
Such an obvious correction, once made, could not be overlooked in
later editions; there is therefore no doubt that the text of *Cb* was set
up before the appearance of *Cc*. Since there is reason to believe that
this error was to be found in the manuscript copy available to Wolfe,
now presumably handed over to Cawood together with the printing
rights, the correction was most probably made by an alert reader.
Other corrections in the text of the 'Complaint' suggest occasional
reference to the manuscript or to a copy of *Ca*, but there is no

a single accidental signing of the fourth leaf of a quarto gathering. The occurrence of
fully signed gatherings in this volume, in the proportion of two fully signed gatherings
to one regularly signed, is almost certainly due to the influence of the copy, *Cb*, in which
one of Windet's compositors signed all leaves.

[1] McDonald, pp. 73–75, 76, 77–78.

[2] Other variants in catchwords may be studied on G1^v, G2, and G2^v, where *Ca* and
Cb take the catchword in each case from the first line of the following poem, and not
from its title; after this point *Cb* takes catchwords from following titles (with an error
on sig. H1^v); the compositor of *Cc* is misled on G1^v, where he gives the first word of the
following poem, but elsewhere he regularly uses the first word of the title.

sign of regular collation, nor of any use of a more authoritative
source.[1] Similar treatment of the text is to be seen in the shorter
poems.[2]

IV

Five subsequent editions of *Saint Peters Complaint* were issued
before any attempt was made to combine its contents with other
items of Southwell's work in verse and prose to make up a more sub-
substantial volume. Rights of publication remained with Cawood,
who continued to employ Roberts to print the successive editions.
The first two, *1597* (*S.T.C.* 22958) and *1599* (*S.T.C.* 22959), are
merely reprints of *Cc*. There are no signs of consistent textual revision in these editions, which are page-by-page reprints, except that
the awkward compression of the page layout in those gatherings
containing the shorter poems in *Cc* was avoided by the re-allocation
of stanzas. The dependence of *1597* upon *Cc*, and of *1599* upon its
predecessor *1597*, is clearly established by textual changes. In the
text of the 'Complaint', for instance, *1597* introduced six variants,
all of which were retained in later editions; in *1599* three slight
changes were made.[3] Few textual changes were made in the shorter
poems in either edition.[4]

Cawood's regular succession of editions at two- or three-year
intervals could not be sustained without some additional incentive

---

[1] Sixteen misprints and manifest errors appearing in the text of the 'Complaint' in
Cb, and a misprint derived from *Ca* (l. 748), are corrected in *Cc*; the reading of the
'uncorrected' state of outer D in *Ca* is recovered at l. 712 (although the error at l. 631
remains undetected). In three instances textual changes in *Cc* give superior readings;
in two of these, at ll. 33 and 638, *Cc* agrees with *A* and *O*, but at l. 85 both manuscripts
reproduce the error of *Ca* and *Cb*. Six textual corruptions are introduced, and a change
of doubtful value, though in agreement with *A*, is made at l. 149; these are perpetuated
in later editions.

[2] Five obvious errors and misprints in *Cb* are corrected, although two are introduced;
other errors first occurring in *Ca* are removed in 'Loves servile lot', ll. 31 and 36 (where
reference to the original manuscript was probably made), and in poems first published
in *Cb* a correction is made in 'At home in Heaven', l. 33. But three obvious errors in
the text of poems in *Ca* remain uncorrected.

[3] Most important of the variants in *1597* is the recovery of the text at l. 484 and of the
regular metrical pattern at l. 615, both changes supported by *A* and *O*.

[4] In *1597* the correction of *dignities* to *dignitie*, as required by the rime, in 'Fortunes
Falsehoode', l. 26, is finally made, but a further change at l. 21, where the ambiguous
waies is spelled *way's*—the form repeated in later editions—may not indicate the correct
interpretation. A spelling correction is made in 'Marie Magdalens complaint', l. 35, but
other changes in both *1597* and *1599* are erroneous.

offered to the buyers. In his last edition, *1602* (*S.T.C.* 22960*a*), he sought to gain renewed public interest by the addition of a further group of seven poems, for which this edition provides a substantive text. This 'newlie augmented' edition includes all the poems now known in the surviving manuscripts, with the exception of those already published in *Mœoniœ*, the short version of 'Saint Peters Complaynte', and a few others containing Catholic doctrine or political reference. This correspondence between the contents of *1602* and the poems in the manuscript copies suggests very strongly that at this time Cawood had come into possession of a manuscript of the same type as those surviving. With this new material, however, he made no attempt to revise the text of poems already printed in his earlier editions; *1599* supplied the copy for this part of the volume (sigs. A–I).[1]

The poems added in this edition (sigs. K1–M2) may have been arranged according to subject. The first chosen is actually the last of the seven in the manuscripts, a parody of Sir Edward Dyer's 'A Fancy', here entitled 'A Phansie turned to a sinners complaint'. From the same group of penitential poems Cawood also printed 'Davids Peccavi', and added the first of the manuscript group based on meditation on Gethsemane, 'Sinnes heavie loade'. The remaining four poems are all concerned with the Nativity: 'Josephs Amazement', and the three still unpublished from the Nativity group in the manuscripts, here printed in reverse order, 'New Prince, new pompe', 'The burning Babe', and 'New heaven, new warre'. These poems were the last to be printed by English publishers until the discovery of the manuscripts in the nineteenth century.

The proportion of errors in the text of these seven additional poems is much higher than in Cawood's earlier editions of *Saint Peters Complaint*; some may be accounted for by the greater difficulty in setting from manuscript than from printed copy, and others, occurring also in one or more of the surviving manuscript copies, were probably already present in the manuscript submitted to Roberts for printing. Even the manifest error of the omission of l. 14 in 'Davids Peccavi' is perhaps not to be attributed to the carelessness

---

[1] Although the change in 'The Epistle Dedicatory' from *censurers* to *censures*, as in *S* and *H*, may have been made after reference to a manuscript copy, the text of *1599* was otherwise closely followed. There are no revisions in the 'Complaint', for which it may be assumed Cawood had no new manuscript material.

of the compositor, but to the state of his copy, since the line was
never recovered in later editions. The total number of instances
where *1602* has no support from any known textual source except
the comparatively late and unreliable *H* and *F* undermines any
confidence in its variants.[1]

After Cawood's death in 1602 his printing rights in *Saint Peters
Complaint* were assigned to William Leake, whose single edition
(*L*; *S.T.C.* 22961), printed by Humphrey Lownes, is undated, but
was probably produced in the period 1607–9.[2] Although there is no
question of authoritative revision, Leake's edition with *1602* as copy-
text has been prepared by an intelligent reader.[3]

The eighth English edition of *Saint Peters Complaint* (*S.T.C.*
22962), printed by William Stansby for William Barrett, is dated
1615, although the entry in the Stationers' Register transferring the
rights of publication from Leake to Barrett was not made until
February 1616/17.[4] By this time the state of the text has deteriorated
considerably; no attempt at revision was made, and the accumulation of errors greatly reduces the interest of the edition. At
fifteen points where the text of the 'Complaint' diverges from
that of *L* errors are introduced, to be duly handed down to the
editions of the collected works in 1620, 1630, and 1636. In a single
instance only, in 'What joy to live?', l. 22, does *1615* recover the text
of the manuscripts, in removing a corruption which had been allowed
to persist rather unaccountably since the first printing of the poem
in *Cb*; the St. Omer edition of 1620 also makes this change, indepen-
dently of the English editions. Elsewhere in the poems *1615* adds
seven more errors to the burden now being borne.

V

Besides the editions published in England, two editions of *Saint
Peters Complaint* came from Scottish presses. The first of these

---

[1] Of five doubtful readings in 'A Phansie turned' one appears in *H* and *F*, and two
more in *F* only; in 'Davids Peccavi', of six variants two are in *H* and *F*, and two in *F*
only; three of the ten variants in 'Josephs Amazement' are in *F*, and one of these
in *H* also; in 'New Prince', two variants occur in *A*, *H*, and *F*, and one is in *H*; in
'Sinnes heavie loade', two variants are found also in *A*, *H*, and *F*, and one in *A* and *F*.

[2] McDonald, p. 89.

[3] In the 'Complaint' the text of *Ca* is recovered at ll. 145, 429, and 631, and in the
shorter poems *L* shows some sensible correction, even though the text supported by the
manuscripts is not regained in every case.

[4] *Stationers' Register*, iii, p. 603.

(*S.T.C.* 22960) was a quarto printed by Robert Waldegrave, who had been granted the title of 'Printer to the Kings Majestie', and who therefore issued the volume '*Cum Privilegio Regio*'. The edition (*W*) is undated, but Father McDonald's suggestion of 1599 as the most likely date is strongly supported by the evidence of the paper and a distinctive ornament on sig. A3.[1]

The contents of this edition are those of the English editions *Cb* to *1599*, with the addition of a sonnet entitled 'A sinfull soule to Christ', signed 'I. I.' and inserted at the end of the 'Complaint'. There is no reason to suppose that this sonnet, beginning 'I lurk, I lowre, in dungeon deepe of mynd', is Southwell's work. The occurrence of the typical readings of *1597* show that this edition provided the copy-text for *W*.

Some of the textual changes in *W* were made on religious grounds. Biblical references in sidenotes were changed to accord with the names of Old Testament books as they appeared in the Bishops' Bible. Other textual revisions in the 'Complaint' suppress references to the Mother of God as intercessor (ll. 577–87), and other points of Catholic doctrine; some changes seem to have been made at the whim of the editor, but alone of all the early editions *W* punctuates l. 161 of the 'Complaint' to indicate correctly the sense of the line.

Waldegrave's printing of the *Complaint*, like his printing of Sidney's *Arcadia* in 1599 (*S.T.C.* 22542), may have been an attempt to gain illicit profits from sales in England of a work he recognized as an established best-seller. Such a hypothesis receives some support from his use of the Bishops' Bible in making sidenote references, where the Geneva Bible, authorized by the Church of Scotland, might be expected. Whether copies were sold in England or not, it is a curious comment on commercial practices to find a printer who had suffered for issuing illegal Puritan tracts now profiting from the work of a Jesuit Mission priest.

The second edition to be issued in Scotland was printed by John Wreittoun in 1634 (*S.T.C.* 22967). It contains the introductory items, the text of the 'Complaint', and 'Content and rich'. Textual variants show it to have been set up from a copy of *1615*; it is of very little bibliographical interest.

---

[1] McDonald, p. 82. The watermark appears to be composed of the letters I R G, and not, as Father McDonald thought, I R C. The ornament, a floral design $7 \cdot 1 \times 1 \cdot 6$ cm., frequently found in books from the press, shows wear, with damage on the lower left side of the central figure, as in other books of 1599 and 1600.

VI

Two other editions of *Saint Peters Complaint* remain to be considered. These were produced by the Jesuit press at St. Omer in 1616 and 1620 (*S.T.C.* 22963 and 22964). The St. Omer edition of 1616 (*SOa*) attempts a new alignment of the poems in the volume of *1602* used as copy-text. The regrouping has been carried out with the intention of imposing some unity upon the previously disconnected lyrics. The material in the volume is arranged in two parts: the first based upon the 'Complaint', and the second upon the prose work here entitled *Saint Mary Magdalens Funerall Teares*. A selection of the shorter poems follows each of these pieces, and in order to clarify the plan of the volume, titles are changed, and in two cases two poems are printed as one. As a result of this editorial activity, in the first part the preliminaries and text of the 'Complaint' are followed by four poems printed as follows:

'Saint Peters Peccavi' (made up of the poems entitled in *1602* 'Davids Peccavi' and 'Sinnes heavie loade')
'S. Peters Returne home' ('Looke home' under a new title)
'Saint Peters Comfort' (made up of the two poems 'Scorne not the least' and 'Times goe by turnes')
'Saint Peters Wish' (the text of 'Life is but Losse').

Following a similar pattern, the second part is made up first of the prose work, *Saint Mary Magdalens Funerall Teares*, then of a group of eight poems to complete the volume:

'S. Mary Magdalens Blush'
'No Joy to live' (elsewhere entitled 'What joy to live?')
'S. Mary Magdalens Traunce' (the text of 'Lewd Love is Losse')
'S. Mary Magdalens farewell' (the text of 'From Fortunes reach')
'At home in Heaven'
'Christs Nativity'
'Christs Childhood'
'The Christians Manna' (entitled in the manuscripts 'Of the Blessed Sacrament of the Aulter').

The selection of poems shows that the editor of *SOa* had available both a copy of *1602* and a manuscript source from which 'The Christians Manna' was set up. His use of *1602* rather than a later edition is clear from the recurrence of textual errors. The recovery of the text of earlier printed editions at two points, and an unsuccessful attempt to correct the grammatical construction of *1602* in

'Sinnes heavie loade', ll. 1 and 2, probably represent only editorial guesses. The lack of any consistent revision suggests that the manuscript material available was very limited.

Nevertheless, the editor of *SOa* had some manuscript material in his possession, and its nature is of particular concern because of some inexplicable additions made in this printing. 'The Christians Manna', published for the first time in this volume, has so many variants in the text as to suggest that the copy used was itself incomplete or damaged, or that the poem had been subjected at some time to both carelessness and editorial irresponsibility. Even more mysterious are the additions to the introductory prose dedication. The letter, appearing without superscription in the manuscripts, is now introduced with the words 'To my worthy good cosen Maister W. S.', and begins 'Worthy Cosen . . .'. It ends with the addition 'Your loving cosen, R. S.' The greater emphasis upon the personal nature of the dedication has led to considerable speculation concerning the identity of 'W. S.'[1] Unfortunately, nothing in this first edition from a Jesuit press points to any source acquired directly from Southwell or his associates on the Mission. The puzzle of 'W. S.' may have its origin in a tradition preserved by the Jesuits of St. Omer, or perhaps only in the imagination of the editor of the poems.

The second edition issued by the St. Omer press four years later (*SOb*) is the first to identify the author of the poems as 'the R. Father Robert Southwell, Priest of the Society of Jesus'. It contains the same material as the first, and is indeed a page-by-page reprint of the poems, with some editorial revision. Obvious misprints, as in the numbering of stanzas in the 'Complaint', are removed, but there is no indication of collation with an independent text, or even with the copy-texts available for the printing of *SOa*.

VII

The little volume *Mœoniæ* represents the second attempt by a London publisher to cull from manuscript sources a group of Southwell's lyrics that would appeal to readers of religious verse without expressing obviously Roman Catholic doctrine. The rights of publication were secured to John Busby by an entry in the Stationers' Register on 17 October 1595;[2] three editions, all dated

---

[1] See, for instance, Devlin, ch. 18.   [2] *Stationers' Register*, iii, p. 50.

1595, were printed for Busby by Valentine Sims.[1] The group of poems was not printed again until the 'collected edition' of Southwell's poetry and prose published by William Barrett in 1620.

The contents of *Mœoniæ*, described on the title-page as 'Certaine excellent Poems and spirituall Hymnes', were apparently selected and arranged by Busby himself, and he is probably also responsible for the classical title, with its reference to Mœonia, the ancient name for part of Lydia, in western Asia Minor, associated with lyric song, and reputedly the birthplace of Homer. In a prefatory letter Busby explained to his reader that his collection was intended to augment and complement the poems in the earlier *Saint Peters Complaint*:

> Having beheld (kind Gentlemen) the numberlesse Judges of not to be reckoned labours, with what kind admiration you have entertained the Divine Complaint of holy Peter; and having in my hands certaine especiall Poems and divine Meditations, full as woorthie belonging to the same, I thought it a charitable deede to give them life in your memories, which els should die in an obscure sacrifice, gently embrace them, gentle censurers of gentle indevors: . . . nor could I other wish, but that the courteous reader of these labors, not having already bought Peters Complaint, would not for so small a mite of money loose so rich a treasure of heavenly wisdome as these two Treatises should minister unto him, the one so needfully depending upon the other.[2]

The contents of the three editions correspond exactly. The first group of lyrics consists of ten poems from the Sequence on Mary and Christ. In his prefatory note Busby continued with the explanation that he had omitted the poem on the Nativity because of its earlier appearance in the *Complaint*; he did not mention that he had also omitted 'Christs Childhoode', which was in the other volume, and the two final poems, 'The death of our Ladie' and 'The Assumption of our Lady'. The poems from the Sequence are followed by nine short lyrics:

> 'Christs bloody sweat' (first two stanzas only)
> 'Christs sleeping friends'
> 'A holy Hymme'
> 'S. Peters afflicted minde'

---

[1] *S.T.C.* lists only two editions, 22954 and 22955; the examination of copies listed as 22955 for their agreement in reading *The* as catchword on sig. B3 (p. 5) showed that three copies were those of a separate and earlier edition.

[2] 'The Printer to the Gentlemen Readers', *Ma*, sig. A2.

'S. Peters remorse'
'A vale of teares'
'The prodigall childs soule wracke'
'Mans civill warre'
'Seeke flowers of heaven'.

These are printed in the order in which they are found in the surviving manuscript collections, but with the omission of all those already published in *Cb*, and of other poems—or, in the case of 'Christs bloody sweat', two stanzas of a poem—that, for reasons sometimes difficult to assess, were considered unsuitable for inclusion in the group. This choice of poems strongly suggests that Busby had a copy of the manuscript compilation. The evidence is supported by his publication about the same time of *The Triumphs over Death*, a prose work which seems to have been habitually included in the manuscripts of the poems, and is now preserved with them in *S*, *VC*, and *A*.

Even more mysterious than the inexplicable omissions from the manuscript compilation is the inclusion of three poems found in the surviving manuscripts only in *F*. The first of these, 'The virgin Mary to Christ on the Crosse', is printed after 'Christs sleeping friends'; the second, 'Man to the wound in Christs side', is printed following 'S. Peters remorse'; it is followed immediately by the third poem, 'Upon the Image of death'.

Although the date *1595* appears on all three of the title-pages of these early editions of *Mœoniæ* it would be unwise to suppose that all three are to be assigned to the brief period between the registration of the copyright in October and the end of the business year in March 1596. It is more reasonable to assume that Busby obtained only the ecclesiastical sanction before the volume was made available to the public. When the sales of *Mœoniæ* revealed an unexpected best-seller, then, like Cawood before him securing his rights to the *Complaint*, Busby registered the title to safeguard his interest, issuing the second and third editions as supplies were needed during the next few years, and retaining the date *1595* on the title-page for its rather uncertain value as the date of Southwell's execution, and the date of the first editions of his poetry. Unless this rather free interpretation of the dates of entry and publication is accepted, it must otherwise be concluded that Busby seriously underestimated the demand for the volume not once, but twice, causing Sims to set up the text three times within a few months. The hypothesis that the issue of the editions was more spaced out than appears from the date on the title-pages is supported by an examination of surviving copies of the editions, which has not produced any example of a copy made up from mixed sheets. What is of greater concern than the precise date of the editions of *Mæoniæ*, however, is their relative importance as textual sources.

Three copies only of Busby's first edition (*Ma*) are known: two copies are in Cambridge, one in the Capell collection at Trinity College, and the other in the Young collection at the University Library; the third is in the library of Wellesley College.[1] This edition bears close resemblance to the other two editions, but it is in fact both an earlier and a more accurate printing than either of the two previously described by Father McDonald.[2] Copies of the later edition with which it has been confused in *S.T.C.* (both listed as 22955) are identified as *Mb*, and copies of *S.T.C.* 22954 as *Mc*.

Ma is a small quarto volume; the measurements of the Capell copy, bound with other items to Edward Capell's own specifications, are 18·2 × 13·7 cm., and those of the Young copy, in a later binding with other items, 17·5 × 12·8 cm. The following distinctive features may be noted on the title-page:

(a) The colon after *Hymnes* (l. 5) is erroneously in italic fount instead of roman;

(b) *as* (l. 8) is ligatured, whereas it is printed in a fount of separate letters in *Mb* and with a broken ligature in *Mc*;

(c) The *N*'s of *LONDON* are swash letters, as in *Mc*.

The collational formula of the volume is as follows:

4°: A² B–E⁴; 18 leaves.

The great number of errors in the volume is indicative of hasty setting from manuscript copy. At least thirty-two textual errors in *Ma* may be attributed to misreading, although not all can be laid to carelessness in the printing-house, for the occurrence of some of them in existing manuscripts, particularly in *A* and *VC*, suggests that they were already present in the printer's copy. The later editions of *Mæoniæ* also supply a poor text. They reproduce many of

---

[1] The copy at Wellesley College lacks the leaf A2, for which leaf A2 from a copy of *Cc* has been substituted; curiously, a corresponding substitution has taken place in the copy of *Cc* at the Huntington Library, in which leaf A2 has been replaced by leaf A2 from a copy of *Ma*.

[2] McDonald, pp. 101, 105.

the errors of the first, without any attempt to correct the text by collation with the copy, and additional errors mar the poems still more severely. More than sixty clear errors are sustained in all three editions; even where blatant nonsense has been produced in *Ma* the succeeding editions merely attempt half-hearted emendation, often no more than changes in the punctuation. Most outstanding of all the errors is the loss of a complete line in 'The Virgins salutation', an omission which would certainly have been corrected with careful proof-reading, unless by chance the line was also lacking in the manuscript available in the printing-house.

The page layout, identical in all three editions, was presumably retained for ease in printing, even though revision is clearly needed. The poems are printed without stanza divisons—an economy which perhaps had its source in the manuscript copy. The reason for crowding pages in sig. E is less explicable. The last three poems in the volume, 'The prodigall childs soule wracke', 'Mans civill warre', and 'Seeke flowers of heaven' (sigs. E3ᵛ–4ᵛ), are printed in small italic fount, with every indication of compression. These pages were not revised in the later editions, in spite of available space on sig. E1ᵛ, and on the previous sheet.

Of the three editions *Ma* has less errors than the other two, and on textual examination is shown to be the earliest. *Mb* contributes six more textual errors and six misprints, while correcting nothing in the text except five obvious misprints. The six errors are variants at points where *Ma* agrees with *S* and other manuscripts. Four of these six readings in *Mb* are obvious errors, and it may be postulated that the correct text would have been recovered if *Ma* had been set up later than *Mb*; the remaining two could only have been recovered in a later printing after collation with a more authoritative source—but there is no evidence of any consultation, much less of systematic collation at points in the text where no error would be suspected.[1] *Ma* was therefore printed first, and served as copy-text for *Mb*.

Mc does not reproduce the errors first appearing in *Mb*, but it adds

---

[1] The four manifest errors occur in 'Her Spousals', l. 13, 'Christs returne out of Egypt', l. 12, 'A vale of teares', l. 50, and 'Mans civill warre', l. 11; the two variants which would be less easily detected are the substitution of *into* for *unto* in 'Christs returne', l. 15, and inversion of *wisdome* and *reason* in 'Mans civill warre', ll. 15 and 17. A copy of *Mb* was used in the preparation of *1620*, when three of the obvious errors were corrected, but the two variants where the sense was not seriously distorted, together with the error in 'A vale of teares', were undetected, and were perpetuated in later editions.

to an already bad text thirty-five errors and two misprints. With such a burden of printing faults it could not have preceded the other two editions. At each one of the six points which are significant in determining the dependence of *Mb* upon *Ma*, *Mc* retains the correct readings of *Ma*; it is therefore clear that *Mc* was also set up from a copy of *Ma*.

The text of *Mc* appears to be the work of a clumsy editor whose attempts at emendation reveal his lack of understanding in his desire to simplify involved syntax or imagery.[1] Of the three errors corrected in *Mc* one is the change of the catchword *The* of sig. B3 to *His*, the first word of the title 'His circumcision' of the following page. It was unfortunate that this catch-word, identical in *Ma* and *Mb*, was used in *S.T.C.* as the touchstone for the recognition of the editions of *Mœoniæ*.

The relationship of the three editions as indicated by textual variants is confirmed by variations in the accidentals of punctuation and spelling. The comparatively sparse punctuation of *Ma* is considerably augmented in the two later editions. At points in the text of the poems the compositors have apparently tried to correct faults by emending the punctuation, but seldom with any improvement.[2]

That *Mb* and *Mc* are later editions than *Ma* may also be illustrated in terms of increasing independence in spelling. Although the relationship of Busby's manuscript copy to Southwell's holograph cannot be determined, distinctive features of his spelling, such as the phonetic 'shortened' forms, appear irregularly in the text of *Ma*. These are reproduced less frequently in the later editions. In *Mc* the general spelling habits resemble those in *Ma* so closely that it must be supposed that the same compositor was responsible for setting both editions. On the other hand, the spelling habits illustrated in the text of *Mb* show striking differences, and indicate that another compositor was at work.

---

[1] Examples of editorial activity may be seen in 'The Virgins salutation', l. 8 (*thee* substituted for *they*); 'The Visitation', ll. 6 (*neighbours* for *neighbour*) and 16 (*did cause* for *did force*); 'The Epiphanie', l. 9 (*their passage they did finde*), with minor changes at ll. 8, 13, and 18.

[2] In 'A holy Hymme', ll. 55–57, a difficulty arose in *Ma* with the omission of the preposition *in* (l. 56), an error which was perhaps in the printer's copy; the compositor has attempted to emend the passage by punctuation at the end of lines. *Mc* follows *Ma* without change, but the compositor of *Mb*, trying to make sense, transferred a colon previously set at the end of l. 56 to l. 57, and used a spate of commas in these and the following lines.

VIII

The first attempt by an English publisher to issue a substantial amount of Southwell's work in a single volume was made by William Barrett in 1620 (*S.T.C.* 22965), when he reprinted the two collections of verse together with the prose works, *Marie Magdalens Funerall Teares*, *The Triumphs over Death*, and the revised form of *A Short Rule of Good Life* (now entitled *Short Rules . . .*). The various items were attributed to the authorship of R. S., and Barrett makes clear reference to the identity of the author in his dedication to Richard, Earl of Dorset, one of the children of Lady Margaret Sackville, whose death in 1591 was the reason for Southwell's writing *The Triumphs over Death*. The title-page of the volume was engraved to illustrate the contents, and was used again in later editions in 1630 and 1636. The printer was Richard Field, whose typical device appears on the inner title-pages; distinctive ornaments and decorated capitals from his stock are used throughout.

This collection of two books of verse and three prose items in a small 12° necessitated an entirely new page layout for both *Saint Peters Complaint* and *Mœoniæ*. The sidenotes added to the 'Complaint' were now abandoned, and long lines of verse were divided into two shorter lines, although the original length was still indicated by the indentation of the second line and the absence of a second initial capital. A copy of *1615* was used to set up the 'Complaint' and the poems regularly printed with it; a copy of *Mb* provided the text for the poems of *Mœoniæ*. The texts of both underwent some editing, and at some points original readings were recovered, but there is no evidence of collation or even of reference to an earlier text, either manuscript or printed book. In the 'Complaint' and the poems with it textual corruptions were removed at three points. In the group of poems printed as *Mœoniæ* the most extensive editing is to be found in the translation of '*Lauda Sion*'— 'A holy Hymme'—where the Catholic doctrine of transubstantiation is excised, and the poem made to conform with the Anglican doctrine of the Eucharist.

The second printing of this collection, again in 12°, was carried out by John Haviland in 1630 (*S.T.C.* 22966). The publication rights were held at this time by John Parker,[1] but his name does not appear. A device used by Haviland is to be found on the inner

---

[1] *Stationers' Register*, iv, p. 128.

title-pages. The poems in *1630* are reproduced as a page-by-page reprint of *1620*, with only slight changes in setting up the dedication, and occasional correction in catchwords.

Haviland undertook a second printing of the volume a few years later, when again there was no indication that Parker was responsible for the edition (*1636*; *S.T.C.* 22968). Although the date 1636 appears on the title-page, it is likely that much of the work of printing was carried out earlier; the date 1634 appears on the inner title-pages of *Mœoniæ*, *Marie Magdalens Funerall Teares*, and *Short Rules of Good Life*.

Neither of these last editions, *1630* and *1636*, is of textual interest. Except for inconsequential variation in page layout in sig. G, *1636* is a page-by-page reprint of the poems in *1630*. Changes in the text of the poems are in every case unauthorized variants introduced in the course of printing; in accordance with contemporary spelling changes the comparative conjunction *then* is consistently altered to *than*.

In 1638 the printing rights were reassigned directly to Haviland and John Wright,[1] but they did not issue another edition. Presumably the growth of Puritan sentiment, particularly strong in the capital, put an end to the succession of English editions of Southwell's work.

IX

The course of the printing history of *Saint Peters Complaint* and *Mœoniæ* illustrates in both cases the publishers' lack of concern with the accuracy of the text; only in the instance of Wolfe's second edition of the *Complaint* (*Cb*) is there any indication of careful revision, and here it is most unlikely that there was consistent collation with the manuscript source. When fresh manuscript materials came into a publisher's hands, as at the time of Cawood's augmented edition of 1602, and the St. Omer edition of 1616, no textual collation of the manuscripts with poems already in print was undertaken. The first appearance of each poem therefore supplies the only substantive text from the abundance of printed copies; subsequent printings offer variant readings which may represent either spot-reference to an earlier source or, in most cases, more-or-less fortunate guesses on the part of editor or proof-reader. These early editions in their turn

---

[1] *Stationers' Register*, iv, p. 432.

supplied the text of poems or parts of poems reproduced in various books of this period of Southwell's greatest popularity. None of these excerpts appears to have been based on any source more authoritative than an earlier printed text.

The brief account of the editions given here includes some estimate of the sensitivity of judgement displayed by the textual editors, but in general their literary perceptivity was limited by the purpose of their revision. With the exception of the St. Omer editions the poetry was printed for its commercial value, not specifically for its religious content, and textual changes were made primarily to appease censors, to satisfy the educated reader by removing obvious errors or cruces in meaning, and in the later editions to increase public interest in volumes whose contents, set out with some concern for elegance, provided variety in subject and style.

IV. CANON AND DATE OF THE POEMS

The preceding account of the manuscript sources of the short lyrics and of the long poem, 'Saint Peters Complaint', and the brief descriptions of the printed collections of the poems have shown that no authoritative text of any of the poems is known. The attribution of them to Southwell is also no more than a traditional assumption of his authorship. The manuscripts contain no direct ascription of the poems to him; the superscription of the Letter to his Father in *S* contains an abbreviated form of his name, *Rob: Sou:*, and prose items in both *S* and *VC* are signed *R. S.* The editions of 1595 were issued anonymously or with the initials *R. S.* The publishers were clearly confident that their readers would be able to associate the poems with Southwell, the object of great public interest at this time, in spite of government policy in keeping the circumstances of his trial and execution secret. The publishers' assumption may have been rashly overconfident; the earliest references to Southwell's poetry in the 1590's do not include any indication of authorship, with the exception of the description of 'Decease release' as 'Des vers de Mr Southwell' in a note dated 1596 among the Bacon Papers—and this poem was not included in the early editions. The attribution of the poems to Southwell was not made directly until his name appeared on the title-page of the St. Omer edition of 1620. The question of the authenticity of the poems is complicated by the related questions of the time and conditions of writing. It is convenient to study first the problem as it applies to the authenticity of the lyrics in the five manuscript copies; second, the question of the more doubtful authenticity of poems included in *Mœoniæ* and in *F*; third, the stronger doubt raised by the poems found only in *F*; and last, the particular problems attaching to the composition of the 'Complaint'.

I

There seems to be no doubt that the compiler of the manuscript collection of short lyrics believed he was assembling Southwell's work and excluding material from other hands; his confidence was transmitted to the later copyists who so scrupulously preserved the whole group of fifty-two lyrics in the order which had been established. Only *F* makes any additions to this compilation. No other similar collection of lyrics has ever been ascribed to the poet. It would follow, therefore, that the poems first collected were believed to represent the whole of Southwell's lyric output to the time of his arrest. But in view of the circumstances under which the collection was made we wonder if any literary executor, however conscientious, could have been sure either of excluding poems which were not Southwell's, though they were found among his papers, perhaps in his hand, or of including all his work. Copies of the poems must have been found in all states of readiness and probably in several places; some poems had already been distributed to friends to whom they had been committed for circulation; some may have been put aside as unsatisfactory, some unrevised or mere drafts of future work. Nevertheless, no serious doubts of the authenticity of the poems in the compilation have ever been expressed. It would appear that the unknown editor worked with extraordinary perseverance and care, and neither his contemporaries nor later critics have questioned his selection. In my own examination of the poems I feel the greatest reluctance in including in the canon 'A holy Hymme', the translation of St. Thomas Aquinas's '*Lauda Sion salvatorem*'; it has kept its place in this volume mainly out of respect for the compiler's judgement.

Within the compilation groups of lyrics distinguished by subject or by metrical form are discernible that indicate parallel developments in lyric writing rather than any clear evolution of a particular style. The existence of these groups serves to confirm the ascription of the poems within a group to a single hand, but they do not enable us to find any order of composition within the larger compilation. Some apparently unsophisticated forms of lyric writing may actually include late work of considerable artistic complexity. Literary parodies of the kind represented by the two poems based on lyrics of Sir Edward Dyer are examples of experimentation in the contemporary fashion of love-poetry adapted for spiritual teaching, but within the form itself the parody may be either an exercise in line-by-line adaptation—as is much of 'A Phansie turned'—or a more sophisticated restatement of idea and phrase—as is 'Content and rich'. Similarly, the group of poems based upon moral admonitions, including 'Times goe by turnes', 'Losse in delaies', and 'Scorne not the least', apparently exercises in the fashion of writing such verse as was printed in popular collections like *The Paradise of Dainty Devices*, may have hidden relevance for the persecuted English Catholics; with this interpretation they are not so dully commonplace as they would seem to be.

A recognizable characteristic of the verse is an extraordinary metrical flexibility. Southwell appears to have had an almost unerring ear, although the effects for which he strove may be no longer pleasing to readers untrained in rhetorical patterns, who may well be irritated by the laboured and sustained balance of phrases, e.g. in 'A childe my Choyce'. At times he is clearly experimenting with unusual metrical structures, as in 'Loves Garden grief'[1] and 'Fortunes Falsehoode'. There are other poems that lack this musical sensitivity and have little stylistic originality; nevertheless, these may not be summarily dismissed from the canon. Such poems may be literary exercises to regain facility in writing English; it is to be expected that his first attempts at writing verse on his return to England would be mainly derivative, traditional in metrical forms, perhaps somewhat archaic in language. These features are to be found in poems such as 'The prodigall childs soule wracke', 'Mans civill warre', 'S. Peters afflicted minde', and 'S. Peters remorse', all printed in *Mœoniæ*. These poems are based on subjects which had occupied his mind in earlier days, when he wrote his Latin poem, '*Filii prodigi porcos pascentis ad patrem epistola*', and worked on the translation of Tansillo's *Le Lagrime di San Pietro*.

---

[1] Father H. Thurston suggested (*The Month*, 1895, p. 239) that Southwell used for his model Nicholas Breton's poem, 'A strange description of a rare Garden plot', published in *The Phoenix Nest*, 1593. Breton's poem, in poulter's measure, begins 'My garden ground of griefe: where selfe wils seeds are sowne . . .'.

While the ascription of these poems to the early years of writing English verse must be purely hypothetical, a stronger case may be made for ascribing to the earlier period two poems which apparently contain references to political events. The poems 'Decease release' and 'I dye without desert' stand out in the compilation for unusual features in subject and treatment. They commemorate the ordeal of two who suffered for their religion, and both appear to have been written under the emotional stress of recent events. The name *Mary* in 'Decease release' (l. 14) in *VC* and *A* associates the poem with the execution of Mary Queen of Scots on 8 February 1587.[1] In the second poem, 'I dye without desert', the speaker pleading his cause is evidently a young man. His identity may be searched for among those who were most notable prisoners for religion at the time of Southwell's work in England; of them all the figure of Philip Howard, Earl of Arundel, is set in relief as one whose virtues Southwell might have extolled with such vigour and whose fate he might have lamented so unrestrainedly. W. Joseph Walter, who first printed these poems in 1817, linked 'Decease release' with the death of the Queen of Scots, and thought that 'I dye without desert' referred also to the same event. J. H. Pollen, publishing materials related to the life of the Earl of Arundel, believed that 'I dye without desert' was an expression of the Earl's suffering during the period of waiting for execution that never came, after his arraignment in April 1589; this interpretation was strongly supported by Professor Janelle.[2] It is more reasonable to suppose that both these occasional poems belong to the earlier period, in 1587, when it is to be expected that the imagination of the young missionary priest might be most moved by the reports of the suffering of Catholics in great place.

With inconclusive evidence of this kind, and hints yielded by stylistic features, the compilation of lyrics offers extremely little ground on which to build any possible chronological sequence, but most of the poems strongly indicate their origin from a single hand. Links in theme and phrase and vocabulary are everywhere to be found, and there are numerous echoes of passages in the prose writings. The compilation as a whole gives the strongest impression

---

[1] This interpretation is confirmed by a notation on a copy of the poem among the Bacon papers in Lambeth Palace (MS. 655, described by Louise Guiney in *Recusant Poets* [New York, 1939], p. 247). *S* and *H* omit any name, indicating only that a name is to be inserted; *F* has the name *Anna*, perhaps with reference to Queen Anne of Denmark.

[2] Walter, pp. 96 and 99; *C.R.S.* xxi. 323; Janelle, p. 160.

of the sense of responsibility shown by the first editor in assembling what he believed to be the corpus of Southwell's lyric writing.

II

This impression of the integrity of the editor of the lyrics necessarily casts doubts upon the ascription to Southwell of other poems not included in his compilation. But his excellent intentions may have been frustrated by the conditions under which he worked. It is not at all unlikely that some of the poems were not included in the collection, and isolated lyrics may yet be brought to light. Additions to the group of lyrics in the early texts include three poems printed in *Mœoniæ*, which also appear in *F*. In both printed book and manuscript the attribution of the poems to Southwell is made simply by implication; the difficulty in accepting them as authentic lies in the comparative irresponsibility of the publisher of *Mœoniæ* and of the compiler of *F*. The attribution rests finally on internal evidence. In this edition the three poems have been accepted in the canon.

The poems in *Mœoniæ*, 'The virgin Mary to Christ on the Crosse', 'Man to the wound in Christs side', and 'Upon the Image of death', appear in *F* with numerous textual variants, indicating an independent source.[1] Two of the poems, 'The virgin Mary to Christ' and 'Man to the wound', are presented in *F* (fols. 44ᵛ and 46) as two of a group of four poems in the same verse form. 'Christes answere' (fol. 45) is a reply to Mary's lament; 'Christ upon the Crosse to man' (fol. 45ᵛ) precedes the address to the wound of Christ. All four poems contain phrases which in imagery, thought, and choice of words are typical of Southwell's work. It is difficult to discard from the canon two poems selected by Busby for *Mœoniæ*, but, as will be shown in the discussion of the poems in *F*, the remaining two poems cannot be accepted as Southwell's with any confidence.

'Upon the Image of death', the third of the poems published in *Mœoniæ*, has been fixed in the canon of Southwell's work by frequent publication as one of the small group of poems appearing in anthologies. But on stylistic evidence it seems unlikely to be Southwell's. In its unpretentious vocabulary and musical structure it has the charm of the work of earlier lyricists who fused the simplicity of the medieval tradition with the musical forms of the Renaissance; it is a *memento mori* written probably in the mid-sixteenth

---

[1] The poems are also found without ascription to Southwell in Thomas Fairfax's Commonplace Book (*B*), in which 'Man to the wound' is copied twice (pp. 15 and 85).

century. Southwell's concern with the theme, in language recalling that of the poem, may be illustrated from his prose writings, as in *An Epistle of Comfort*: 'If any thing make death tedious, it is the wante of the consideration of it. The old men have it right before them, the yonge men hard behinde them, all men daylye over them, and yet we forget it. . . . If therfore we wilbe out of all feare of death, lett us continuallye remember it.' (sig. P7ᵛ.) The ground of his strongest appeal to his father in the letter published with *A Short Rule* is that he should remember the imminence of death. But Southwell's concern with the theme, even to the point of stylistic echo, does not prove his authorship of the poem. The resemblance of the stanza structure, subject, and tone of the poem to '*Respice finem*' in *The Paradise of Dainty Devices* has been pointed out by Professor Martz.[1] Both poems are in the tradition of the hymn of the Vanity of the World, '*Cur mundus militat*', attributed to St. Bernard, a translation of which also appears in the *Paradise*. In the seventeenth century 'Upon the Image of death' was handled as a separate poem without any ascription of authorship. Although rights to the publication of *Mœoniæ* were held by John Parker in 1624, on 14 December the rights to 128 ballads, including 'Before my face the picture', presumably 'Upon the Image of death', were assigned to a group of other publishers.[2] It was appended to Simon Wastell's *Microbiblion* (for Robert Mylbourne, 1629), sig. z3ᵛ, as a means of filling the last sheet in the volume. It is admitted to the canon of the poems in this edition, together with the other poems of *Mœoniæ*, mainly on the grounds of its traditional ascription to Southwell, and because proof of another hand is still lacking.

III

Besides these three poems, *F* includes eleven lyrics not found in the other manuscripts and printed books. In this edition these have been excluded from the main body of the poems. No external evidence exists to strengthen the attribution of any of them to Southwell, and their presence in a manuscript that is remarkable for the freedom with which the compiler edited his text as he copied the poems prejudices their acceptance in the canon. The frequent changes the compiler made in his manuscript and in the copy of the *Complaint* (*Ca*) to which it is appended are not evident in these poems; it is

---

[1] Martz, p. 207.
[2] *Stationers' Register*, iv, p. 131.

possible that the condition of the text from which the compiler worked imposed the necessity of revisions as he copied, and led him in some instances to complete rewriting or imitation. After careful stylistic study it is clear that some of the poems are almost certainly not Southwell's, but imitations of his style; others, on the other hand, are typical expressions of some of his favourite themes, and may be early drafts or examples of work later discarded. None can be summarily dismissed. They are examined briefly here to indicate the varying degrees of doubt which the poems raise in a consideration of the problem of their attribution.

Three of the lyrics resemble those of the Sequence. Two are inscribed on a separate leaf (fol. 2) preceding the section of the manuscript containing the Sequence and the other lyrics; the third, 'The Annuntiation altered from that before', is in the group of poems appended to those of the manuscript compilation (fol. 49ᵛ). The two poems preceding the Sequence are given Latin titles, a feature typical of several of the poems in the manuscript. The first, '*Conceptio B. Virginis sub porta aurea*', is on a subject included in the Sequence with the English title 'The Virgine Maries conception'; the third stanzas of both poems are very similar. The '*Conceptio*' has the appearance of an earlier version, later substantially rewritten. The second poem, '*Præsentatio B. Virginis*', may also be Southwell's work, and may have been intended for inclusion in the Sequence, where there is no poem on this subject.[1]

The third poem, 'The Annuntiation altered', must be considered in a very different light. It is not an early version, but a revision of the poem on the same subject in the Sequence, 'The Virgins salutation'. The poem is far inferior to the version in the Sequence, where in three closely connected stanzas a most delicately controlled line of thought presents the Church's teaching on the way of restitution offered in the Incarnation. The 'altered' form of the poem in *F* has weaknesses which must cast serious doubts on its authenticity. Not least is the reversal of the second and third stanzas of the poem. The weakening effect of unnecessary verbal changes may be illustrated from the final lines of what is now the second stanza:

> Man by aspiring did procure our fall,
> God by descending freëd us from thrall.

---

[1] Although the feast of the Presentation of the Virgin had been reintroduced into the Roman calendar on 1 September 1585, it had not yet the general recognition of the other feasts of the Virgin which are the subjects of some of the other poems.

If there were not more serious reasons to doubt the authenticity of the poem the use of the ugly *freëd* would make it suspect, since such a diæresis is rare in Southwell's verse. (Other examples occur in 'I dye without desert', l. 33, and 'S. Peters complaint', l. 28.) But the chief cause to suspect the authorship of the 'altered' poem lies in what is now the third stanza, in the form of a colloquy addressed to 'O Virgin blest'. In his earlier copying of 'The Virgins salutation' the compiler of *F* first wrote 'O virgin brest', but later inexplicably changed 'brest' to 'blest', making nonsense of the rest of the stanza, when it is said in the fourth line, with reference to the womb ('brest') of Mary, and not of Mary herself, 'Whose chaste receit God more then heaven did prize'. The corruption recurs in the 'altered' version; the fourth line is permitted to stand without change, but the last two lines are changed to sustain the reference to Mary. It is obvious the changes are not authoritative revisions but clumsy substitutions. By this rewriting the poem has lost much of the intensity of thought and expression that characterizes the version in the Sequence, and the smooth versification has been awkwardly roughened. It seems very probable that it is the work of the compiler himself; if so, he is shown to be not only an unreliable editor, but also a thoroughgoing textual reviser.

This hypothesis, which necessarily restricts the value of the manuscript as a textual source, is supported by the passage of twelve lines inserted after the first stanza of the poem 'Christs bloody sweat'.[1] The interpolation extends the basic Christian paradox which is the subject of the poem, the mystery of the blood (as symbol of life) that does not extinguish but increases the power of fire (as symbol of love). The first six lines of the insertion expand two images of blood—as a stream in which sinners may wash, and as a cloud pouring health-giving showers upon earth. In these lines a clumsy change is made from the objective contemplation of Christ in Gethsemane to Christ as speaker. The second stanza of the interpolation, in which the poet is again speaker, interprets the events in Gethsemane as a sacrifice; this imagery is developed in the concluding stanzas of the poem, where it is worked out with reference to Elijah's sacrifice to demonstrate the power of God. The question asked in the final two lines of the interpolated passage is also repeated in another form in the version of the poem in the other manuscripts. The insertion adds neither stylistic grace nor theological

[1] See Commentary, p. 126.

clarity to the poem, and it must be regarded as either an early draft or an attempt, probably by the compiler of *F*, to expand a poem of unusual compression of imagery.

The two poems, 'Christes answere' (fol. 45) and 'Christ upon the Crosse to man' (fol. 45ᵛ), pose a similar problem. They are linked in style and subject to the two appearing with them in the manuscript and printed in *Mœoniæ*, 'The virgin Mary to Christ' and 'Man to the wound in Christs side', but they are clearly inferior in development of thought and in expression. In argument they tend to present a series of tangential points, none of which is intensively developed, and metrically there are occasional lines of unusual roughness. They appear to be early drafts or attempts by another writer to recapture the tone of the other two poems.

Other lyrics in the group of poems added in *F* also suggest the possibility that some early work may have survived. Five brief lyrics, in a variety of verse forms, are translations or adaptations of scriptural themes: '*Ubi est Deus meus?*' (fol. 41ᵛ) in fourteeners; '*Optima Deo*' (fol. 42), a translation from Tasso (*Gerusalemme Liberata*, xvi. 14, 15) in which the final lines, a summons to sensual love, have been transformed to an appeal to 'Yeld God the prime of youth'; 'Unworthy receaving' (fol. 42ᵛ) in awkward iambic hexameter couplets on one of the themes of 'A holy Hymme' and 'Of the Blessed Sacrament of the Aulter'; '*Beatus vir qui non abiit etc.*' (fol. 43), a free translation of Psalm 1; and a version of 'S. Peters complaint' (fol. 43ᵛ) in eleven four-lined stanzas.

There are also grounds for attributing to Southwell the poem yet to be considered, 'The Complaint of the B. Virgin having lost her Sonne in Hierusalem' (fol. 46ᵛ). It has close affinities in theme with the other 'complaint' poems, and in style with the twelve-stanza version of 'Saint Peters Complaynte' in the manuscripts. The speaker throughout the poem, as in the other complaints, expresses her concern for the Son whom she believes lost, as Peter regrets the loss through his sin of his close relationship with God, and as Mary Magdalen mourns the death of her Lover. In each the irony of the situation is clear to the reader, and each would have particular significance for the English Catholic reader who must also have endured the torments of loss, cut off from the Sacraments of his Church, and afraid that he was also forgotten of God; to him the complaint poems spoke with the voice of the Mission priest. Nevertheless, 'The Complaint of the B. Virgin' is a poem that a more objective reader must find laboured, and its passages of pleasantly melodious verse are marred by a narrative of confused tenses, inverted constructions, conventional phrases, and sudden bathos, as after seventeen sorrowful stanzas Mary exclaims: 'And to be short I lacke my Saviour swete.' (l. 102)[1]

No simple solution can be reached concerning the authenticity of these additional poems in *F*. There are some grounds for believing that the compiler had access to another manuscript, or perhaps a collection of single poems from which he copied. He may even have been fortunate enough to have come across drafts of some of Southwell's earliest English lyrics, later set aside as he progressed in literary skills. Although some of the poems suggest Southwell's hand very strongly, in view of the extremes of trust and mistrust aroused in an examination of the poems as a group they have been relegated to an appendix of poems of doubtful authorship in this edition.

IV

A special interest attaches to the textual study of the 'Complaint' for the materials bearing upon the composition of the poem which have survived. A version of a poem on the subject of Peter's sorrow after his denial of Christ, headed 'Peeter Playnt', a draft of a translation of part of Luigi Tansillo's *Le Lagrime di San Pietro*, is found in the holograph papers preserved in Stonyhurst MS. A. v. 4.[2] Two other versions may indicate stages in the gradual emergence of the long poem. One of these ('S. Peters complaint'), a poem of 11 four-lined stanzas, is extant only in *F*; the second ('Saint Peters Complaynte') is a poem of 12 six-lined stanzas, found in all the manuscripts. The long poem, of 132 six-lined stanzas, is found in *A* and *O*, and in the successive printed editions from 1595. There can be no doubt that Southwell was responsible for the rough translation in his hand, but the stages by which it was developed into the long 'Complaint' can only be hypothetically reconstructed from internal evidence provided by the poems.

Tansillo's poem bears little resemblance to Southwell's three original versions. It is a comparatively leisurely reconstruction of Peter's spiritual experiences during the three days that followed his denial of Christ. The stanzas Southwell translated sustain an

---

[1] Seven stanzas are transcribed in *B*, without attribution of authorship. This section concludes with the stanzas on the Nativity; in *B* a four-line doxology is appended.

[2] Printed in Appendix I. The first page is reproduced as frontispiece to this volume.

objective and narrative point of view; the events in the courtyard are recalled as in the immediate past, while with the privilege of omniscience, reference is also made to the suffering Peter must know in the future. In contrast, in each of the three original versions, Peter is the speaker throughout; both time and place are left deliberately indeterminate as the re-creation in memory of the sin in the courtyard merges with the agony of present suffering, and, in the longer poems, with greater spiritual insight which comes with the growing awareness of sin as an offence against a loving God.

The Christian paradox at the base of the thought structure of all three versions is expressed at the beginning of the version in *F*:

> How can I live, that have forsaken life,
> And dasht with dreade denied my sovereigne Lord?

Viewed in its place as a stage in the development of the 'Complaint' the poem appears to be Southwell's work. Father McDonald believed that it was a recasting of portions of the other versions,[1] but an examination of the relevant passages shows with considerable certainty that the poems were written in the reverse order, the four-lined stanza form of the poem in *F* being refashioned into the six-lined stanza form that was later to be used for the greatly expanded version of the poem. Passages providing ground for comparison in phrase or in thought in the two short versions are as follows:

'S. Peters complaint' (*F*)	'Saint Peters Complaynte' (MSS.)
ll. 1–4	ll. 1–4
5–10, 15–16	7–10
17–20	25–28
21–24	31–34
25–27	36–39
28	41–42
31	55
37–44	18, 62–66

A comparison of these passages clarifies their relationship with each other and with parallel passages in the long version of the poem. At most points an increasing dramatic intensity is felt in the successive versions, a development attained by changes not only in phrase but in the order of thought, as in ll. 5–10 of the version in *F*, compared with ll. 7–10 of the 'Complaynte', and ll. 61–64 of the long

---

[1] McDonald, p. 41.

'Complaint'. The debt of the later versions to the poem in F is not felt at every point, nor always with the direct progression seen in this instance. The rather disconcerting imagery of wild beasts (ll. 41–44) at the climax of the poem in F is dropped (except for an echo in a different context at l. 594 of the long poem); the imagery of enchantment (ll. 33–36), closely echoed in 'A prodigall childs soule wracke', ll. 41–48, does not recur in the 'Complaynte', but reappears in the long poem, ll. 664, 667–72.

Much of the material of the 'Complaynte' is incorporated into the long poem without significant change. Passages of similar content are as follows:

'Complaynte'	'Complaint'
ll. 1–12	ll. 55–66
13–24	163–74
25–30	79–84
31–36	97–102
37–39	151–6
41–42	179–80
45–54	121–32
55–58	115–18
61–66	133–8
67–72	781–6

While the early redactions of the poem are of interest chiefly for the information they yield regarding Southwell's method of preparation for his longest work, the text of the 'Complaint' is of particular importance for the evidence it offers of his most mature craftsmanship.[1] The sustained structural pattern, the manipulation of several levels of meaning, the musical felicities of phrase, and the extraordinary variety within the stanza form, all point to a mastery which is found rarely in the lyric compilation.

The theme of the poem as fully worked out in the long form would have particular relevance to the circumstances of Southwell's life in the year before his arrest in the summer of 1592. At that time of persecution the work of ministering to Catholics scattered widely in the country was considerably curtailed. The 'Complaint', embodying the Catholic doctrine of penance as defined by the Council of

---

[1] The earliest reference to the poem that can be dated occurs in the examination of John Bolt, the musician, 20 March 1594 (*Calendar, S.P., Dom., 1591–4*, p. 467), when he admitted borrowing a manuscript from William Wiseman, of Broad Oaks, Essex, who made his house a centre for local Catholic life. Inevitably this reference to a manuscript circulating in East Anglia suggests a link with *O*.

Trent, which explicitly stated that when no priest was available reconciliation with God might be obtained through perfect contrition,[1] offered to English Catholics spiritual consolation and strength.

A political undercurrent in the poem may be seen in the surprisingly vicious taunts Peter levels at the woman in the courtyard. The emphasis laid upon the part she played in his denial of Christ is not found in the earlier versions, and it is very likely that Southwell was aware of a parallel between her questions and the actions of the Queen, whose demands for an Oath of Supremacy and a show of allegiance tempted Catholics to deny their religious loyalty to Rome.

The uneven quality of the poem has led to some serious critical censures, and where it has been admired, as in Professor Janelle's critical survey, it has been assigned to an earlier period of experimentation.[2] But unevenness may be a sign of unpolished work, and not of youthful inexperience. The hypothesis advanced here, therefore, is that the poem is one of Southwell's last works, left in an unrevised state at the time of his arrest.

No doubt the text is near its final form, and the accompanying poem of introduction, an address to the reader, indicates that Southwell was already considering its circulation, although the substance of the address does not in this case imply that he was finished with the work. He defends his choice of subject, and ends with the hope that modern writers, habitually choosing subjects of profane love, should select instead subjects more worthy of their gifts. He uses a precisely similar argument in his dedicatory letter introducing *Marie Magdalens Funerall Teares*, first printed by John Wolfe for Gabriel Cawood in 1591:

> Yet shall I thinke my indevors well apaide, if it may wooe some skilfuller pennes from unworthy labours, either to supply in this matter my want of abilitie, or in other of like pietie, (whereof the scripture is full) to exercise theyr happier talents. . . . Sith the finest wits are now given to write passionat discourses, I would wish them to make choise of such passions, as it neither should be shame to utter, nor sinne to feele.[3]

---

[1] *Canons and Decrees of the Council of Trent*, ed. and trans. H. J. Schroeder, O.P. (St. Louis, Mo., and London, 1941), Doctrine of the Sacrament of Penance, ch. iv, 'Contrition', p. 91.

[2] Janelle, pp. 160–6.

[3] Edition of 1592, sig. A6. (An edition also printed by Wolfe for Cawood, unrecorded in *S.T.C.*, surviving in a copy in the Folger Shakespeare Library.)

This theme is further developed in the prose address to the reader that follows the letter. Such a close correspondence in thought and expression as is discernible in these preliminaries to both works suggests that preparations for issuing copies of both the *Funerall Teares* and the 'Complaint' were made within a short period of time, possibly not long before the public appearance of the prose work.

In spite of the existence of the introductory poem, the text of the 'Complaint' has several features that suggest that final revisions have not been made, but that an editor—perhaps the same editor who was responsible for the compilation of lyrics—has been at pains to extract the text from a holograph working draft. A little information regarding the state of Southwell's drafts may be gathered from the few holograph pages that have survived in Stonyhurst College MS. A. v. 4. 'Peeter Playnt', for instance, reveals Southwell's tendency to interline his draft with alternative words and phrases, to add other phrases in margins, and at the same time to indicate words he wished to omit only by the most casual crossing-out. It seems likely that the draft of the 'Complaint' was in a similar state of unreadiness.

Four textual problems illustrate this contention. The first has arisen from Southwell's rewriting of the shorter six-lined version, the 'Complaynte'. In the earlier poem Peter asks:

> Was life so deare and Christ become so base, . . .

and in the same stanza he compares his sin with that of Judas:

> Yett Judas deemed thirtye pence his price:
> I, worse then he, for nought deny'd him thrice.
>
> (ll. 31, 35–36)

In the long poem Peter speaks only of his concern for his own life:

> And could I rate so high a life so base?

He then compares his sin with the sins of Judas and Caiaphas:

> Yet they esteemed thirty pence his price:
> I, worse then both, for nought denied him thrise.
>
> (ll. 97, 101–2)

In the rewriting, the removal of the name of Christ in the first line of the stanza has left the pronouns *his* and *him* of the final lines without antecedent reference; this slight inconsistency might have been removed with revision.[1]

At two points there are more serious textual blemishes when it appears that alternative versions of passages in the poem have both been included—errors which might have been caused by Southwell's too casual method of indicating deletions. The first instance of this faulty copying occurs in the section of the poem on the eyes of Christ. At the point where the error occurs the imagery has been formulated into strictly parallel statements: in ll. 367–72 it is concerned with sight and reflection; in ll. 379–81 with feeling and the response engendered by it; in ll. 382–4 with sound and its echo; in ll. 385–90 with speech and understanding. The stanza interjected into this pattern of imagery, ll. 373–8, restates the thought content of the previous stanza—that dealing with sight and reflection—but curtails the full development of thought. It seems most likely that this stanza was inserted in error by the original copyist, overlooking a deletion in the holograph.

A later passage of four stanzas provides evidence of a similar error. The stanzas at ll. 673 and 679 are both built up on a rhetorical framework, but whereas in the first stanza the first five lines are of identical structure and rhythm, emphasizing the artificiality of the figure, an attempt has been made in the second stanza to vary the rhythm, and to condense the figure into the final four lines. The two following stanzas are both based on imagery of shopkeeping; the argument of the first, ll. 685–90, is concentrated into the final two lines of the second, ll. 695–6. The addition in the second stanza of the ironical expression of pleasure in displeasure, the acceptance of suffering as satisfaction for sin, introduces the thought dominant in the next stage of the poem:

> My comfort now is comfortlesse to live. . . .   (l. 697)

There seems to be good reason to accept the second of each of these pairs of stanzas as revised forms of the preceding stanzas. The earlier and less polished versions, the stanzas at ll. 673 and 685, should perhaps be discarded.

The most obvious textual error is the transposition of a group of sixteen stanzas (ll. 235–330) to a place after l. 714, an error found in *A* and *O*, and also in *Ca* and *Cb*. Its occurrence can be most easily

---

[1] The unusual metrical roughness of l. 101 in *Ca* and *A*, where the shortened form *esteem'd* is found, also points to lack of revision in this part of the poem.

explained by the accidental misplacement of sheets of manuscript as they were gathered together for copying, and once again the evidence of the surviving holograph pages in Stonyhurst College MS. A. v. 4 offers some support for this hypothesis. The leaves of paper Southwell prepared for his writing were generally very small; the six leaves of the single gathering in which the 'Peeter Playnt' is transcribed measure 14·4 × 10·6 cm. The home-made gathering, with chain-lines running vertically, would appear to have been made by folding a half-sheet twice to form the four outer leaves, and then by inserting another quarter-sheet, folded once. On the three pages, fols. 50, 50ᵛ, and 51, which he completely filled with his translation, Southwell wrote roughly 33, 32, and 28 lines of verse, allowing only very narrow stanza divisions. For comparison, the Latin poem '*Filii prodigi . . . ad patrem epistola*' is transcribed on eight leaves, a gathering made up of a single sheet folded as for 8° printing, each leaf measuring 14·3 × 10·8 cm. The lines of verse are spaced with some care, eighteen to each page. These holograph leaves are slight evidence from which to deduce Southwell's writing habits, but they give some ground for the possibility that his holograph of the 'Complaint' averaged four stanzas—twenty-four lines of verse—to the page. The sixteen stanzas would therefore have taken up four pages, or two leaves, which, if they were conjugate leaves from the centre of a gathering of six leaves, might have slipped out of their correct place, and so initiated the error retained in later copies.

In view of this serious error in the illogical transposition of such a long passage, and other errors less glaring but damaging in a critical estimate of the poet's achievement, it is reasonably certain that whatever the state of the manuscript from which all copies of the poem descend, it was not the final copy that Southwell would have wished to leave. This evidence of the unrevised condition of the text of the 'Complaint' also points to a time of composition shortly before Southwell's arrest, and reaffirms the argument for such a date based on a study of the development of the theme in the four successive versions of the poem.

V. THE ORDER OF THE LYRICS

Although *S*, *VC*, *A*, and *H* have been examined with emphasis on points of variation and on their relative value as textual sources, their importance lies in their obvious similarities. It has been shown

that all are copies of copies, at some remove from the first copy of
the assembled lyrics; in each the whole body of the lyrics in the
order in which they had been arranged was scrupulously transcribed.
Such respect for the integrity of the compilation may have arisen
first from a conviction that in the accurate copying of the whole
number of poems the work of the English martyr was sustained and
carried forward, and second from a recognition of the religious and
didactic purpose which lay behind the compilation. Even a cursory
reading would have revealed that the brief lyrics were not unrelated
and disordered verses, but poems set in an intelligible series, so that
the impact of the spiritual teaching they contained might be intensi-
fied. This order, so carefully preserved by the earliest copyists, was
dismembered by the publishers of the printed collections. Although
no authority can be claimed for the manuscript order of the poems,
and it is impossible to tell what preliminary arrangement had been
made by Southwell himself, in the successful establishment of a
traditional pattern the chief concern of both author and editor was
achieved with the presentation of the poems in an effective order for
spiritual reading.

    Southwell's intentions for the dissemination of his poetry are
expressed in the introductory letter to his 'Cosen' and the verse
address to the reader. In setting these items at the head of the
larger compilation the editor allows Southwell's hopes to justify
his own actions in planning the copying and distribution of the
lyrics. From this point it is impossible to distinguish between the
work of the editor and the plans Southwell had made. It is quite
certain that Southwell's original gift of poems did not comprise the
group of fifty-two lyrics, but there are no clear indications of what
was included in it. The suggestion made in the letter that a musical
accompaniment was to be added does not aid in making a more
precise identification of the 'ditties', since even 'Saint Peters Complaint' was set to music, as is recorded in a chapter heading of Elizabeth Grymeston's *Miscelanea. Meditations. Memoratives.*: '*Morning
Meditation, with sixteene sobs of a sorowfull spirit, which she used for
mentall prayer, as also an addition of sixteene staves of verse taken out
of* Peters complaint*; which she usually sung and played on the winde
instrument.*'[1] The contents of Southwell's gift of poems must remain
a matter of guesswork.

    It may well have included the first poems in the compilation, the

---

[1] *Miscelanea. . . .* (Melchior Bradwood for Felix Norton, 1604), ch. xi.

Sequence on the Virgin Mary and Christ. It comprises fourteen meditative lyrics closely linked in mood and style, and clearly planned as a unit by Southwell himself.[1] Even this unity was broken in the earliest publication of the poems. Wolfe selected two of the lyrics, 'The Nativitie of Christ' and 'Christs Childhoode', for inclusion in *Ca*; later in 1595 Busby included in *Ma* the remaining poems of the Sequence, except the last two, 'The death of our Ladie' and 'The Assumption of our Lady'. These last poems were not published until Turnbull's edition of 1856, when they were printed from *A*; Grosart printed them from *S* in 1872. This edition presents the Sequence for the first time as a single unit and with the poems in their original order.

A group of four poems (15–18) on the Nativity follows the Sequence in the manuscripts. Their place there is probably the work of the editor, aware of the link supplied by the subject matter. His error in treating 'New heaven, new warre' as a single poem suggests that this group was not part of the collection made by Southwell. It consists in fact of two meditative poems, linked only by subject and metrical form.[2] The two parts are clearly distinguished by their strikingly different tone: the first four stanzas develop a pleasant conceit in the form of a direct appeal to the Angels to come to the newly born Child in the manger, their 'new heaven'; the second part, of equal length, enlarges an image of the most powerful associations for the Jesuit missionary, with the contemplation of 'This little Babe so few dayes olde', who is yet a warrior 'come to ryfle sathans folde', and the final exhortation to his own soul to fight beside the Child in the battle against evil. These images of the Angels and of the battle undertaken by the 'Almightie babe' are also found together in the final stanza of 'A childe my Choyce', one of the other poems in the group, and the one first published, appearing among the lyrics in *Ca*. This poem, in which every line is broken into smaller elements and the construction of every sentence tormented by rhetorical tricks, nevertheless sets out with the utmost compression themes

---

[1] For discussion of the Sequence as a unit, see Martz, pp. 101–7.

[2] Miss Helen Gardner noted the two separate poems when she included 'New heaven, new warre' in her anthology *The Metaphysical Poets* (Penguin Books, Ltd., 1957), p. 37. She suggests that they are parallel poems on the Nativity, or on the Nativity and the Circumcision. The distinct character of the second part is brought out in the musical setting by Benjamin Britten in *A Ceremony of Carols* (1942). Professor Martz has suggested that the first four stanzas comprise a 'Preludium', followed by three stanzas of 'application' and analysis, and a final colloquy. (*The Meditative Poem* [Anchor Books, 1963], note, pp. 524–5.)

echoing through the whole of Southwell's writing, and reiterated in the lyrics that follow:

Loves sweetest mark, Lawdes highest theme, mans most desired light:
To love him, life: to leave him, death: to live in him, delight.

(ll. 5–6)

The next group, three poems (19–21) on the agony in Geth-semane, is also not without textual difficulty. The second and third poems, 'Christs bloody sweat' and 'Christs sleeping friends', are of the same meditative character and in the same six-lined stanza form as the poems of the Sequence, and probably for these reasons they were published immediately following the group of the Sequence poems in *Ma*. Busby's omission of two stanzas of 'Christ's bloody sweat' is unaccountable unless the manuscript from which the text was set up had suffered some damage; it is not likely that he felt any objection to the baroque imagery of the final lines. The stanzas are included in all manuscript copies of the poem, and they were pub-lished from *A* by Turnbull in 1856. (*F* supplies two further stanzas, of doubtful authenticity.) The first poem of the group, 'Sinnes heavie loade', although in the same metrical form, is a meditation of the kind enjoined in the First Week of the Spiritual Exercises when the retreatant contemplates his own sin; here the suffering of Christ in Gethsemane is seen as imposed by the poet's sin:

O Lord my sinne doth over-charge thy brest,
The poyse thereof doth force thy knees to bow. . . .

(ll. 1–2)[1]

Once again it is impossible to guess for what reason the poem was excluded from its place among the poems of Gethsemane when the contents of *Ma* were selected; together with the three unpublished poems on the Nativity it was first printed in *1602*, the augmented edition of the *Complaint*.

It is easier to account for the delay in publication of the next poem, an unusually prolonged and tedious study of 'Josephs Amazement' (22), also included in *1602*. The following two poems may be grouped together: a translation of '*Lauda Sion salvatorem*', entitled on its first printing in *Ma* 'A holy Hymme' (23), and 'Of the Blessed Sacrament of the Aulter' (24), first published with many

---

[1] Martz discusses 'Sinnes heavie loade' and 'Christs sleeping friends' as companion-poems, pp. 40–43.

editorial changes in the St. Omer edition of 1616. The translation of '*Lauda Sion*', which attempts to retain the rhythm and verse form of the medieval Latin, is doubtfully Southwell's, unless it is a rough draft made in preparation for the composition of his own poem on the same subject, 'Of the Blessed Sacrament', which reproduces the Thomistic doctrine expressed in the hymn.

The following eight poems (25–32) in the compilation explore various aspects of remorse. The variety of treatment and style in this group is indicative of Southwell's intense concern with the theme in his writing. The first of the poems is the twelve-stanza version of 'Saint Peters Complaynte', much of which was incorporated later into the long form of the poem. This version was set aside in the early printed volumes; it remained unpublished until Father McDonald printed it from *S* in his *Bibliographical Study*. Other poems within this group are also based on the figures of St. Peter and of those other repentant sinners whose examples were constantly set before the erring flock, but precise reference is confined to titles, and these are probably not Southwell's. The text of these poems—'S. Peters afflicted minde', 'Mary Magdalens blush', 'S. Peters remorse', 'Davids Peccavi', 'The prodigall childs soule wracke'—have doctrinal effectiveness not because of the Biblical references of the titles but because of their general application to all sinners, in a variety of states of sin. 'S. Peters afflicted minde', for instance, makes a general statement of the causes of grief—sickness, loneliness, injury, imprisonment—summed up in the troubled heart described in ll. 5–6. The speaker's personal sorrow is then examined in terms of each one of these sorrows, with the concluding rhetorical question, ll. 23–24, emphasizing the extremity of his suffering. The treatment of the subject suggests no obvious application to Peter. On the other hand, 'S. Peters remorse' has many affinities with the last section of the 'Complaint', and the poem may represent a preparatory exploration of this theme. Two poems in the group, 'A Phansie turned to a sinners complaint' and 'A vale of teares', make no such attempt at Biblical identification. 'A Phansie turned' is a parody of Sir Edward Dyer's lament for the loss of his lady's love; in such exercises Southwell demonstrates the manner in which the language and metrical forms of popular verse may be adapted to the higher themes of spiritual love. Similarly, 'A vale of teares', a poem of astonishing imaginative power, is the development of a single conceit, in the manner of the love poets. The influence of the Ignatian Exercises is clear;[1] the mood and language of the poem recall various conventional love lyrics in which the despairing lover turns away from the world, as in the sonnet 'Let me go seeke some solitarie place' ('The complaint of a forsaken lover') in *Brittons Bowre of Delights*, 1591.

The twenty poems completing the collection (32–52) reiterate some of the themes already expressed. 'Marie Magdalens complaint at Christs death' (33) is another parody of the Elizabethan lyric theme of the loss of the lover, here transferred to the loss felt by the Magdalen before the empty tomb, seeing earthly life a mere shadow of life in the presence of God. The treatment of the subject closely resembles a section of the holograph sermon on Mary Magdalen:

> She had lost her master whome she so singulerlye loved that besyde him she could love nothynge she could hope nothynge She had lost the lyfe of her soule and now she thought it better to dye then to lyve for peradventure she myght fynd dyynge whome she could not fynd lyvynge and without whome lyve she could not. (fol. 56ᵛ)

The theme also impregnates much of the printed prose, as in *The Triumphs over Death*: 'What is the daily lessening of our life, but a continual dying?' (*TD*, sig. D2.) In *An Epistle of Comfort* Southwell restates the paradox:

> Every daye we dye, and howrely loose some parte of our life, and even then when we grow we decrease. . . . For while we live, we dye, and then we leave dyeinge, when we leave livinge. Better therfore it is to dye to lyfe, then to live to death: because our mortal lyfe is no thing, but a living death. (sig. P6)

The theme of death-in-life and of physical death as the means to life is recurrent in the group of lyrics including, besides 'Marie Magdalens complaint', 'Life is but Losse' (37), 'Seeke flowers of heaven' (38), 'I die alive' (39), 'What joy to live?' (40), and 'Lifes death loves life' (41), and it is implicit in others in this final section of the compilation.

The related theme, that of the conflict fought in man's soul between things of this world and the joys of heaven is also predominant in poems in this group. It is expressed directly in 'Mans civill warre' (36), in which the soul, strengthened by wisdom, aspires towards heavenly beauty and goodness; 'At home in Heaven' (42) and 'Looke home' (43) present other aspects of this neo-Platonic

---

[1] See Martz, pp. 207-10.

progression, as the soul is exhorted to realize its true nature as
the image of God. Similar exposition of the theme is to be found
in Diego de Estella's *A Hundred Meditations on the Love of God*,
which Southwell translated.[1] Opposing the soul's growth in heavenly
love, the power of the senses to mislead and corrupt is expressed in
poems of this group, such as 'Loves servile lot' (46), 'Lewd Love is
Losse' (47), and 'Loves Garden grief' (48); and the transitory nature
of the joys of this world, together with the expression of confidence
in the life directed by the three Christian virtues towards heavenly
joys, is the subject of the group of four lyrics concluding the compilation, 'Fortunes Falsehoode' (49), 'From Fortunes reach' (50),
'Content and rich' (51), and 'Scorne not the least' (52).

   Besides these poems which, after the lyrics of remorse, draw the
reader's sensibility to an understanding of spiritual values and a life
enriched by the hope of heaven, there are other poems apparently
less integrated into the thematic pattern. As has been shown in the
discussion of the date of the poems, 'Decease release' (34) and 'I dye
without desert' (35) clearly contain reference to events of the religious persecution. But although their relevance to particular occurrences makes them distinctive in the group of lyrics with universal
application, by setting them after 'Marie Magdalens complaint' at
the beginning of this last section of the compilation, the editor
emphasized the manner in which the suffering of these two, no
doubt identified by many contemporary readers, illustrates the
themes of the group of poems, as in 'Decease release' the speaker
asserts that her dying day 'Beganne my joy and termed fortunes
spite' (l. 12), and in 'I dye without desert' the second voice declares
again:

> Thus fortunes favors still are bent to flight,
> Thus worldly blisse in finall bale doth end.
>
> (ll. 31–32)

Finally, a few of the poems are of apparently sober moral character,
including 'Times goe by turnes' (44), 'Losse in delaies' (45), and
the poems enjoining the retired life of virtue, 'Content and rich' (51)
and 'Scorne not the least' (52). Their place in this section of the
compilation, when the insistence upon moral and spiritual discipline
must be related to the circumstances of the life of the Catholic

---

[1] See, for instance, Meditation V, in the 1873 edition of Southwell's translation by
John Morris, S.J.

in England, points strongly to a more precise application of the precepts than would normally be contained in a recitation of these pious platitudes. 'Times goe by turnes', with this connotation, offers comfort to those much distressed by oppression; 'Losse in delaies' exhorts the Catholic to take positive and immediate steps to maintain his spiritual independence by refusing to compromise with the new Babylon (see l. 42); and most strongly of all, 'Scorne not the least' advocates endurance, silence, and the hope of a time of relief 'When sunne is set' (l. 6), a phrase which in its political context may look to a time after the death of Elizabeth.

From this survey it may be seen that the fifty-two lyrics have been arranged with sensitive awareness of the place of each in a framework of training in the spiritual life. In this order the poems supply a stimulus to the imagination and strength to the wavering spirit, as they exemplify the ministry of the priests to the English Catholics: first, meditation upon familiar incidents in the life of the Virgin and of Christ, with traditional emphasis upon the Incarnation and the Passsion; second, commentary on the doctrine inherent in the Sacraments of the Holy Eucharist and of Penance, both recently defined at the Council of Trent; and in the final long section, an exposition of the way of life for the Catholic facing not only the temptations of spiritual laxity, but actual persecution. Although, no doubt, Southwell's hand may be seen in the arrangement of the more closely integrated groups of poems, the skilful presentation of the whole collection must be attributed to his unknown editor. It is a matter of conjecture whether Southwell had formulated any plan for the collection of his work in the event of his arrest, but the method of manuscript dissemination which he had inaugurated in the preparation of the group of poems sent to his 'Cosen' was in the work of his editor extended to strengthen and sustain his intentions in his apostolate of letters.

VI. CONCLUSIONS

In an examination of the surviving manuscript copies of the poems and of the printed books it becomes quite clear that two different traditions have been established. The manuscripts preserve a record of spiritual teaching set in an effective order designed specifically to guide the English Catholic. On the other hand, the printed books are designed for a wider public, and their contents ordered with thought for the approval of the ecclesiastical censor and for their appeal to the purchasers.

Since Southwell's own plans for his poetry cannot be known, it seems preferable to accept the pattern of spiritual teaching imposed by his first editor than to reproduce the poems in the order in which they appeared in the earliest printed collections. The disintegration of the manuscript order in the printed books may be illustrated in tabular form, when the numbering of the poems from 1 to 52 represents the order in the manuscripts. Within the larger group poems 1–14 comprise the Sequence on the Virgin and Christ; 15–22, meditative poems on incidents drawn from the Nativity and the Passion; 23–32, poems on the Sacraments; 33–52, poems of moral and spiritual instruction and example.

Ca: 27, 33, 44, 43, 49, 52, 6, 12, 15, 51, 45, 46 (part), 38 (part).
Cb: includes the poems in Ca, completing 46, omitting defective 38, and adding: 37, 39, 40, 41, 42, 47, 48, 50.
1602: includes poems of Ca (omitting defective 38) and Cb, and adds: 30, 29, 19, 22, 18, 17, 16.
Ma: 1, 2, 3, 4, 5, 7, 8, 9, 10, 11, 20 (part), 21, x, 23, 26, 28, x, x, 31, 32, 36, 38. (The three poems indicated by x are not found in any manuscript except F.)

Besides the group of twelve short lyrics, Ca published also the prose dedicatory letter and the accompanying poem 'To the Reader', found at the beginning of the manuscript compilation, and the introductory poem and the long form of 'Saint Peters Complaint', items independent of the lyric collection. From internal evidence, presented above in an account of the composition of the poem, it would seem most likely that the 'Complaint' was written shortly before Southwell's imprisonment. It has therefore been placed in this edition after the group of lyrics, most of which are of earlier composition.

It remains to make a final comment on the relative textual value of manuscripts and printed books as it has emerged in the process of editing both the short lyrics and the 'Complaint'.

I

The copyists' concern for the accurate transmission of the short lyrics is most obvious in the care taken not only to preserve the original order without additions or subtractions, but to reproduce the text without editorial change. The four copies *S*, *VC*, *A*, and *H* are substantially true to the compiler's intentions, although a number of careless errors gradually accumulate to mar the text of the poems; *F*, however, reveals a departure from this scribal scrupulosity, in numerous textual revisions, and in additions made to the original group of poems. *S* and *VC* are of greatest interest as they supply early readings in texts which have been copied with unusual care; *A*, *H*, and *F* are of importance as they confirm readings found in the more responsible manuscripts.

The printed books, lacking the pious motivation of the Catholic copyists, are of more textual significance than may be supposed from the manipulation of their contents for commercial purposes. The four volumes listed above supply substantive texts of early date for all but six of the poems in the manuscript compilation; of these only one, 'Of the Blessed Sacrament', printed in the St. Omer edition of 1616, appeared before the discovery of the manuscripts in the nineteenth century. In the absence of any manuscript of out-standing superiority, the text of the poems as they appear in these substantive editions gains significant value. Each volume provides evidence that the text has been set up from copy-texts which either antedated the manuscript compilation or derived from it at points in the transmission of the text at least as close to the common ancestor as the best of the surviving manuscript copies. On the basis of this textual evidence, the recovery of the text of the short poems in this edition has been attempted from the printed substantive texts, corrected as the weight of alternative manuscript readings indicates flaws in the compositors' work or in their copy-texts.

II

As in the case of the short poems, the two manuscript copies of 'Saint Peters Complaint' and the earliest printed copy, *Ca*, derive from a common textual tradition. The introductory poem 'Deare eie that daynest to let fall a looke' precedes the poem in each instance; even more significantly, in all three texts an obvious error, the transposition of sixteen stanzas, points to a common ancestor in which the misplacement had already occurred. Other errors in all three texts, suggesting an unrevised state of the holograph, have been discussed in a reconstruction of the composition of the poem.

Although there are many variant readings in the three texts, at only three points are all manifestly corrupt, and of these, only one, at l. 85, offers a serious corruption by supplying an acceptable alternative reading.[1] The copy-text from which the text of *Ca* was set up was clearly of a textual authority at least equal to that of *A*, the more reliable of the two manuscript copies.[2]

In the second edition of the poem, *Cb*, considerable textual revision was undertaken and corrections made after consultation of the original manuscript copy used in the preparation of *Ca*. The sidenotes ignored in the first hasty printing were set in the margins. These changes in *Cb* do not, however, imply consistent collation; in spite of its numerous flaws *Ca* remains the only substantive text of the printed volumes. In this attempt to recover the text of the poem *Ca* is followed, corrected from *Cb*, and consideration is also given to the alternative readings offered by the two manuscript copies surviving, by *Cc*, and by the compiler of *F* as he made changes in his copy of *Ca* (*F*).

III

The present edition, therefore, is a selective text based on that of the earliest printed collections for all the poems they include; *S*, the best of the surviving manuscript copies, has provided the basis for the text of the six and a half poems not included in the early English editions. To these the two poems in the prose works, *The Triumphs over Death* and *An Epistle of Comfort*, have been added; the texts of both poems are similarly based on those of their earliest editions, collated with the manuscripts and later editions. The source of the text of each poem is given first in the critical apparatus, followed by reference to other witnesses used in the establishment of the text, and, where relevant, the listing of manuscripts and editions not of comparable textual value, but useful as they lend support to variant readings. Further details concerning the state of the text in manuscripts and printed books are to be found in the Commentary.

In presenting the fifty-two short lyrics in the order not of the printed books but of the manuscript tradition, it is inevitable that the characteristic spelling and punctuation and the use of accidentals

---

[1] Other errors occur at l. 235, where *Ca*'s error is probably a misprint, and at l. 351, where all three reveal misunderstanding. The readings at ll. 50 and 418 may also be corrupt. A few lines show metrical irregularity.

[2] *A* offers readings superior to either *Ca* or *O* at three points, ll. 278, 522, and 548; *O* is superior at l. 201, and achieves a smoother line at l. 101.

of the various compositors and of the copyist of *S* will be found to occur irregularly throughout the group of poems, according to the source used as basis for the text. This variation is to be regretted, but it seemed preferable to the acceptance either of the order of the poems in the printed collections or of the text of any of the manuscripts, all of which are marked by eccentricities of spelling and scribal idiosyncrasies.

The critical apparatus of the short lyrics records all deviations from the copy-text, including misprints, except for minor printing errors such as reversed letters, letters dropped in making press-corrections, and irregularities in the use of type founts—details which are of bibliographical interest only. All variant readings in *S* are recorded, unless they are clearly scribal errors; variants occurring elsewhere in a single manuscript are not listed, except when they are of particular interest, as when an emendation of a corrupt passage is offered. The numerous revisions in *F* are cited only at points where there is no general agreement on a textual reading. In the text of the 'Complaint' variants in *A* and *O* are given whenever they offer a possible reading, and changes made by the compiler of *F* in the printed text of the copy of *Ca* with which his manuscript is bound are included as further evidence in support of such readings.

Variant readings in early editions are cited where there is some evidence of consultation of an earlier text, as in *Cb*, but textual changes clearly without authority are omitted.

The spelling and capitalization of the copy-texts have been retained, except that the use of *i/j*, *u/v*, and *U/V* has been modernized. Some ambiguous spellings have been changed to forms which are less likely to distract the reader; these include the change of *weight* to *wight*, *soone* to *sonne* or *sunne*, *powers* to *pours*, *poure* to *powre* (a monosyllabic form of modern *power*), *to* or *two* to *too*. The original spelling form is recorded in the apparatus. Prefixes printed as independent elements, such as *a sleepe*, *a floate*, *in consolable*, have been silently incorporated according to modern spelling. Contracted forms have been expanded unless the contraction appears to have some textual significance. Readings in the text supplied from sources other than the copy-text have been reproduced to accord in spelling with the habitual spelling in the copy-text. Variant readings appearing in the critical apparatus are cited in the spelling of the manuscript or printed book first listed after the lemma.

The punctuation of the copy-text has been reproduced except at those points where changes were necessary to remove difficulties for the reader. Since the punctuation of neither the manuscripts nor the printed editions may be considered in any way authoritative no variations other than changes made in the copy-text have been recorded in the apparatus. Because marks of punctuation are very rare in the poems for which S provided the copy-text, light punctuation in accordance with the methods of the printing-houses responsible for the printed texts has been supplied.

LIST OF SIGLA

I. MANUSCRIPTS

S^1 Stonyhurst College Library MS. A. v. 27
VC Virtue and Cahill Library, MS. 8635
A British Museum, Additional MS. 10422
H British Museum, MS. Harleian 6921
F^2 Harmsworth MS., Folger Shakespeare Library
O Commonplace Book of Peter Mowle, St. Mary's College, Oscott
B Commonplace Book of Thomas Fairfax, Bodleian MS. Eng. Poet. b. 5

II. EDITIONS

A. *Saint Peters Complaint, With other Poemes*

Ca	Wolfe, 1595	*S.T.C.* 22957 (*ii*)
Cb	Wolfe, 1595	*S.T.C.* 22957 (*i*)
Cc	Cawood, 1595	*S.T.C.* 22956
1597	Cawood, 1597	*S.T.C.* 22958
1599	Cawood, 1599	*S.T.C.* 22959
W	Waldegrave, ?1599	*S.T.C.* 22960
1602	Cawood, 1602	*S.T.C.* 22960[2]
L	Leake, ?1608	*S.T.C.* 22961
1615	Barrett, 1615	*S.T.C.* 22962
1634	Wreittoun, 1634	*S.T.C.* 22967

B. *Mœoniæ*

Ma	Busby, 1595	} *S.T.C.* 22955
Mb	Busby, 1595	}
Mc	Busby, 1595	*S.T.C.* 22954

C. 'Collected' Works

1620	Barrett, 1620	*S.T.C.* 22965
1630	Haviland, 1630	*S.T.C.* 22966
1636	Haviland, 1636	*S.T.C.* 22968

---

[1] *S(b.c.)*: *S* before correction by a second scribe; these earlier readings, when not manifest copying errors, may be assumed to have been present in the manuscript copy used by the first transcriber.

[2] *F compiler*: This indicates a change made by the compiler of *F* in the printed text of *Ca* (*F*), with which *F* is bound.

C. *'Collected' Works* (contd.)

SOa	St. Omer, 1616	*S.T.C.* 22963
SOb	St. Omer, 1620	*S.T.C.* 22964

D. *Prose Works*
i. *The Triumphs over Death*

1595	Busby, 1595	*S.T.C.* 22971

ii. *An Epistle of Comfort*

EC	Printed secretly in England, 1587–88	*S.T.C.* 22946

III. LIBRARIES CITED AS HOLDING PARTICULAR COPIES OF EARLY EDITIONS

F	Folger Shakespeare Library, Washington, D.C.
HEH	Henry E. Huntington Library and Art Gallery, San Marino, California
TC	Trinity College, Cambridge
VC	Virtue and Cahill Library, Diocese of Portsmouth (R.C.)

I

POEMS IN MANUSCRIPTS

The Author to his loving Cosen

POETS by abusing their talent, and making the follies and fayninges of love, the customary subject of their base endevours, have so discredited this facultie, that a Poet, a Lover, and a Liar, are by many reckoned but three wordes of one signification. But the vanity of men, cannot counterpoyse the authority of God, who delivering 5 many partes of Scripture in verse, and by his Apostle willing us to exercise our devotion in Himnes and Spirituall Sonnets, warranteth the Arte to bee good, and the use allowable. And therefore not onely among the Heathens, whose Gods were chiefly canonized by their Poets, and their Painim Divinitie Oracled in verse: But even in the 10 Old and New Testament it hath bene used by men of greatest Pietie, in matters of most devotion. Christ himselfe by making a Himne, the conclusion of his last Supper, and the Prologue to the first Pageant of his Passion, gave his Spouse a methode to immitate, as in the office of the Church it appeareth, and all men a paterne to 15 know the true use of this measured and footed stile. But the Divell as hee affecteth Deitie, and seeketh to have all the complements of Divine honor applied to his service, so hath he among the rest possessed also most Poets with his idle fansies. For in lieu of solemne and devout matter, to which in duety they owe their abilities, they 20 now busy themselves in expressing such passions, as onely serve for testimonies to how unwoorthy affections they have wedded their wils. And because the best course to let them see the errour of their workes, is to weave a new webbe in their owne loome; I have heere layd a few course threds together, to invite some skillfuller wits to 25 goe forward in the same, or to begin some finer peece, wherein it may be seene, how well verse and vertue sute together. Blame me not (good Cosen) though I send you a blame-woorthy present, in

The Author to his loving Cosen. Ca; *S*, *H*; *F compiler*
  9 Heathens *S*, *H*, *F compiler*: Heathen *Ca*   15 and all *S*, *H*: and to all *Ca*

which the most that can commend it, is the good will of the writer,
30 neither Arte nor invention, giving it any credite. If in mee this be a
fault, you cannot be faultlesse that did importune mee to committe
it, and therefore you must beare parte of the pennance, when it shall
please sharpe censures to impose it. In the meane time with many
good wishes I send you these few ditties, add you the Tunes, and
35 let the Meane, I pray you, be still a part in all your Musicke.

To the Reader

DEARE eye that doest peruse my muses style,
With easie censure deeme of my delight:
Give sobrest countnance leave sometime to smyle,
And gravest wits to take a breathing flight:
Of mirth to make a trade may be a crime,   5
But tyred spirites for mirth must have a time.

The lofty Eagle soares not still above,
High flightes will force her from the wing to stoupe,
And studious thoughtes at times men must remove,
Least by excesse before their time they droupe.   10
In courser studies tis a sweete repose,
With Poets pleasing vaine to temper prose.

Prophane conceites and fayning fits I flie,
Such lawlesse stuffe doth lawlesse speeches fit:
With *David* verse to vertue I apply,   15
Whose measure best with measured wordes doth sit
It is the sweetest note that man can sing,
When grace in vertues key tunes natures string.

33 censures *S, H*: censurers *Ca*
To the Reader. Ca; *S, A, H*; *F compiler*
16 sit *S, F compiler*: fit *Ca, A, H*

THE SEQUENCE ON THE
VIRGIN MARY AND CHRIST

i. *The Virgine Maries conception*

OUR second *Eve* puts on her mortall shroude,
Earth breeds a heaven, for Gods new dwelling place,
Now riseth up *Elias* little cloude
That growing, shall distill the showre of grace:
Her being now begins, who ere she end,   5
Shall bring the good that shall our ill amend.

Both Grace and Nature did their force unite,
To make this babe the summe of all their best,
Our most, her least, our million, but her mite:
She was at easiest rate worth all the rest,   10
What grace to men or Angels God did part,
Was all united in this infants heart.

Four only wights bred without fault are namde
And al the rest conceived were in sinne,
Without both man and wife was *Adam* framde,   15
Of man, but not of wife did *Eve* beginne,
Wife without touch of man Christs mother was,
Of man and wife this babe was bred in grace.

ii. *Her Nativity*

JOY in the rising of our Orient starre,
That shal bring forth the Sunne that lent her light,
Joy in the peace that shall conclude our warre,
And soone rebate the edge of Sathans spight,
Load-starre of all engolfd in worldly waves,   5
The card and compasse that from ship-wracke saves.

The Virgine Maries conception. Ma; *S, VC, A, H, F*
  6 the *S, VC, H, F*: our *Ma, A*   amend.] amend, *Ma*   13 wights] weights *Ma*
14 sinne,] sinne *Ma*   15 framde,] framde *Ma*   18 bred *MSS.*: borne *Ma*
Her Nativity. Ma; *S, VC, A, H, F*
  5 engolfd *MSS.*: inclosed *Ma*   6 card *MSS.* (*A torn*): care *Ma*   saves.] saves, *Ma*

The Patriarchs and Prophets were the flowers,
Which Time by course of ages did distill,
And cul'd into this little cloud the showers,
Whose gratious drops the world with joy shall fil,   10
Whose moisture suppleth every soule with grace,
And bringeth life to *Adams* dying race.

For God on earth she is the royall throne,
The chosen cloth to make his mortall weede,
The quarry to cut out our corner stone,   15
Soile ful of fruit, yet free from mortall seede,
For heavenly flowre shee is the *Jesse* rod,
The child of man, the parent of a god.

iii. *Her Spousals*

WIFE did she live, yet virgin did she die,
Untoucht of man yet mother of a sonne,
To save her selfe and child from fatall lie,
To end the web wherof the thred was sponne
In mariage knots to *Joseph* shee was tide,   5
Unwonted workes with wonted veiles to hide.

God lent his Paradise to *Josephs* care
Wherein he was to plant the tree of life,
His sonne of *Josephs* child the title bare:
Just cause to make the mother *Josephs* wife.   10
O blessed man betroth'd to such a spouse,
More bless'd to live with such a childe in house.

No carnall love this sacred league procurde,
All vaine delights were farre from their assent,
Though both in wedlocke bandes themselves assurde,   15
Yet streite by vow they seald their chast intent.

9 cul'd S, VC, F: cal'd Ma, H   this MSS. (A torn): his Ma   13 on] in H, F
14 his (changed from this A)] this S, VC   weede,] weede Ma   17 Jesse S, VC, H,
F: Jessa Ma: Jesses A
Her Spousals. Ma; S, VC, A, H, F
2 Untoucht MSS.: Untaught Ma   5 tide,] tide Ma   6 veiles MSS.: wiles
Ma   hide.] hide Ma   10 wife.] wife Ma   11 to such MSS.: too much Ma
12 house.] house Ma   14 assent,] assent Ma   15 in wedlocke bandes themselves
S, A, H, F: themselves in wedlocke bandes Ma, VC   16 streite S, VC, H, F: chast
Ma, A   intent.] intent Ma

Thus had she Virgins, wives, and widowes crowne
And by chast child-birth dubled her renowne.

iv. *The Virgins salutation*

SPELL *Eva* backe and *Ave* shall you finde,
The first began, the last reverst our harmes,
An Angels witching wordes did *Eva* blinde,
An Angels *Ave* disinchants the charmes,
Death first by womans weakenes entred in,   5
In womans vertue life doth now begin.

O virgin breast the heavens to thee incline,
In thee their joy and soveraigne they agnize,
Too meane their glory is to match with thine,
Whose chaste receit God more then heaven did prize,   10
Haile fairest heaven, that heaven and earth dost blisse,
Where vertues starres God sunne of justice is.

With hauty minde to godhead man aspirde,
And was by pride from place of pleasure chac'de,
With loving minde our manhood God desired,   15
And us by love in greater pleasure plac'de,
Man labouring to ascend procurde our fall,
God yeelding to discend cut off our thrall.

v. *The Visitation*

PROCLAIMED Queene and mother of a God,
The light of earth, the soveraigne of Saints,
With Pilgrim foote, up tyring hils she trod,
And heavenly stile with handmaids toile acquaints,
Her youth to age, her health to sicke she lends,   5
Her heart to God, to neighbour hand she bends.

17 she *MSS*.: the *Ma*   18 her *MSS*.: their *Ma*
The Virgins salutation. Ma; *S, VC, A, H, F*
   3 *Omitted Ma*   7 virgin *S, H, F*: virgines *Ma, VC, A*   8 their *MSS*.: they
Ma   joy] joy, *Ma*   11 dost *S, VC, F*: doe *Ma*: did *A*: doth *H*   12 starres
S, VC, H, F: starre *Ma, A*   God *S, VC, H, F*: Gods *Ma, A*   is.] is, *Ma*
15 manhood] manhead *S, H, F*
The Visitation. Ma; *S, VC, A, H, F*
   4 acquaints,] acquaints *Ma*   5 health *S, VC, H, F*: selfe *Ma, S(b.c.), A*   6 bends.]
bends *Ma*

A prince she is, and mightier prince doth beare,
Yet pompe of princely traine she would not have,
But doubtles heavenly Quires attendant were,
Her child from harme her selfe from fall to save,   10
Word to the voice, song to the tune she brings,
The voice her word, the tune her dittie sings.

Eternal lights inclosed in her breast,
Shot out such piercing beames of burning love,
That when her voice her cosens eares possest,   15
The force thereof did force her babe to move,
With secret signes the children greet each other,
But open praise each leaveth to his mother.

✓ vi. *The Nativitie of Christ*

BEHOLDE the father, is his daughters sonne:
The bird that built the nest, is hatched therein:
The olde of yeares, an houre hath not out runne:
Eternall life, to live doth now beginne.
The word is dumme: the mirth of heaven doth weepe: 5
✓ Might feeble is: and force doth faintly creepe.

O dying soules, beholde your living spring:
O dasled eyes, behold your sonne of grace:
Dull eares, attend what word this word doth bring:
Up heavie hartes: with joye your joye embrace.   10
From death, from darke, from deafenesse, from dispaires:
This life, this light, this word, this joy repaires.

Gift better then himselfe, God doth not know:
Gift better then his God, no man can see:
This gift doth here the gever geven bestow: 15
Gift to this gift let each receiver bee.
God is my gift, himselfe he freely gave me:
Gods gift am I, and none but God shall have me.

---

12 sings.] sings, *Ma*

The Nativitie of Christ. Ca; *S*, *VC*, *A*, *H*, *F*
  8 sonne] summe *S*   18 shall have] can save *VC*

Man altered was by sinne from man to beast:
Beastes foode is haye, haye is all mortall flesh: 20
Now God is flesh, and lies in Manger prest:
As haye, the brutest sinner to refresh.
O happie fielde wherein this fodder grew,
Whose tast, doth us from beasts to men renew.

vii. *His circumcision*

THE head is launst to worke the bodies cure,
With angring salve it smarts to heal our wound,
To faultlesse sonne from all offences pure
The faulty vassals scourges do redound,
The Judge is cast the guilty to acquite,   5
The sonne defac'd to lend the starre his light,

The vein of life distilleth drops of grace,
Our rocke gives issue to an heavenly spring,
Teares from his eies, blood runnes from wounded place,
Which showers to heaven of joy a harvest bring,   10
This sacred dew let angels gather up,
Such dainty drops best fit their nectared cup.

With weeping eies his mother rewd his smart,
If blood from him, teares ran from her as fast,
The knife that cut his flesh did pierce her heart,   15
The paine that Jesus felt did *Mary* taste,
His life and hers hung by one fatall twist,
No blow that hit the sonne the mother mist.

His circumcision. Ma; *S, VC, A, H, F*
   2 angring *S, A, H, F*: angry *Ma, VC*   wound,] wound *Ma*   3 sonne] soone *Ma*
pure] pure, *Ma*   7 vein *MSS.*: vine *Ma*   9 eies,] eies *Ma*   place,] place *Ma*
10 heaven . . . bring,] heaven, . . . bring *Ma*   12 cup.] cup, *Ma*   14 ran *S*,
VC, H, F: came *Ma, A*   15 her *MSS.*: his *Ma*   16 felt *MSS.*: set *Ma*

viii. *The Epiphanie*

To blaze the rising of this glorious sunne
A glittering starre appeareth in the east
Whose sight to pilgrim toyles three sages wun,
To seeke the light they long had in request,
And by this star to nobler starre they pace,   5
Whose armes did their desired sunne imbrace.

Stall was the sky wherein these plannets shinde,
And want the cloud that did eclipse their raies,
Yet through this cloud their light did passage finde,
And pierc'd these sages hearts by secret waies,   10
Which made them know the ruler of the skies
By infant tongue and lookes of babish eies.

Heaven at her light, earth blusheth at her pride,
And of their pompe these peeres ashamed be,
Their crowns, their robes, their traine they set aside   15
When Gods poore cottage, clouts, and crew they see,
All glorious things their glory now despise
Sith God Contempt doth more then Glory prise.

Three giftes they bring, three giftes they beare away,
For incense, mirre, and gold, faith, hope, and love,   20
And with their gifts the givers hearts do stay,
Their mind from Christ no parting can remove,
His humble state, his stall, his poore retinew
They fancy more then all their rich revenew.

The Epiphanie. Ma; *S, VC, A, H, F*

   3 pilgrim toyles *MSS.*: pilgrims toyle *Ma*   4 request,] request *Ma*   6 sunne
MSS.: sinne *Ma*   imbrace.] imbrace: *Ma*   7 these *MSS.*: those *Ma*
12 infant] infantes *VC, A*   eies.] eies, *Ma*   15 traine *S, VC, H, F*: traines *Ma,*
A (changed from trayne)   18 prise.] prise *Ma*   19 away,] away *Ma*   20 incense,]
incense *Ma*   21 stay,] stay *Ma*   22 Christ] Christ, *Ma*   remove,] remove *Ma*

ix. *The Presentation*

To be redeemd the worlds Redeemer brought,
Two silly turtle doves for ransome paies,
O ware with empires worthy to be bought,
This easie rate doth sound not drowne thy praise,
For sith no price can to thy worth amount,   5
A dove, yea love, due price thou doest account.

Old *Simeon,* cheape penny worth and sweete
Obteind when thee in armes he did imbrace,
His weeping eies thy smiling lookes did meete,
Thy love his heart, thy kisses blest his face,   10
O eies, O hart, meane sights and loves avoyde,
Base not your selves, your best you have enjoyde.

O virgin pure thou dost these doves present
As due to law, not as an equall price,
To buy such ware thou wouldst thy life have spent,   15
The world to reach his worth could not suffice,
If God were to be bought, not worldly pelfe,
But thou wert fittest price next God himselfe.

x. *The flight into Egypt*

ALAS our day is forst to flie by night,
Light without light, and sunne by silent shade,
O nature blush that suffrest such a wight,
That in thy sunne this darke eclipse hath made,
Day to his eies, light to his steps denie,   5
That hates the light which graceth every eie.

The Presentation. Ma; *S, VC, A, H, F*
   3 ware *MSS.*: wares *Ma*   6 account.] account, *Ma*   7 sweete] sweete, *Ma*
11 loves] love *VC, H*   12 enjoyde.] enjoyde, *Ma*   13 these *MSS.*: those *Ma*
15 life *S, VC, H, F*: selfe *Ma* (felfe *A*)
The flight into Egypt. Ma; *S, VC, A, H, F*
   1 night,] night *Ma*   4 this *MSS.*: thy *Ma*   hath *S, A, H, F*: hast *Ma, VC*
6 eie.] eie, *Ma*

Sunne being fled the starres do leese their light,
And shining beames, in bloody streames they drench.
A cruell storme of *Herods* mortall spight
Their lives and lightes with bloody showers doth quench,   10
The tyrant to be sure of murdring one,
For feare of sparing him doth pardon none.

O blessed babes, first flowers of christian spring,
Who though untimely cropt faire garlandes frame,
With open throats and silent mouthes you sing   15
His praise whom age permits you not to name,
Your tunes are teares, your instruments are swords,
Your ditty death, and blood in liew of wordes.

xi. *Christs returne out of Egypt*

WHEN death and hell their right in *Herod* claime,
Christ from exile returnes to native soile:
There, with his life more deepely death to maime
Then death did life by all the infantes spoile.
He shewed the parents that their babes did mone,   5
That all their lives were lesse then his alone.

But hearing *Herods* sonne to have the crowne,
An impious offspring of a bloudy sire,
To *Nazareth* (of heaven beloved) towne,
Flowre to a flowre he fitly doth retire.   10
For flower he is and in a flower he bred,
And from a thorne now to a flowre he fled.

And wel deservd this flower his fruit to view
Where he invested was in mortall weede,
Where first unto a tender bud he grew   15
In virgin branch unstaind with mortall seede.
Young flower, with flowers, in flower well may he be:
Ripe fruit he must with thornes hang on a tree.

---

7 leese *MSS.*: loose *Ma*   10 doth *MSS.*: doe *Ma*   quench,] quench *Ma*
14 frame,] frame *Ma*   15 sing] sing, *Ma*

Christs returne out of Egypt. Ma; S, VC, A, H, F
    5 their *MSS.*: the *Ma*   8 An *MSS.*: The *Ma*   11 flower he is *MSS.*: he is
a flower *Ma*   15 unto] into H, F

xii. *Christs Childhoode*

TILL twelve yeres age, how Christ his childhood spent,
All earthly pennes unworthy were to write,
Such acts, to mortall eyes hee did present:
Whose worth, not men, but Angels must recite.
No natures blots, no childish faults defilde,   5
Where grace was guide, and God did play the childe.

In springing lockes laye couched hoary wit:
In semblant young, a grave and auncient port:
In lowly lookes, high Majestie did sit:
In tender tongue, sound sense of sagest sort.   10
Nature imparted all that shee could teach:
And God supplied, where nature could not reach.

His mirth, of modest meane a mirrour was:
His sadnesse, tempered with a milde aspect:
His eye, to trie each action was a glasse: 15
Whose lookes, did good approve, and bad correct.
His natures gifts, his grace, his word, and deede
Well shewed that all did from a God proceede.

xiii. *The death of our Ladie*

WEEPE living thinges, of life the mother dyes,
The world doth loose the summ of all her blisse,
The Quene of Earth, the Empresse of the skyes,
By maryes death mankind an orphan is,
Lett nature weepe, yea lett all graces mone,   5
Their glory, grace, and giftes dye all in one.

Christs Childhoode. Ca; S, VC, A, H, F   8 semblant S, VC, A H: semblance
Ca, F

The death of our Ladie. S; VC, A, H, F
  Punctuation supplied, *except in* 4 *and* 18 (*in* S).
  2 summ] sunne VC, H

It was no death to her but to her woe,
By which her joyes beganne, her greives did end,
Death was to her a frende, to us a foe,
Life of whose lives did on her life depende,   10
Not pray of death but praise to death she was,
Whose uglye shape seemd glorious in her face.

Her face a heaven, two planettes were her eyes
Whose gracious light did make our clearest day,
But one such heaven there was, and loe it dyes,   15
Deathes darke Eclipse hath dymmed every ray.
Sunne hide thy light, thy beames untymely shine,
Trew light sith wee have lost we crave not thine.

xiv. *The Assumption of our Lady*

IF sinne be captive grace must finde release,
From curse of synne the innocente is free,
Tombe prison is for sinners that decease,
No tombe but throne to guiltles doth agree.
Though thralles of sinne lye lingring in their grave   5
Yet faultles cors with soule rewarde must have.

The daseled eye doth dymmed light require
And dying sightes repose in shrowdinge shades,
But Eagles eyes to brightest light aspire
And living lookes delite in loftye glades.   10
Faynte winged foule by grounde doth fayntly flye,
Our Princely Eagle mountes unto the skye.

Gemm to her worth, spouse to her love ascendes,
Prince to her throne, Queene to her heavenly kinge,
Whose court with solemne pompe on her attends,   15
And Quires of Saintes with greeting notes do singe.
Earth rendreth upp her undeserved praye,
Heaven claymes the right and beares the prize awaye.

The Assumption of our Lady. S; VC, A, H, F
    Punctuation supplied, except full stops at end of stanzas.
    11 doth] do *A, H*

A childe my Choyce

LET folly praise that fancie loves, I praise and love that child,
Whose hart, no thought: whose tong, no word: whose hand no deed
    defiled.
I praise him most, I love him best, all praise and love is his:
While him I love, in him I live, and cannot live amisse.

Loves sweetest mark, Lawdes highest theme, mans most desired
    light: 5
To love him, life: to leave him, death: to live in him, delight.
He mine, by gift: I his, by debt: thus each, to other due:
First friend he was: best friend he is: all times will try him true.

Though young, yet wise: though smal, yet strong: though man,
    yet God he is:
As wise, he knowes: as strong, he can: as God, he loves to blisse. 10
His knowledge rules: his strength, defends: his love, doth cherish all:
His birth, our Joye: his life, our light: his death, our end of thrall.

Alas, he weepes, he sighes, he pants, yeat doo his Angels sing:
Out of his teares, his sighes and throbs, doth bud a joyfull spring.
Almightie babe, whose tender armes can force all foes to flie: 15
Correct my faultes, protect my life, direct me when I die.

New heaven, new warre

    COME to your heaven you heavenly quires,
    Earth hath the heaven of your desires;
    Remove your dwelling to your God,
    A stall is now his best abode;
    Sith men their homage doe denie,   5
    Come Angels all their fault supplie.

A childe my Choyce. Ca; *S, VC, A, H*
  3 his] this *S, VC*   7 other *MSS.*: others *Ca*
New heaven, new warre. 1602; *S, VC, A, H, F*
  6 fault] faults *A, H*

His chilling cold doth heate require,
Come Seraphins in liew of fire;
This little Arke no cover hath,
Let Cherubs wings his body swath: 10
Come Raphaell, this Babe must eate,
Provide our little Tobie meate.

Let Gabriell be now his groome,
That first took up his earthly roome;
Let Michaell stand in his defence,   15
Whom love hath linck'd to feeble sence,
Let Graces rock when he doth crie,
And Angels sing his lullabie.

The same you saw in heavenly seate,
Is he that now sucks Maries teate;   20
Agnize your King a mortall wight,
His borrowed weede lets not your sight:
Come kisse the maunger where he lies,
That is your blisse above the skies.

    .   .   .   .   .

This little Babe so few dayes olde,   25
Is come to ryfle sathans folde;
All hell doth at his presence quake,
Though he himselfe for cold doe shake:
For in this weake unarmed wise,
The gates of hell he will surprise.   30

With teares he fights and winnes the field,
His naked breast stands for a shield;
His battring shot are babish cryes,
His Arrowes lookes of weeping eyes,
His Martiall ensignes cold and neede,   35
And feeble flesh his warriers steede.

His Campe is pitched in a stall,
His bulwarke but a broken wall:
The Crib his trench, hay stalks his stakes,
Of Sheepheards he his Muster makes;   40

18 And *MSS.*: Let *1602*   26 come *MSS.*: com'd *1602*   33 battring *A*,
H, F: battering *1602, S, VC*

And thus as sure his foe to wound,
The Angells trumps alarum sound.

My soule with Christ joyne thou in fight,
Sticke to the tents that he hath pight;
Within his Crib is surest ward,   45
This little Babe will be thy guard:
If thou wilt foyle thy foes with joy,
Then flit not from this heavenly boy.

The burning Babe

As I in hoarie Winters night
  Stoode shivering in the snow,
Surpris'd I was with sodaine heate,
  Which made my hart to glow;

And lifting up a fearefull eye,   5
  To view what fire was neare,
A pretty Babe all burning bright
  Did in the ayre appeare;

Who scorched with excessive heate,
  Such floods of teares did shed,   10
As though his floods should quench his flames,
  Which with his teares were fed:

Alas (quoth he) but newly borne,
  In fierie heates I frie,
Yet none approach to warme their harts,   15
  Or feele my fire, but I;

My faultlesse breast the furnace is,
  The fuell wounding thornes:
Love is the fire, and sighs the smoake,
  The ashes, shame and scornes;   20

42 trumps] trumpet *A*, *H*   44 pight *MSS.*: dight *1602*   48 this *MSS.*:
the *1602*

The burning Babe. 1602; *S*, *VC*, *A*, *H*, *F*
  12 fed *MSS.*: bred *1602*   **20** shame *MSS.*: shames *1602*

The fewell Justice layeth on,
   And Mercie blowes the coales,
The metall in this furnace wrought,
   Are mens defiled soules:

For which, as now on fire I am   25
   To worke them to their good,
So will I melt into a bath,
   To wash them in my blood.

With this he vanisht out of sight,
   And swiftly shrunk away,   30
And straight I called unto minde,
   That it was Christmasse day.

New Prince, new pompe

BEHOLD a silly tender Babe,
   In freesing Winter night;
In homely manger trembling lies,
   Alas a pitteous sight:

The Innes are full, no man will yeeld   5
   This little Pilgrime bed;
But forc'd he is with silly beasts,
   In Crib to shrowd his head.

Despise not him for lying there,
   First what he is enquire: 10
An orient pearle is often found,
   In depth of dirty mire,

Waigh not his Crib, his wooden dish,
   Nor beasts that by him feede:
Waigh not his Mothers poore attire,   15
   Nor Josephs simple weede.

New Prince, new pompe. 1602; *S, VC, A, H, F*
  2 Winter] winters *VC, F*   9 not him *S, VC*: him not *1602, A, H, F*   11 An
MSS.: As *1602*

This stable is a Princes Court,
 The Crib his chaire of state:
The beasts are parcell of his pompe,
 The wooden dish his plate. 20

The persons in that poore attire,
 His royall livories weare,
The Prince himselfe is come from heaven,
 This pompe is prized there.

With joy approach o Christian wight, 25
 Doe homage to thy King;
And highly prise this humble pompe,
 Which he from heaven dooth bring.

Sinnes heavie loade

O LORD my sinne doth over-charge thy brest,
 The poyse thereof doth force thy knees to bow;
Yea flat thou fallest with my faults opprest,
 And bloody sweat runs trickling from thy brow:
But had they not to earth thus pressed thee, 5
Much more they would in hell have pestred mee.

This Globe of earth doth thy one finger prop,
 The world thou doo'st within thy hand embrace;
Yet all this waight of sweat drew not a drop,
 Ne made thee bow, much lesse fall on thy face: 10
But now thou hast a loade so heavy found,
That makes thee bow, yea flat fall to the ground.

O sinne, how huge and heavie is thy waight,
 Thou wayest more then all the world beside,
Of which when Christ had taken in his fraight 15
 The poyse thereof his flesh could not abide;
Alas, if God himselfe sinke under sinne,
What will become of man that dies therein?

23 come *MSS.*: com'd *1602* 27 prise *S, VC*: praise *1602, A, H, F* this *S,*
VC, A, F: his *1602, H*

Sinnes heavie loade. 1602; *S, VC, A, H, F*
 1 sinne *S, VC, H, F*: sinnes *1602, A* 6 pestred] pressed *VC, F* 7 one]
owne *VC, F* 12 flat fall *S, VC*: fall flat *1602, A, H, F* 14 Thou *S, VC*:
That *1602, A, H, F* beside,] beside? *1602* 18 therein?] therein. *1602*

811841   C

First, flat thou fel'st, when earth did thee receave,
  In closet pure of Maries virgin brest;   20
And now thou fall'st of earth to take thy leave,
  Thou kissest it as cause of thy unrest:
O loving Lord that so doost love thy foe,
As thus to kisse the ground where he doth goe.

Thou minded in thy heaven our earth to weare,   25
  Doo'st prostrate now thy heaven our earth to blisse;
As God, to earth thou often wert severe,
  As man, thou seal'st a peace with bleeding kisse:
For as of soules thou common Father art,
So is she Mother of mans other part.   30

She shortly was to drink thy dearest blood,
  And yeeld thy soule a way to sathans cave;
She shortly was thy corse in tombe to shrowd,
  And with them all thy deitie to have:
Now then in one thou joyntly yeeldest all,   35
That severally to earth should shortly fall.

O prostrate Christ, erect my crooked minde,
  Lord let thy fall my flight from earth obtaine;
Or if I still in earth must needes be shrinde,
  Then Lord on earth come fall yet once againe: 40
And eyther yeeld with me in earth to lie,
Or else with thee to take me to the skie.

Christs bloody sweat

FAT soile, full spring, sweete olive, grape of blisse,
That yeelds, that streams, that pours, that dost distil,
Untild, undrawne, unstampt, untoucht of presse,
Deare fruit, cleare brookes, faire oile, sweete wine at will:

28 seal'st *S, A, H, F*: call'st *1602*: seald'st *VC*   32 a way *S, A, H, F*: away *1602*,
VC   35 one *MSS.*: me *1602*   39 still . . . needes *S, VC*: needes must still
in earth *1602, A, F*: still must needs in earth *H*   41 with me in earth *MSS.*: in
earth with me *1602*

Christs bloody sweat. 1–12: *Ma*; 13–24: *S*; *S, VC, A, H, F*
  2 pours] powers *Ma*   distil,] distil *Ma*

Thus Christ unforst prevents in shedding blood 5
The whips, the thornes, the nailes, the speare, and roode.

He Pelicans, he Phenix fate doth prove,
Whom flames consume, whom streames enforce to die,
How burneth bloud, how bleedeth burning love?
Can one in flame and streame both bathe and frie? 10
How could he joine a Phenix fiery paines
In fainting Pelicans still bleeding vaines?

Elias once to prove gods soveraigne powre
By praire procur'd a fier of wondrous force
That blood and wood and water did devoure, 15
Yea stones and dust, beyonde all natures course:
Such fire is love that fedd with gory bloode
Doth burne no lesse then in the dryest woode.

O sacred Fire come shewe thy force on me
That sacrifice to Christe I maye retorne, 20
If withered wood for fuell fittest bee,
If stones and dust, yf fleshe and blood will burne,
I withered am and stonye to all good,
A sacke of dust, a masse of fleshe and bloode.

Christs sleeping friends

WHEN Christ with care and pangs of death opprest
From frighted flesh a bloody sweate did raine,
And full of feare without repose or rest
In agony did pray and watch in paine
Three sundrie times he his disciples findes 5
With heavy eies, but farre more heavy mindes,

5 shedding *S*, *VC*, *A*, *H*: sheeding *Ma*: sweating *F*　　6 nailes *MSS.*: naile *Ma*　　8 consume,] consume *Ma*　　whom streames *MSS.*: when streames *Ma*　10 flame] flame, *Ma*　11 could *MSS.*: would *Ma*　13-24 *Punctuation supplied.*　13 powre] poure *S*　　23 good,] good. *S*
Christs sleeping friends. Ma; *S*, *VC*, *A*, *H*, *F*
　4 pray . . . paine *MSS.*: watch and pray in vaine *Ma*

With milde rebuke he warned them to wake:
Yet sleepe did still their drousie sences hold:
As when the sunne the brightest shew doth make
In darkest shrouds the night birdes them infolde.   10
His foes did watch to worke their cruell spight,
His drousie friendes slept in his hardest plight.

As *Jonas* sayled once from *Joppaes* shoare
A boystrous tempest in the aire did broile,
The waves did rage, the thundring heavens did roare,   15
The stormes, the rockes, the lightnings threatned spoile,
The shippe was billows gaine, and chaunces pray,
Yet carelesse *Jonas* mute and sleeping lay:

So now though *Judas* like a blustring gust,
Doe stirre the furious sea of Jewish ire,   20
Though storming troopes in quarrels most unjust
Against the barke of all our blisse conspire,
Yet these disciples sleeping lie secure,
As though their wonted calme did still endure.

So *Jonas* once his weary limmes to rest,   25
Did shrowd himselfe in pleasant ivy shade,
But lo, while him a heavy sleep opprest,
His shadowy bowre, to withered stalke did fade,
A cankered worme had gnawen the root away,
And brought the glorious branches to decay.   30

O gratious plant, O tree of heavenly spring,
The paragon for leafe, for fruit and flower,
How sweete a shadow did thy braunches bring
To shrowd these soules that chose thee for their bower,
But now while they with *Jonas* fall asleepe,   35
To spoile their plant an envious worme doth creepe.

Awake ye slumbring wightes lift up your eies,
Marke *Judas* how to teare your roote he strives,
Alas the glorie of your arbor dies,
Arise and guarde the comforte of your lives.   40

8 hold:] hold. *Ma*   10 infolde.] infolde, *Ma*   12 plight *MSS.*: night *Ma*
17 gaine *S*, *VC*: game *Ma*, *A*, *H*, *F*   18 sleeping *MSS.*: slumbring *Ma*   24 did still]
still did *S*   25 weary *MSS.*: heavy *Ma*   26 pleasant ivy *MSS.*: ivy pleasant *Ma*
29 had gnawen *MSS.*: did gnaw *Ma*   37 ye *S*, *A*, *H*, *F*: you *Ma*, *VC*

No *Jonas* ivy, no *Zacheus* tree,
Were to the world so great a losse as he.

Josephs Amazement

WHEN Christ by growth disclosed his desent,
    Into the pure receipt of Maries brest;
Poore Joseph stranger yet to Gods intent,
    With doubts of jealous thoughts was sore opprest:
And wrought with divers fits of feare and love,   5
He neither can her free, nor faulty prove.

Now sence the wakefull spie of jealous minde,
    By strong conjectures deemeth her defilde;
But love in doome of things best loved blinde,
    Thinks rather sence deceav'd, then her with childe: 10
Yet proofes so pregnant were, that no pretence
Could cloake a thing so cleare and plaine to sence,

Then Joseph daunted with a deadly wound,
    Let loose the raines to undeserved griefe,
His hart did throb, his eyes in teares were drownd,   15
    His life a losse, death seem'd his best reliefe:
The pleasing rellish of his former love,
In gaulish thoughts to bitter tast doth prove.

One foote he often setteth forth of dore,
    But t'others loath uncertaine wayes to tread;   20
He takes his fardle for his needefull store,
    His casts his Inne where first he meanes to bed:
But still ere he can frame his feete to goe,
Love winneth time, till all conclude in no.

Josephs Amazement. 1602; *S, VC, A, H, F*
    7 sence *S, A, F*: since *1602, VC, H*   8 defilde] with childe *S(b.c.)*: a childe *H*
10 her] shee *VC*   with childe] defilde *S(b.c.), H*   12 to] in *?S(b.c.), A*   14 to
MSS.: of *1602*   19 forth *MSS.*: out *1602*   20 t'others *S, VC, A, H*: t'other
1602: th'other's *F*

Sometime griefe adding force he doth depart,   25
  He will against his will keepe on his pace;
But straight remorse so racks his ruing hart,
  That hasting thoughts yeeld to a pausing space:
Then mighty reasons presse him to remaine,
She whom he flies doth winne him home againe.   30

But when his thought by sight of his aboade,
  Presents the signe of misesteemed shame;
Repenting every step that back he troade,
  Teares drowne the guides, the tong the feet doth blame:
Thus warring with himselfe a field he fights,   35
Where every wound upon the giver lights.

And was (quoth he) my love so lightly pris'd,
  Or was our sacred league so soone forgot;
Could vowes be voyd, could vertues be dispis'd;
  Could such a spouse be stain'd with such a spot?   40
O wretched Joseph that hast liv'd so long,
Of faithful love to reape so greevous wrong.

Could such a worme breed in so sweet a wood,
  Could in so chast demeanure lurke untruth;
Could vice lie hid where Vertues image stood,   45
  Where hoarie sagenesse graced tender youth:
Where can affiance rest to rest secure?
In vertues fairest seate faith is not sure.

All proofes did promise hope a pledge of grace,
  Whose good might have repay'd the deepest ill;   50
Sweet signes of purest thoughts in saintly face,
  Assur'd the eye of her unstayned will,
Yet in this seeming lustre, seeme to lie
Such crimes for which the law condemnes to die.

But Josephs word shall never worke her woe,   55
  I wish her leave to live, not doome to die;
Though fortune mine, yet am I not her foe,
  She to her selfe lesse loving is then I:

The most I will, the least I can is this,
Sith none may salve, to shunne that is amisse.   60

Exile my home, the wildes shall be my walke,
   Complaint my joy, my musick mourning layes;
With pensive griefes in silence will I talke,
   Sad thoughts shall be my guides in sorrowes wayes:
This course best sutes the care of curelesse minde,   65
That seekes to loose, what most it joy'd to finde.

Like stocked tree whose branches all doe fade,
   Whose leaves doe fall, and perisht fruite decay;
Like hearbe that growes in cold and barren shade,
   Where darknes drives all quickning heate away: 70
So die must I, cut from my roote of joy,
And throwne in darkest shades of deepe annoy.

But who can flie from that his hart doth feele?
   What change of place can change implanted paine?
Removing, moves no hardnes from the steele,   75
   Sicke harts that shift no fits, shift roomes in vaine:
Where thought can see, what helps the closed eye?
Where hart pursues, what gaines the foote to flie?

Yet still I tread a maze of doubtfull ende;
   I goe, I come, she drawes, she drives away,   80
She wounds, she heales, she doth both marre and mende,
   She makes me seeke, and shunne, depart, and stay:
She is a friend to love, a foe to loth,
And in suspence I hang between them both.

A holy Hymme

PRAISE, O Sion, praise thy Saviour,
Praise thy Captaine and thy pastour,
With hymnes and solemne harmony.
What power affords performe indeede,
His worthes all praises farre exceede: 5
No praise can reach his dignity.

65 curelesse S, VC, A: carelesse *1602*, H, F
A holy Hymme. Ma; S, VC, A, H, F
5 worthes *MSS.*: workes *Ma*

A speciall theame of praise is read,
A living and life giving bread
Is on this day exhibited
Which in the supper of our Lord,   10
To twelve disciples at his bord,
None doubtes but was delivered.

Let our praise be loud and free,
Full of joy and decent glee,
With mindes and voices melody.   15
For now solemnize we that day,
Which doth with joy to us display
The prime use of this mistery.

At this borde of our new ruler,
Of new Law, new pascall order,   20
The ancient rite abolisheth.
Old decrees by new annulled,
Shadows are in trueths fulfilled:
Day former darknes finisheth.

That at supper Christ performed   25
To be done he straightly charged
For his eternall memory.
Guided by his sacred orders
Bread and wine upon our altars
To saving host we sanctifie,   30

Christians are by faith assured
That to flesh the bread is changed,
The wine to blood most pretious,
That no wit nor sence conceiveth
Firme and grounded faith believeth   35
In strange effects not curious.

---

10 Which in *MSS.*: Within *Ma*   12 None doubtes but was *MSS.* (but] *omitted A*
was] t'was *VC*): As doubtlesse twas *Ma*   13 loud *MSS.*: *misprinted* lou'd *Ma*
18 prime *MSS.*: privy Ma   mistery.] mistery *Ma*   21 abolisheth.] abolisheth
Ma   22-23 annulled . . . fulfilled *MSS.*: annilld . . . fulfilld *Ma*   23 trueths
S, A, H, F: trueth *Ma, VC*   36 effects *MSS.*: affects *Ma*

Under kindes two in appearance
Two in shew but one in substance,
Lie thinges beyond comparison:
Flesh is meat, blood drinke most heavenly: 40
Yet is Christ in each kinde wholy
Most free from al division.

None that eateth him doth chew him,
None that takes him doth divide him,
Received he whole persevereth.   45
Be there one or thousandes housled
One as much as all received,
He by no eating perisheth.

Both the good and bad receive him,
But effectes are divers in them,   50
True life, or dewe destruction,
Life to the good, death to the wicked:
Marke how both alike received
With farre unlike conclusion.

When the priest the hoast devideth,   55
Know that in each part abideth
All that the whole hoast covered,
Forme of bread not Christ is broken,
Not of Christ but of his token
Is state or stature altered.   60

Angels bread made *Pilgrimes* feeding,
Truly bread for childrens eating
To dogs not to be offered:
Signd by *Isack* on the altar,
By the Lambe and pascall supper,   65
And in the manna figured.

Jesu food and feeder of us
Heere with mercy feede and friend us,
Then grant in heaven felicity,
Lord of all whom heere thou feedest,   70

39 Lie *MSS.*: Be *Ma*   44 him . . . him,] him, . . . him *Ma*   45 persevereth.]
persevereth *Ma*   46 housled *S, A, H*: housoled *Ma, F* (*omitted VC*)   51 dewe
MSS.: true *Ma*   56 in *MSS.*: *omitted Ma*   abideth] abideth: *Ma*   64 altar,]
altar *Ma*

Fellow heires, guests with thy dearest,
Make us in heavenly company.

Of the Blessed Sacrament of the Aulter

IN paschall feast the end of aunciENT rite
An entraunce was to never endinge grace,
Tipes to the truth, dymm glymses to the light,
Performinge Deede presageing signes did chase,
Christes Final meale was fountayne of our good: 5
For mortall meate he gave immortall foode.

That which he gave he was, o peerelesse gifte,
Both god and man he was, and both he gave,
He in his handes him self did trewelye lifte:
Farre off they see whome in them selves they have.   10
Twelve did he feede, twelve did their feeder eate,
He made, he dressd, he gave, he was their meate.

They sawe, they harde, they felt him sitting nere,
Unseene, unfelt, unhard, they him receiv'd,
No diverse thinge though divers it appeare,   15
Though sences faile, yet faith is not deceivd'.
And if the wonder of the worke be newe,
Beleive the worke because his worde is trewe.

Here truth beleefe, beleefe inviteth love,
So sweete a truth love never yett enjoy'd,   20
What thought can thincke, what will doth best approve
Is here obteyn'd where no desire ys voyde.
The grace, the joy, the treasure here is such
No witt can wishe nor will embrace so much.

Selfelove here cannot crave more then it fyndes,   25
Ambition to noe higher worth aspire,
The eagrest famyn of most hungry myndes
May fill, yea farre exceede their owne desire:

71 Fellow] Fellows *S, A, H*

Of the Blessed Sacrament of the Aulter. S; VC, A, H, F; SOa
  Punctuation supplied to augment very rare marks in S.
  10 off] of *S*

In summ here is all in a summ expressd,
Of much the most, of every good the best.   30

To ravishe eyes here heavenly bewtyes are,
To winne the eare sweete musicks sweetest sound,
To lure the tast the Angells heavenly fare,
To sooth the sent divine perfumes abounde,
To please the touch he in our hartes doth bedd,   35
Whose touch doth cure the dephe, the dumm, the dedd.

Here to delight the witt trewe wisdome is,
To wooe the will of every good the choise,
For memory a mirrhor shewing blisse,
Here all that can both sence and soule rejoyce: 40
And if to all all this it do not bringe,
The fault is in the men, not in the thinge.

Though blynde men see no light, the sunne doth shyne,
Sweete Cates are sweete, though fevered tasts deny it,
Perles pretious are, though trodden on by swyne,   45
Ech truth is trewe, though all men do not trye it:
The best still to the badd doth worke the worste,
Thinges bredd to blisse do make them more accurst.

The Angells eyes whome veyles cannot deceive
Might best disclose that best they do descerne,   50
Men must with sounde and silent faith receive
More then they can by sence or reason lerne:
Gods powre our proofes, his workes our witt exceede,
The doers might is reason of his deede.

A body is endew'd with ghostly rightes,   55
A natures worke from natures law is free,
In heavenly sunne lye hidd eternall lightes,
Lightes cleere and neere yet them no eye can see,
Dedd formes a never dyinge life do shroude,
A boundlesse sea lyes in a little cloude.   60

31–36 *Omitted SOa*   32 musicks] musicke *S*(*b.c.*), *A*   40 Here all] Here is all
VC: Here's al *F*, *SOa*   53 powre] poure *S*

The god of hoastes in slender hoste doth dwell,
Yea god and man, with all to ether dewe:
That god that rules the heavens and rifled hell,
That man whose death did us to life renewe,
That god and man that is the Angells blisse,   65
In forme of bredd and wyne our nurture is.

Whole may his body be in smallest breadd,
Whole in the whole, yea whole in every crumme,
With which be one or be Tenn thowsand fedd
All to ech one, to all but one doth cumme,   70
And though ech one as much as all receive,
Not one too much, nor all too little have.

One soule in man is all in everye parte,
One face at once in many mirrhors shynes,
One fearefull noyse doth make a thowsand start,   75
One eye at once of countlesse thinges defynes:
If proofes of one in many nature frame,
God may in straunger sort performe the same.

God present is at once in everye place,
Yett god in every place is ever one,   80
So may there be by giftes of ghostly grace
One man in many roomes yett filling none.
Sith Angells may effects of bodyes shewe,
God Angells giftes on bodyes maye bestowe.

What god as auctour made he alter may,   85
No change so harde as making all of nought:
If Adam framed was of slymye claye,
Bredd may to Christes most sacred flesh be wrought.
He may do this that made with mighty hande
Of water wyne, a snake of *Moyses* wande.   90

---

66 nurture (*changed from* nature *A*)] Nurriture *VC, F* (*H illegible*)   72 too . . .
too] to . . . to *S*   87 was] were *A, H, F, SOa*

Saint Peters Complaynte

How can I live, that have my life deny'de?
What can I hope, that lost my hope in feare?
What trust to one that trewth it self defyde?
What good in him that did his god forsweare?
O synne of synnes, of evells the very worste,   5
O synfull wretch, of synners most accurste.

I vaunted erst though all his frendes had fayld',
Alone with Christe all fortunes to have try'de:
And loe I craven first of all was quaild:
Excellinge none but in Untrewth and pride.   10
Such distance is betwene highe wordes and deedes:
In proofe the greatest vaunter seldome speedes.

If tyrans bloody thretts had me dismay'd:
Or smart of cruell torments made me yelde,
There had bene some pretence to be afray'de,   15
I should have fought before I lost the feilde.
But o infamous foyle: a maydens breathe
Did blowe me downe, and blast my soule to death.

Was I to stay the Churche a Chosen rocke
That with so soft a gale was overthrowen?   20
Was I cheife pastour of the faithfull flocke,
To guide their soules that murdred thus my owne?
A rocke of ruyne, not a reste to staye:
A pastour, not to feede but to betraye.

Could servile feare of rendring natures dewe,   25
Which grouth in yeres was shortly like to clayme,
So thrall my love, that I should thus eschewe
A vowed death and mysse so faire an ayme?
Dye: dye: disloyall wretch, thy life detest:
For saving thyne, thow hast forsworne the best.   30

Saint Peters Complaynte. S; VC, A, H, F (lacks 1–4)
   Punctuation supplied; S has a mid-line comma at 65 and occasional full stops.
  8 fortunes] tortures *S(b.c.), A, H*   12 greatest] greater *VC, H*   22 thus]
his *A*: first *H*

Was life so deare and Christ become so base,
I of so greate, god of so small accounte:
That Peter nedes must followe Judas race,
And all the Jewes in Crueltye surmounte?
Yett Judas deemed thirtye pence his price: 35
I, worse then he, for nought deny'd him thrice.

Where was the hart that did so little feare
The armed troupes that him did apprehende?
Where was the sworde that strooke off Malchus eare?
Where was the faith of Christes professed frende?   40
O Adams childe, it was a selye Eve
That thee of faith and force did thus bereave.

I once designed Judge to loose and bynde
Now pleade at mercyes barr as guilty thrall.
Doves sonne was once to me for name assign'd: 45
My stony name now better sutes my fall.
My othes were stones: my cruell tongue the slynge:
My god the marke at which my spite did flynge.

Were all the Jewesh tyrannyes too fewe
To glutt thy hungry lookes with his disgrace: 50
That thow more mallice then they all must shewe:
And spitt thy poyson in thy makers face?
Didst thowe to spare his foes putt up thy sworde
To brandish now thy tongue againste thy lorde?

Is this thy best deservinge maysters meede?   55
Is this the wage he earn'd with all his toyle?
And didst thow vow thy helpe at every neede
Thus at the first encounter to recoyle?
O impious tongue, no tongue but vipers stinge,
That could with cursinge othes forsweare thy kinge. 60

O tongue, the first that did his godhedd sounde,
How couldst thow utter such detestinge wordes,
That every word was to his hart a wounde,
And lawncd him deeper then a thowsand swordes?
What Jewish rage, yea what infernall sprite,   65
Could have disgor'gd against him greater spite?

38 him did] did him *VC, F*   39 off] of *S*   42 thee] the *S*   45 sonne]
soonne *S*   49 too] to *S*   65 rage *VC, A, H, F:* race *S*

With mercye, Jesu, measure my offence:
Lett deepe remorse thy due revenge abate:
Lett teares appeace when trespas doth incense:
Lett myldnes temper thy deserved hate.   70
Lett grace forgive, lett love forgett my fall:
With feare I crave, with hope I humbly call.

S. Peters afflicted minde

IF that the sicke may grone,
Or Orphane morne his losse:
If wounded wretch may rue his harmes,
Or caitife shew his crosse:

If heart consumde with care   5
May utter signes of paine,
Then may my brest be sorrowes home,
And tongue with cause complaine.

My maladie is sinne,
And languor of the minde,   10
My body but a lazars couch,
Wherein my soule is pinde.

The care of heavenly kinne
Is dead to my reliefe,
Forlorne and left like Orphan child   15
With sighs I feede my griefe.

My woundes with mortall smart
My dying soule torment,
And prisoner to mine owne mishaps
My follies I repent.   20

My hart is but the haunt
Where all dislikes doe keepe:
And who can blame so lost a wretch,
Though teares of blood he weepe.

69 appeace] appeare *S(b.c.)*, *A*, *H*

S. Peters afflicted minde. Ma; *S*, *VC*, *A*, *H*, *F*
13 kinne *S*, *VC*, *A*, *H*: kinde *Ma*: King *F*   15 Forlorne] Forborne *S*

Mary Magdalens blush

THE signes of shame that staine my blushing face
Rise from the feeling of my raving fits,
Whose joy, annoy: whose guerdon, is disgrace:
Whose sollace, flies: whose sorrow, never flits:
Bad seed I sow'd: worse fruite is now my gaine: 5
Soone dying mirth begat long living paine.

Now pleasure ebbes: revenge beginnes to flow:
One day doth wreake the wrath that many wrought:
Remorse doth teach my guiltie thoughts to know,
How cheape I sould, that Christ so dearely bought.   10
Faults long unfelt doth conscience now bewraye,
Which cares must cure, and teares must wash awaye.

All ghostly dynts that grace at me did dart,
Like stubborne rocke I forced to recoyle:
To other flights an ayme I made my hart,   15
Whose wounds, then wel-come, now have wrought my foyle.
Woe worth the bow, woe worth the archers might,
That drave such arrowes to the marke so right.

To pull them out, to leave them in, is death:
One, to this world: one, to the world to come: 20
Wounds may I weare, and draw a doubtfull breath:
But then my wounds will worke a dreadfull dome.
And for a world, whose pleasures passe away:
I lose a world, whose joyes are past decay.

O sence, O soule, O had, O hoped blisse,   25
You wooe, you weane, you draw, you drive me back.
Your crosse-encountring, like their combate is,
That never end but with some deadly wrack.
When sense doth winne, the soule doth loose the field,
And present happes, make future hopes to yeeld.   30

Mary Magdalens blush. Ca; *S, VC, A, H*
    15 To] *misprinted* Lo *Ca*   17 woe] *misprinted* who *Ca*   18 drave] drawe
A: drew *H*   30 happes, make future hopes] happ makes future hopes *S*: happes
makes future hope *VC*: haps makes future hopes *A*: happ, makes futures hopes *H*

O heaven, lament: sense robbeth thee of Saints:
Lament O soules, sense spoyleth you of grace.
Yet sense doth scarse deserve these hard complaints,
Love is the theife, sense but the entring place.
Yet graunt I must, sense is not free from sinne,   35
For theefe he is that theefe admitteth in.

S. Peters remorse

REMORSE upbraids my faults,
    Selfe blaming conscience cries,
Sinne claimes the hoast of humbled thoughtes,
    And streames of weeping eies.

Let penance Lorde prevaile,   5
    Let sorrow sue release,
Let love be umpier in my cause,
    And passe the doome of peace.

If doome go by desert,
    My least desert is death,   10
That robs from soule immortall joies,
    From body mortall breath.

But in so high a God,
    So base a wormes annoy
Can adde no praise unto thy power,   15
    No blisse unto thy joy.

Well may I frie in flames
    Due fuell to hell fire,
But on a wretch to wreake thy wrath
    Can not be worth thine ire.   20

Yet sith so vile a woorme
    Hath wrought his greatest spight,
Of highest treasons well thou maist
    In rigor him endite.

S. Peters remorse. Ma; *S, VC, A, H, F*
  23 treasons *MSS.*: treason *Ma*
811841   D

But mercy may relent   25
  And temper justice rod:
For mercy doth as much belong
  As Justice to a God.

If former time or place
  More right to mercy winne,   30
Thou first wert author of my selfe,
  Then umpier of my sinne.

Did mercy spin the thread
  To weave in justice loome,
Wert thou a father to conclude   35
  With dreadfull Judges doome?

It is a small reliefe
  To say I was thy child,
If as an ill deserving foe
  From grace I be exilde.   40

I was, I had, I could,
  Are wordes importing want:
They are but dust of dead supplies,
  Where needfull helpes are scant.

Once to have beene in blisse   45
  That hardly can returne,
Doth but bewray from whence I fell,
  And wherefore now I mourne.

All thoughts of passed hopes
  Encrease my present crosse: 50
Like ruins of decaied joies
  They still upbraide my losse.

O milde and mighty Lord,
  Amend that is amisse:
My sinne my soare, thy love my salve,   55
  Thy cure my comfort is.

Confirme thy former deede,
   Reforme that is defilde:
I was, I am, I will remaine
   Thy charge, thy choice, thy childe.   60

Davids Peccavi

IN eaves, sole Sparrowe sits not more alone,
   Nor mourning Pellican in Desert wilde:
Then silly I, that solitarie mone,
   From highest hopes to hardest hap exilde:
Sometime (ô blisful time) was vertues meede,   5
Ayme to my thoughts, guide to my word and deede.

But feares now are my Pheares, griefe my delight,
   My teares my drink, my famisht thoughts my bread;
Day full of dumps, Nurse of unrest the night,
   My garments gyves, a bloody field my bed,   10
My sleepe is rather death, then deaths allie,
Yet kill'd with murd'ring pangues, I cannot die.

This is the change of my ill changed choyse,
   Ruth for my rest, for comforts cares I finde;
To pleasing tunes succeedes a plaining voyce,   15
   The dolefull ecchoe of my wayling minde:
Which taught to know the worth of vertues joyes,
Doth hate it selfe for loving fancies toyes.

If wiles of wit had over-wrought my will,
   Or subtle traines misled my steppes awrie,   20
My foile had found excuse in want of skill,
   Ill deede I might, though not ill doome denie:
But wit and will must now confesse with shame,
Both deede and doome, to have deserved blame.

57 deede *MSS.*: deedes *Ma*

Davids Peccavi. 1602; S, VC, A, H, F
4 hap]happes *VC,H*   7 now are S, VC, A: are now *1602*,H,F.   13 change
S, VC, A, H: chaunce *1602*, F   15 pleasing S, VC, A, H: pleasant *1602*, F

I Fansie deem'd fit guide to leade my way, 25
 And as I deem'd, I did pursue her track;
Wit lost his ayme, and will was Fancies pray,
 The Rebell wan, the Ruler went to wrack:
But now sith fansie did with folly end,
Wit bought with losse, will taught by wit, will mend. 30

A Phansie turned to a sinners complaint

Hee that his mirth hath lost,
Whose comfort is to rue,
Whose hope is fallen, whose faith is cras'de,
Whose trust is found untrue:

If he have held them deere, 5
And cannot cease to mone;
Come, let him take his place by me,
He shall not rue alone.

But if the smallest sweete,
Be mixt with all his sower; 10
If in the day, the moneth, the yeare,
He feele one lightning hower,

Then rest he with himselfe,
He is no mate for me;
Whose time in teares, whose race in ruth, 15
Whose life a death must be.

Yet not the wished death,
That feeles no plaint or lack:
That making free the better part,
Is onely Natures wrack. 20

O no, that were too well,
My death is of the minde;
That alwayes yeelds extreamest pangues,
Yet threatens worse behinde.

28 Rebell *MSS.*: Rebels *1602* Ruler *S, VC, A*: Rulers *1602, H, F*
A Phansie turned to a sinners complaint. 1602; S, VC, A, H, F

As one that lives in shewe,   25
And inwardly dooth die;
Whose knowledge is a bloody field,
Where vertue slaine doth lie.

Whose hart the Altar is,
And hoast a God to move: 30
From whom my ill doth feare revenge,
His good doth promise love.

My phansies are like thornes,
In which I goe by night;
My frighted wits are like an hoast,   35
That force hath put to flight.

My sence is passions spie,
My thoughts like ruines olde,
Which shew how faire the building was,
While grace did it upholde.   40

And still before mine eyes,
My mortall fall they lay;
Whom grace and vertue once advaunc'd
Now sinne hath cast away.

O thoughts, no thoughts but wounds,   45
Sometime the seate of joy,
Sometime the store of quiet rest,
But now of all annoy.

I sow'd the soyle of peace,
My blisse was in the spring;   50
And day by day the fruite I eate,
That Vertues tree did bring.

To Nettles now my corne,
My field is turn'd to flint;
Where I a heavie harvest reape,   55
Of cares that never stint.

41 mine *MSS.*: my *1602*   56 Of] *misprinted* Off *1602*

The peace, the rest, the life,
That I enjoy'd of yore,
Were happy lot, but by their losse,
My smart doth sting the more.   60

So to unhappy men,
The best frames to the worst:
O time, ô place, where thus I fell,
Deere then, but now accurst.

In was, stands my delight,   65
In is, and shall my woe,
My horrour fastned in the yea,
My hope hangd in the no.

Unworthy of releefe
That craved it too late;   70
Too late I finde, (I finde too well)
Too well, stoode my estate.

Behold, such is the end,
That pleasure doth procure,
Of nothing else but care and plaint,   75
Can she the minde assure.

Forsaken first by grace,
By pleasure now forgotten,
Her paine I feele, but graces wage,
Have others from me gotten.   80

Then grace, where is the joy
That makes thy torments sweete;
Where is the cause that many thought,
Their deaths through thee but meete?

Where thy disdaine of sinne,   85
Thy secret sweete delight;
Thy sparks of blisse, thy heavenly rayes,
That shined erst so bright?

68 hangd *S, VC, A*: hangs *1602, H, F*   84 meete?] meete. *1602*   87 rayes
S, VC, A, H: joyes *1602, F*

O that they were not lost,
Or I could it excuse;   90
O that a dreame of fained losse,
My judgement did abuse.

O fraile inconstant flesh,
Soone trapt in every ginne;
Soone wrought thus to betray thy soule,   95
And plunge thy selfe in sinne.

Yet hate I but the fault,
And not the faulty one:
Ne can I rid from me the mate,
That forceth me to moane.   100

To moane a sinners case,
Then which, was never worse;
In Prince or poore, in young or olde,
In bliss'd, or full of curse.

Yet Gods must I remaine,   105
By death, by wrong, by shame;
I cannot blot out of my hart,
That grace wrought in his name.

I cannot set at naught
Whom I have held so deere: 110
I cannot make him seeme afarre,
That is in deede so neere.

Not that I looke hence-forth
For love that earst I found;
Sith that I brake my plighted truth,   115
To build on fickle ground.

Yet that shall never faile,
Which my faith bare in hand:
I gave my vow, my vow gave me,
Both vow and gift shall stand.   120

97 hate] have *S(b.c.)*, *A*   108 wrought *MSS.*: writ *1602*

But since that I have sinn'd,
And scourge none is too ill;
I yeeld me captive to my curse,
My hard fate to fulfill.

The solitarie Wood   125
My Cittie shall become,
The darkest dennes shall be my Lodge,
In which I rest or come.

A sandie plot my board,
The wormes my feast shall be,   130
Where-with my carcasse shall be fed,
Untill they feede on me.

My teares shall be my wine,
My bed a craggy Rock;
My harmonie the Serpents hisse,   135
The screeching Owle my clock.

My exercise remorse,
And dolefull sinners layes,
My booke remembrance of my crimes,
And faults of former dayes.   140

My walke the path of plaint,
My prospect into hell;
Where Judas and his cursed crue,
In endlesse paines doe dwell.

And though I seeme to use   145
The faining Poets stile,
To figure forth my careful plight,
My fall, and my exile:

Yet is my greefe not fain'd,
Wherein I starve and pine,   150
Who feeleth most, shall think it least,
If his compare with mine.

---

127 dennes] denne *VC*   151 feeleth *S, VC, A, H*: feeles the *1602, F*

A vale of teares

A VALE there is enwrapt with dreadfull shades,
Which thicke of mourning pines shrouds from the sunne,
Where hanging clifts yeld short and dumpish glades,
And snowie floud with broken streames doth runne,

Where eie-roume is from rockes to cloudie skie,   5
From thence to dales with stonie ruines strow'd,
Then to the crushed waters frothie frie,
Which tumbleth from the tops where snow is thow'd:

Where eares of other sound can have no choice,
But various blustring of the stubburne winde   10
In trees, in caves, in straits with divers noise,
Which now doth hisse, now howle, now roare by kinde:

Where waters wrastle with encountring stones,
That breake their streames, and turne them into foame,
The hollow clouds full fraught with thundring groans,   15
With hideous thumps discharge their pregnant wombe.

And in the horror of this fearfull quier,
Consists the musicke of this dolefull place:
All pleasant birds their tunes from thence retire,
Where none but heavy notes have any grace.   20

Resort there is of none but pilgrim wights,
That passe with trembling foot and panting heart,
With terror cast in cold and shivering frights,
They judge the place to terror framde by art:

Yet natures worke it is of arte untoucht,   25
So strait indeed, so vast unto the eie,
With such disordred order strangely coucht,
And so with pleasing horror low and hie,

A vale of teares. Ma; S, VC, A, H, F
  2 sunne,] sunne *Ma*   4 floud *S, VC, A*: flouds *Ma, H, F*   doth *S, VC, A, H*:
doe *Ma, F*   5 rockes *S, A, H, F*: rocke *Ma, VC*   6 with . . . strow'd *S, A,*
H, F: which stormie ruines shroud *Ma*: which stony ruines strowde *VC*   13 encountring *MSS.*: encountering *Ma*   15 fraught with] fraught of *VC*: fraight
with *H*   thundring *MSS.*: thundering *Ma*   23 shivering *MSS.*: shruddring *Ma*
24 They (The *VC*) judge *MSS.*: And all *Ma*

That who it viewes must needs remaine agast,
Much at the worke, more at the makers might,   30
And muse how Nature such a plot could cast,
Where nothing seemed wrong, yet nothing right:

A place for mated minds, an onely bower,
Where every thing doth sooth a dumpish mood.
Earth lies forlorne, the cloudie skie doth lower,   35
The wind here weepes, here sighes, here cries aloude.

The strugling floud betweene the marble grones,
Then roring beates upon the craggie sides,
A little off amidst the pibble stones,
With bubling streames and purling noise it glides.   40

The pines thicke set, hie growne, and ever greene,
Still cloath the place with sad and mourning vaile.
Here gaping cliffe, there mossie plaine is seene,
Here hope doth spring, and there againe doth quaile.

Huge massie stones that hang by tickle stay,   45
Still threaten fall, and seeme to hang in feare,
Some withered trees ashamde of their decay,
Beset with greene, are forcde gray coats to weare.

Here christall springs crept out of secret vaine,
Strait finde some envious hole that hides their grace.   50
Here seared tufts lament the want of raine,
There thunder wracke gives terror to the place.

All pangs and heavie passions here may find
A thousand motives suitly to their griefes,
To feed the sorrowes of their troubled minde,   55
And chase away dame pleasures vaine reliefes.

To plaining thoughts this vaile a rest may bee,
To which from worldly joyes they may retire.
Where sorrow springs from water, stone and tree,
Where everie thing with mourners doth conspire.   60

36 here sighes, here *MSS*.: her sighes, her *Ma*   40 and *MSS*.: a *Ma*
42 sad *S, VC, H, F*: shade *Ma, A* (*changed from* sadd)   43 cliffe *MSS*.: cliffes
Ma   mossie *MSS*.: mosse growne *Ma*   46 fall *MSS*.: foule *Ma*   48 are
MSS.: and *Ma*   50 grace *MSS*.: graine *Ma*   51 want of raine *MSS*.: wants
of grace *Ma*   58 joyes *MSS*.: toyes *Ma*

Set here my soule maine streames of teares afloate,
Here all thy sinfull foiles alone recount,
Of solemne tunes make thou the dolefulst note,
That to thy ditties dolor may amount.

When *Eccho* doth repeat thy plainfull cries,   65
Thinke that the verie stones thy sinnes bewray,
And now accuse thee with their sad replies,
As heaven and earth shall in the latter day,

Let former faults be fuell of the fire,
For griefe in Limbecke of thy heart to still   70
Thy pensive thoughts, and dumps of thy desire,
And vapoure teares up to thy eies at will.

Let teares to tunes, and paines to plaints be prest,
And let this be the burdon of thy song,
Come deepe remorse, possesse my sinfull brest: 75
Delights adue, I harbourd you too long.

The prodigall childs soule wracke

DISANKERD from a blisfull shore,
And lancht into the maine of cares,
Grown rich in vice, in vertue poore,
From freedom faln in fatal snares

I found my selfe on every side   5
Enwrapped in the waves of wo,
And tossed with a toilesome tide,
Could to no port for refuge go.

The wrastling winds with raging blasts
Still hold me in a cruell chace.   10
They broke my anchors, sailes, and masts,
Permitting no reposing place.

61 Set . . . maine *MSS.*: Sit here my soule, mourne *Ma*   63 dolefulst] dolefull
VC, A, H   65 plainfull *S, H*: painfull *Ma, VC, A, F*   70 still] still. *Ma*
74 burdon *MSS.*: burthen *Ma*   of *MSS.*: to *Ma*   76 adue,] adue *Ma*   too] to *Ma*
The prodigall childs soule wracke. Ma; S, VC, A, H, F
2 maine *MSS.*: meane *Ma*   cares,] cares *Ma*   3 poore,] poore *Ma*   10 hold]
helde *H, F*   11 broke *S, A, H, F*: breake *Ma, VC*   sailes *MSS.*: saile *Ma*

The boistrous seas with swelling flouds,
On every side did work their spight,
Heaven overcast with stormie clouds,   15
Denide the Planets guiding light.

The hellish furies lay in wait,
To winne my soule into their power,
To make me bite at every bait,
Wherein my bane I might devoure.   20

Thus heaven and hell, thus sea and land,
Thus stormes and tempests did conspire,
With just revenge of scourging hand,
To witnes Gods deserved ire.

I plunged in this heavie plight,   25
Found in my faults just cause of feares:
By darkenes taught to know my light,
The losse thereof enforced teares.

I felt my inward bleeding sores,
My festred wounds began to smart,   30
Stept far within deaths fatall doores,
The pangs thereof were nere my hart.

I cried truce, I craved peace,
A league with death I would conclude,
But vaine it was to sue release,   35
Subdue I must or be subdude.

Death and deceit had pitcht their snares
And put their wicked proofes in ure
To sinke me in despairing cares,
Or make me stoupe to pleasures lure: 40

They sought by their bewitching charmes,
So to enchant my erring sense,
That when they sought my greatest harmes,
I might neglect my best defence.

14 spight,] spight *Ma*   26 of feares *H, F*: to feare *Ma*: of feare *S, A*: to feares
VC   27 By *S, A, H, F*: My *Ma VC*   38 wicked *MSS.*: wonted *Ma*

My dazled eies could take no view,   45
No heed of their deceiving shifts,
So often did they alter hew,
And practise new devised drifts:

With Sirens songs they fed my eares,
Till luld asleepe in errors lap,   50
I found these tunes turnd into teares,
And short delights to long mishap.

For I inticed to their lore
And soothed with their idle toies
Was trained to their prison doore,   55
The end of all such flying joies:

Where chaind in sinne I lay in thrall,
Next to the dungeon of despaire,
Till mercy raisde me from my fall,
And grace my ruines did repaire.   60

Marie Magdalens complaint at Christs death

SITH my life from life is parted:
    Death come take thy portion.
Who survives, when life is murdred,
    Lives by meere extortion.
All that live, and not in God: 5
Couch their life in deaths abod.

Seely starres must needes leave shining,
    When the sunne is shaddowed.
Borrowed streames refraine their running,
    When head springs are hindered.   10
One that lives by others breath,
Dieth also by his death.

46 deceiving] *misprinted* receiving *Ma*   49 my *MSS*.: mine *Ma*   50 in *MSS*.:
on *Ma*   51 these *S, VC, A, H*: their *Ma*: those *F*   53 lore] lore; *Ma*
Marie Magdalens complaint at Christs death. Ca; *S, VC, A, H*; *F compiler, Cb*

O true life, sith thou hast left me,
　Mortall life is tedious.
Death it is to live without thee,　　　　　　　　15
　Death, of all most odious.
Turne againe or take me to thee,
Let me die or live thou in mee.

Where the truth once was, and is not,
　Shaddowes are but vanitie:　　　　　　　　20
Shewing want, that helpe they cannot:
　Signes, not salves of miserie.
Paynted meate no hunger feedes,
Dying life each death exceedes.

With my love, my life was nestled　　　　　　　25
　In the sonne of happinesse:
From my love, my life is wrested
　To a world of heavinesse.
O, let love my life remove,
Sith I live not where I love.　　　　　　　　30

O my soule, what did unloose thee
　From thy sweete captivitie?
God, not I, did still possesse thee:
　His, not mine, thy libertie.
O, too happie thrall thou wart,　　　　　　　35
When thy prison, was his hart.

Spitefull speare, that breakst this prison,
　Seate of all felicitie,
Working thus, with double treason,
　Loves and lifes deliverie:　　　　　　　　40
Though my life thou drav'st away,
Maugre thee my love shall stay.

13 sith *MSS.*: since *Ca*　　26 sonne] somme *S, VC, H, F compiler, Cb*　　35 too]
two *Ca*　　37 breakst *MSS., Cb*: brakest *Ca*　　39 thus *S, VC*: this *Ca, A (H*
illegible)　　40 lifes *S, VC, H*: lives *Ca*: life *A*　　41 drav'st] drawst *A, H*

Decease release

Dum morior orior

THE pounded spice both tast and sent doth please,
In fading smoke the force doth incense shewe,
The perisht kernell springeth with encrease,
The lopped tree doth best and soonest growe.

Gods spice I was and pounding was my due,   5
In fadinge breath my incense savored best,
Death was the meane my kyrnell to renewe,
By loppinge shott I upp to heavenly rest.

Some thinges more perfect are in their decaye,
Like sparke that going out gives clerest light,   10
Such was my happ whose dolefull dying daye
Beganne my joy and termed fortunes spite.

Alive a Queene, now dead I am a Sainte,
Once N: calld, my name nowe Martyr is,
From earthly raigne debarred by restraint,   15
In liew whereof I raigne in heavenly blisse.

My life my griefe, my death hath wrought my joye,
My frendes my foyle, my foes my weale procur'd,
My speedy death hath shortned longe annoye,
And losse of life an endles life assur'd.   20

My skaffold was the bedd where ease I founde,
The blocke a pillowe of Eternall reste,
My hedman cast me in a blisfull swounde,
His axe cutt off my cares from combred breste.

Rue not my death, rejoyce at my repose,   25
It was no death to me but to my woe,
The budd was opened to lett out the Rose,
The cheynes unloo'sd to lett the captive goe.

Decease release. S; VC, A, H, F
  Punctuation supplied.
  14 N: (*interlineation 2nd hand S*)] Mary *VC, A*: Anna *F*   24 off] of *S*

A prince by birth, a prisoner by mishappe,
From Crowne to crosse, from throne to thrall I fell,   30
My right my ruthe, my titles wrought my trapp,
My weale my woe, my worldly heaven my hell.

By death from prisoner to a prince enhaunc'd,
From Crosse to Crowne, from thrall to throne againe,
My ruth my right, my trapp my stile advaunc'd,   35
From woe to weale, from hell to heavenly raigne.

I dye without desert

If orphane Childe enwrapt in swathing bands
Doth move to mercy when forlorne it lyes,
If none without remorse of love withstands
The pitious noyse of infantes selye cryes,
Then hope, my helplesse hart, some tender eares   5
Will rue thy orphane state and feeble teares.

Relinquisht Lamb in solitarye wood
With dying bleat doth move the toughest mynde,
The gasping pangues of new engendred brood,
Base though they be, compassion use to finde,   10
Why should I then of pitty doubt to speede,
Whose happ would force the hardest hart to bleede?

Left orphane like in helpelesse state I rue,
With onely sighes and teares I pleade my case,
My dying plaints I daylie do renewe,   15
And fill with heavy noyse a desert place.
Some tender hart will weepe to here me mone,
Men pitty may, but helpe me god alone.

Rayne downe, yee heavens, your teares this case requires,
Mans eyes unhable are enough to shedd,   20
If sorow could have place in heavenly quires
A juster ground the world hath seldome bredd.
For right is wrong'd, and vertue wag'd with blood,
The badd are blissd, god murdred in the good.

I dye without desert. S; VC, A, H, F
    Punctuation supplied; S has mid-line comma in 23, and occasional full stops only.
    19 yee] you *VC*: yea *H*

A gracious plant for fruite, for leafe, and flower, 25
A peereles gemm for vertue, proofe, and price,
A noble peere for prowesse, witt, and powre,
A frend to truth, a foe I was to vice,
And loe, alas, nowe Innocente I dye,
A case that might even make the stones to crye. 30

Thus fortunes favors still are bent to flight,
Thus worldly blisse in finall bale doth end,
Thus vertue still pursued is with spight,
But let my fall though ruefull none offend.
God doth sometymes first cropp the sweetest floure, 35
And leaves the weede till tyme do it devoure.

Mans civill warre

MY hovering thoughts would flie to heaven
    And quiet nestle in the skie,
Faine would my ship in vertues shore
    Without remove at anchor lie:

But mounting thoughts are hailed downe 5
    With heavie poise of mortall load,
And blustring stormes denie my ship
    In vertues haven secure aboade.

When inward eie to heavenly sights
    Doth draw my longing harts desire, 10
The world with jesses of delights
    Would to her pearch my thoughts retire,

Fond fancie traines to pleasures lure,
    Though reason stiffely do repine.
Though wisdome wooe me to the saint, 15
    Yet sense would win me to the shrine,

25 and] for *VC, F*   27 powre] poure *S*   34 fall] fate *A, H, F*
Mans civill warre. Ma; *S, VC, A, H, F*
  5 mounting *MSS.*: mounted *Ma*   7 ship] ship, *Ma*   8 secure *MSS.*: sure
Ma   11 jesses *MSS.*: lesses *Ma*   delights] delights, *Ma*

Where reason loathes, there fancie loves,
  And overrules the captive will,
Foes senses are to vertues lore,
  They draw the wit their wish to fill.   20

Neede craves consent of soule to sence,
  Yet divers bents breed civil fray,
Hard hap where halves must disagree,
  Or truce of halves the whole betray,

O cruell fight where fighting frend   25
  With love doth kil a favoring foe,
Where peace with sense is warre with God,
  And selfe delight the seede of woe,

Dame pleasures drugges are steept in sinne,
  Their sugred tast doth breede anoy,   30
O fickle sense beware her ginne,
  Sell not thy soule for brittle joy.

Life is but Losse

BY force I live, in will I wish to die,
  In plaint I passe the length of lingring daies,
Free would my soule from mortall body flie,
  And treade the tracke of deaths desired waies;
Life is but losse, where death is deemed gaine,   5
And loathed pleasures breede displeasing paine.

Who would not die to kill all murdring greeves,
  Or who would live in never dying feares?
Who would not wish his treasure safe from theeves,
  And quit his hart from pangues, his eyes from teares?   10
Death parteth but two ever fighting foes,
Whose civill strife doth worke our endlesse woes.

---

18 overrules *MSS.*: ever rules *Ma*   will,] will *Ma*   19 senses are *MSS.*: senses,
and *Ma*   22 breed *S, VC, A, H*: breeds *Ma, F*   24 truce *MSS.*: trust *Ma*
whole] hole *Ma*

Life is but Losse. Cb; S, VC, A, H, F
  1 live,] live *Cb*   4 tracke] tracke, *Cb*   7 murdring *S, A, H, F*: murdering
Cb, VC   11 two] two, *Cb*   12 strife] strife, *Cb*

Life is a wandring course to doubtfull rest,
  As oft a cursed ryse to damning leape
As happie race to winne a heavenly crest,   15
  None being sure, what finall fruites to reape.
And who can like in such a life to dwell,
Whose waies are straite to heav'n, but wyde to hell.

Come cruell death why lingrest thou so long,
  What doth withholde thy dint from fatall stroake?   20
Now prest I am, Alas thou doest me wrong,
  To let me live more anger to provoke:
Thy right is had, when thou hast stopt my breath,
Why shouldst thou stay, to worke my double death?

If *Saules* attempt in falling on his blade,   25
  As lawful were, as ethe to put in ure:
If *Sampsons* leave, a common law were made,
  Of *Abels* lot if all that would were sure,
Then cruell death thou should'st the tyrant play,
With none but such as wished for delay.   30

Where life is lov'd, thou ready art to kill,
  And to abridge with sodaine pangues their joy,
Where life is loath'd thou wilt not worke their will,
  But dost adjourne their death to their annoy,
To some thou art a fierce unbidden guest,   35
But those that crave thy helpe thou helpest least.

Avant O viper, I thy spight defie,
  There is a God that over-rules thy force,
Who can thy weapons to his will apply,
  And shorten or prolong our brittle course: 40
I on his mercie, not thy might relye,
To him I live, for him I hope to dye.

14 a cursed] accursed *VC*   leape] leape; *Cb*   17 like] like, *Cb*   21 am,]
am *Cb*   28 sure,] sure. *Cb*

Seeke flowers of heaven

SOARE up my soule unto thy rest,
  Cast off this loathsome loade:
Long is the date of thy exile,
  Too long thy strait abode.

Graze not on worldly withered weede,   5
  It fitteth not thy taste,
The flowers of everlasting spring
  Doe grow for thy repast.

Their leaves are staind in beauties die,
  And blazed with their beams,   10
Their stalks inameld with delight,
  And limbde with glorious gleames.

Life giving juice of living love
  Their sugred vaines doth fill,
And watred with eternall showers,   15
  They nectared drops distill.

These flowers do spring from fertile soile,
  Though from unmanurde field,
Most glittering gold in lieu of glebe
  These fragrant flowers doth yeeld: 20

Whose soveraigne sent surpassing sense
  So ravisheth the minde,
That worldly weedes needs must he loath,
  That can these flowers find.

I die alive

O LIFE what lets thee from a quicke decease?
  O death what drawes thee from a present pray?
My feast is done, my soule would be at ease,
  My grace is said, O death come take away.

Seeke flowers of heaven. Ma; S, VC, A, H, F
  4 thy strait *S, VC, H, F*: the strickt *Ma*: thy stricte *A*   7 spring] spring, *Ma*
10 their] her *A, H, F*   13 love] love, *Ma*   19 glebe] glebe, *Ma*   20 doth *S, F*:
do *Ma, S(b.c.), VC, A, H*   21 sense] sense, *Ma*
I die alive. Cb; S, VC, A, H, F
  1-4 *Transferred to end of poem H*   3 done,] done *Cb*

I live, but such a life as ever dies,   5
    I die but such a death, as never ends,
My death to end my dying life denies,
    And life my living death no whit amends.

Thus still I die, yet still I do revive,
    My living death by dying life is fedd: 10
Grace more then nature keepes my hart alive,
    Whose Idle hopes and vaine desires are dead.

Not where I breath, but where I love I live,
    Not where I love, but where I am I die:
The life I wish, must future glory give,   15
    The deathes I feele, in present dangers lie.

What joy to live?

I WAGE no warre yet peace I none enjoy,
    I hope, I feare, I frye, in freesing cold:
I mount in mirth still prostrate in annoy,
    I all the world embrace yet nothing holde.
All wealth is want where cheefest wishes faile,   5
Yea life is loath'd, where love may not prevaile.

For that I love I long, but that I lacke,
    That others love I loath, and that I have:
All worldly fraights to me are deadly wracke,
    Men present hap, I future hopes doe crave.   10
They loving where they live, long life require,
To live where best I love, death I desire.

Heere love is lent for loane of filthy gaine,
    Most frends befriend themselves with frendships shew,
Here plentie perill, want doth breede disdaine,   15
    Cares common are, joyes faultie, short and few.

9 revive] remayne *S(b.c.)*, *A*
What joy to live? Cb; *S, VC, A, H, F*
   Title live?] live. *Cb*
9 fraights] frightes *S(b.c.)*, *A*   13 loane] love *S(b.c.)*, *VC, A*   14 them-
selves] *misprinted* themselvs *Cb*   shew,] shew *Cb*   16 faultie,] faultie *Cb*

Here honour envide, meanenesse is dispis'de,
Sinne deemed solace, vertue little pris'de.

Heere beautie is a baite that swallowed choakes,
   A treasure sought still to the owners harmes: 20
A light that eies to murdring sights provokes,
   A grace that soules enchants with mortall charmes,
A luring aime to Cupids fiery flights,
A balefull blisse that damnes where it delights.

O who would live so many deathes to trye?   25
   Where will doth wish, that wisedome doth reprove:
Where nature craves, that grace must needes denie,
   Where sence doth like, that reason cannot love,
Where best in shew, in finall proofe is worst,
Where pleasures upshot is to die accurst.   30

Lifes death loves life

Who lives in love, loves least to live,
   And long delaies doth rue:
If him he love by whom he lives,
   To whom all love is due.

Who for our love did choose to live,   5
   And was content to die:
Who lov'd our love more then his life
   And love with life did buy.

Let us in life, yea with our life,
   Requite his living love: 10
For best we live when least we live,
   If love our life remove.

Where love is hot, life hateful is,
   Their groundes doe not agree:
Love where it loves, life where it lives,   15
   Desireth most to be.

18 solace,] solace *Cb*   pris'de.] pris'de *Cb*   21 murdring] murthering *VC*: murdering *A*   sighs *MSS.*: sighs *Cb*   provokes,] provokes. *Cb*   22 enchants *MSS.*: enchant *Cb*   charmes,] charmes. *Cb*   23 aime] gayne *S(b.c.)*, *A* 26 wish,] wish *Cb*   27 craves,] craves *Cb*   29 worst,] worst. *Cb*
Lifes death loves life. Cb; *S, VC, A, H, F*
  1 least] best *A, H*

And sith love is not where it lives,
  Nor liveth where it loves:
Love hateth life, that holdes it backe,
  And death it best approves.   20

For seldome is he wonne in life,
  Whom love doth most desire:
If wonne by love yet not injoyde,
  Till mortall life expire.

Life out of earth hath no aboad,   25
  In earth love hath no place,
Love setled hath her joyes in heav'n,
  In earth life all her grace.

Mourne therefore no true lovers death:
  Life onely him annoyes.   30
And when he taketh leave of life,
  Then love beginnes his joyes.

At home in Heaven

FAIRE soule, how long shall veyles thy graces shroud?
  How long shall this exile with-hold thy right?
When will thy sunne disperse this mortall cloud,
  And give thy gloryes scope to blaze their light?
O that a Starre more fit for Angels eyes,   5
Should pyne in earth, not shine above the skyes.

Thy ghostly beautie offred force to God,
  It cheyn'd him in the lynckes of tender love.
It woon his will with man to make abode:
  It stai'd his Sword, and did his wrath remove.   10
It made the rigor of his Justice yeeld,
And Crowned mercye Empresse of the feelde.

25 earth] earth, *Cb*   no *MSS.*: not *Cb*
At home in Heaven. Cb; *S, VC, A, H, F*
  2 right?] right, *Cb*   3 cloud,] cloud? *Cb*   4 light?] light. *Cb*

This lull'd our heavenly *Sampson* fast asleepe,
    And laid him in our feeble natures lapp.
This made him under mortall load to creepe: 15
    And in our flesh his god head to enwrap.
This made him sojourne with us in exile:
    And not disdayne our tytles in his style.

This brought him from the ranckes of heaven'ly quires,
    Into this vale of teares, and cursed soyle: 20
From flow'rs of grace, into a world of bryers:
    From life to death, from blisse to balefull toyle.
This made him wander in our Pilgrim weede,
    And tast our tormentes, to relieve our neede.

O soule do not thy noble thoughtes abase   25
    To lose thy loves in any mortall wight:
Content thy eye at home with native grace,
    Sith God him selfe is ravisht with thy sight.
If on thy beautie God enamored bee:
Base is thy love of any lesse then hee.   30

Give not assent to muddy minded skill,
    That deemes the feature of a pleasing face
To be the sweetest baite to lure the will:
    Not valewing right the worth of Ghostly grace:
Let Gods and Angels censure winne beliefe,   35
That of all bewties judge our soules the chiefe.

Queene *Hester* was of rare and pearlesse hew,
    And *Judeth* once for beauty bare the vaunt,
But he that could our soules endowments vew,
    Would soone to soules the Crowne of beautie graunt,   40
O soule out of thy selfe seeke God alone:
Grace more then thine, but Gods, the world hath none.

---

25 abase] abase? *Cb*   26 wight] weight *Cb*   27 thy *S, VC, A, H*: thyne
Cb, F   30 is] be *S, VC*   32 face] face, *Cb*   33 lure] *misprinted* live *Cb*

Looke home

RETYRED thoughts enjoy their owne delights,
As beawtie doth in selfe beholding eye:
Mans mind a myrrour is of heavenly sights,
A breefe wherein all marvailes summed lye.
Of fayrest formes, and sweetest shapes the store,   5
Most gracefull all, yet thought may grace them more.

The mind a creature is, yet can create,
To natures paterns adding higher skill:
Of finest workes wit better could the state,
If force of wit had equall power of will.   10
Devise of man in working hath no end,
What thought can thinke another thought can mend.

Mans soule of endles beauties image is,
Drawne by the worke of endlesse skill and might:
This skilfull might gave many sparkes of blisse,   15
And to discerne this blisse a native light.
To frame Gods image as his worthes requirde:
His might, his skill, his word, and will conspirde.

All that he had his image should present,
All that it should present he could afford: 20
To that he could afford his will was bent,
His will was followed with performing word.
Let this suffice, by this conceive the rest,
He should, he could, he would, he did the best.

Times goe by turnes

THE lopped tree in time may grow againe,
Most naked plantes renew both fruit and flower:
The soriest wight may find release of paine,
The dryest soyle sucke in some moystning shower.

Looke home. Ca; S, VC, A, H
  23 rest,] rest *Ca*   24 would,] would *Ca*

Times goe by turnes. Ca; S, VC, A, H
  1 lopped] lypped *Ca*   3 soriest *MSS.*: sorest *Ca*   4 sucke] suckes *VC, H*

Times goe by turnes, and chaunces chaunge by course: 5
From fowle to faire: from better happe, to worse.

The sea of fortune doth not ever flowe,
She drawes her favours to the lowest ebbe:
Her tyde hath equall times to come and goe,
Her Loome doth weave the fine and coursest webbe.   10
No joye so great, but runneth to an end:
No hap so hard, but may in fine amend.

Not alwaies fall of leafe, nor ever spring,
No endles night, yet not eternall day:
The saddest birds a season find to sing,   15
The roughest storme a calme may soone alay.
Thus with succeeding turnes God tempereth all:
That man may hope to rise, yet feare to fall.

A chaunce may winne that by mischaunce was lost,
The net that holdes no great, takes little fish: 20
In some things all, in all things none are crost,
Fewe, all they neede: but none, have all they wish,
Unmedled joyes here to no man befall,
Who least, hath some, who most hath never all.

Losse in delaies

SHUN delaies, they breede remorse:
Take thy time, while time doth serve thee,
Creeping Snailes have weakest force;
Flie their fault least thou repent thee:
Good is best when soonest wrought,   5
Lingred labours come to nought.

Hoise up saile, while gale doth last;
Tide and wind stay no mans pleasure:
Seeke not time, when time is past,
Sober speede is wisedomes leasure: 10

9 tyde *S, VC, H*: tydes *Ca*: tyme *A*

Losse in delaies. Ca; *S, VC, A, H*
  Title Losse] *misprinted* Lose *Ca*   delaies] Delaye *S, A, H*
  6 Lingred *MSS.*: Lingring *Ca*   7 Hoise] Hoist *VC, A*

After wits are dearely bought,
Let thy fore wit guide thy thought.

Time weares all his lockes before,
Take thy hold upon his fore head,
When he flies he turnes no more,   15
And behinde his scalpe is naked,
Workes ajournd have many stayes,
Long demurres breede new delaies.

Seeke thy salve while sore is greene,
Festred wounds aske deeper Launcing;   20
After cures are seeldome seene,
Often sought scarce ever chauncing,
Time and place give best advise,
Out of season out of prise.

Crush the Serpent in the head,   25
Breake ill egges ere they be hatched:
Kill bad Chickins in the tread,
Fligge they hardly can be catched.
In the rysing stifle ill,
Least it grow against thy will.   30

Droppes doe pearse the stubborne flint,
Not by force but often falling:
Custome kils with feeble dint,
More by use then strength prevailing.
Single sandes have little waight,   35
Many make a drowning fraight.

Tender twigges are bent with ease,
Aged trees doe breake with bending:
Young desires make little prease,
Grought doth make them past amending.   40
Happie man that soone doth knocke,
Bable babes against the rocke.

---

12 thy fore wit] thy farewell ?S(b.c), A: therefore witte VC   14 thy MSS.:
thou Ca   20 deeper MSS.: deepe Ca   41 doth knocke MSS.: can nocke Ca

Loves servile lot

LOVE mistris is of many mindes,
Yet few know whome they serve:
They recken least how little love
Their service doth deserve.

The will shee robbeth from the wit: 5
The sence from reasons lore,
Shee is delightfull in the rine,
Corrupted in the core.

Shee shroudeth vice in vertues vaile,
Pretending good in ill: 10
Shee offreth joy, affordeth griefe,
A kisse where shee doth kill.

A honnie shower raines from her lippes,
Sweete lights shine in her face:
Shee hath the blush of virgine mild,   15
The mind of viper race.

Shee makes thee seeke, yet feare to find:
To find, but not enjoy,
In many frounes some gliding smiles
Shee yeeldes to more anoy.   20

Shee wooes thee to come neere her fire:
Yet doth shee draw it from thee:
Farre off shee makes thy hart to frie,
And yet to freeze within thee.

Shee letteth fall some luring baites: 25
For fooles to gather up.
Too sweete to some, to every tast
Shee tempereth her cup.

Loves servile lot. 1–48: *Ca*, 49–76: *Cb*; *S, VC, A, H; Cb*
    3 love] love, *Ca*   10 good in ill *MSS., Cb*: much good will *Ca*   11 offreth
MSS.: offereth *Ca*   15 virgine] virgines *VC, A*   mild] mind *MSS., Cb*
19 smiles] smiles, *Ca*   22 shee] *omitted A: interlineated by 2nd hand S*   27 some]
sowre *S, VC, H, Cb*   some,] some *Ca*   tast] tast, *Ca*

Soft soules shee bindes in tender twist,
Small Flees in spinners webb,   30
She settes afloote some luring streames,
But makes them soone to ebb.

Her watrie eyes have burning force:
Her clouds and flames conspire.
Teares kindle sparkes, sobbes fuell are: 35
And sighes doe blow her fire.

May never was the Month of love,
For May is full of flowers,
But rather Aprill wet by kind,
For love is full of showers.   40

Like tyrant cruell wounds shee geves,
Like Surgeon salve shee lends,
But salve and sore have equall force,
For death is both their ends.

With soothing wordes, inthralled soules   45
Shee chaines in servile bands,
Her eye in silence hath a speach,
Which eye best understands.

Her little sweete hath many sowres,
Short hap immortall harmes,   50
Her loving lookes, are murdring dartes,
Her songs bewitching charmes.

Like winter rose, and sommer ise
Her joyes are still untimely,
Before her hope, behinde remorse,   55
Faire first, in fine unseemely.

Moodes, passions, phancies jelous fits,
Attend upon her traine;
She yeeldeth rest without repose,
A heav'n in hellish paine.   60

---

31 luring *MSS.*: turning *Ca, Cb*   36 her *MSS.*: the *Ca, Cb*   45 soothing
S, H, Cb: soothed *Ca, S(b.c.), VC, A*   soules] soules: *Ca*   49-76 *omitted Ca*
57 Moodes,] Moodes *Cb*

Her house is slouth, her doore deceite,
And slipperie hope her staires,
Unbashfull boldnesse bids her guestes,
And every vice repaires.

Her diet is of such delights,   65
As please till they be past,
But then the poyson kils the hart,
That did entise the tast.

Her sleepe in sinne, doth end in wrath,
Remorse rings her awake,   70
Death cals her up, shame drives her out,
Dispaires her up-shot make.

Plowe not the Seas, sow not the sands,
Leave off your Idle paine,
Seeke other mistres for your minds,   75
Loves service is in vaine.

Lewd Love is Losse

MISDEEMING eye that stoupest to the lure
     Of mortall worthes not worth so worthy love:
All beauties base, all graces are impure:
     That do thy erring thoughtes from God remove.
Sparkes to the fire, the beames yeelde to the sunne,   5
All grace to God from whom all graces runne.

If picture move, more should the paterne please,
     No shaddow can with shaddowed thing compare,
And fayrest shapes whereon our loves do seaze:
     But seely signes of Gods high beauties are.   10
Go sterving sense, feede thou on earthly mast,
True love in Heav'n, seeke thou thy sweet repast.

65 delights *MSS*.: delight *Cb*

Lewd Love is Losse. Cb; *S, VC, A, H, F*
     7 move, more] move more, *Cb*   8 can] can, *Cb*   thing *S, VC, A, H*: things
Cb, F   10 beauties] beautie *S*(*b.c.*), *A, H*

Gleane not in barren soyle these offall eares,
   Sith reap thou maiest whole harvestes of delight.
Base joyes with griefes, bad hopes do end in feares: 15
   Lewd love with losse, evill peace with deadly fight:
Gods love alone doth end with endlesse ease:
Whose joyes in hope, whose hope concludes in peace.

Let not the luring traine of phansies trap,
   Or gracious features proofes of natures skill,   20
Lull reasons force asleepe in errors lap,
   Or draw thy wit to bent of wanton will;
The fayrest flowers have not the sweetest smell,
A seeming heaven proves oft a damming hell.

Selfe pleasing soules that play with beauties bayte,   25
   In shining shroud may swallow fatall hooke.
Where eager sight, or semblant fayre doth wayte,
   A locke it proves that first was but a looke.
The fish with ease into the Net doth glide,
But to get out the way is not so wide.   30

So long the flie doth dallie with the flame,
   Untill his singed winges doe force his fall:
So long the eie doth follow fancies game,
   Till love hath left the hart in heavie thrall.
Soone may the mind be cast in Cupids jayle,   35
But hard it is imprisoned thoughts to baile.

O loath that love whose final ayme is lust,
   Moth of the mind, Eclypse of reasons light:
The grave of grace, the mole of natures rust,
   The wracke of wit, the wrong of every right.   40
In summe an evill whose harmes no tong can tel,
In which to live is death, to dye is hell.

---

13 Gleane *MSS.*: O leave *Cb*   18 peace.] peace, *Cb*   19 trap,] trap. *Cb*
23 flowers] flowers, *Cb*   24 heaven] heaven, *Cb*   25–30, 31–36 *In S these*
stanzas are numbered to indicate that 31–36 *should precede* 25–30; *the stanzas are*
reversed in VC   37 loath] loath, *Cb*   40 wit,] wit *Cb*   42 hell.] hell, *Cb*

Loves Garden grief

VAINE loves avaunt, infamous is your pleasure,
    Your joy deceit:
Your jewels jests, and worthelesse trash your treasure,
    Fooles common bait.
Your pallace is a prison that allureth   5
To sweet mishap, and rest that paine procureth,

Your garden griefe, hedg'd in with thornes of envie,
    And stakes of strife:
Your Allyes errour graveled with Jelosie,
    And cares of life.   10
Your bankes are seates enwrapt with shades of sadnes,
Your Arbours breed rough fittes of raging madnes.

Your beds are sowne with seedes of all iniquitie,
    And poys'ning weeds:
Whose stalkes evill thoughts, whose leaves words full of vanity, 15
    Whose fruite misdeedes.
Whose sap is sinne, whose force and operation,
To banish grace, and worke the soules damnation.

Your trees are dismall plantes of pyning corrosives,
    Whose roote is ruth.   20
Whose barke is bale, whose tymber stubborne fantasyes:
    Whose pyth untruth.
On which in liewe of birdes whose voyce delighteth:
Of guiltie conscience screeching note affrighteth.

Your coolest summer gales are scalding sighings,   25
    Your shoures are teares,
Your sweetest smell the stench of sinfull livyng,
    Your favoures feares,
Your gardener Sathan, all you reape is misery:
Your gaine remorse and losse of all felicitie.   30

Loves Garden grief. Cb; *S, VC, A, H, F*
   1 avaunt,] *misprinted* avaunts *Cb*   14 poys'ning] poysening *MSS.*   28 feares,]
feares *Cb*

Fortunes Falsehoode

IN worldly meriments lurketh much miserie,
Slie fortunes subtilties in baites of happinesse
Shrowde hookes, that swallowed, without recoverie
Murder the innocent with mortall heavinesse.

She sootheth appetites with pleasing vanities,   5
Till they be conquered with cloaked tyrannie,
Then, chaunging countenaunce, with open enmities,
She triumphes over them, scorning their slaverie.

With fawning flatterie deathes doore she openeth,
Alluring passengers to bloudie destenie: 10
In offers bountifull, in proofe she beggereth:
Mens ruines registring her false felicitie.

Her hopes are fastened in blisse that vanisheth,
Her smart inherited with sure possession:
Constant in crueltie, shee never altereth,   15
But from one violence, to more oppression.

To those that follow her, favoures are measured,
As easie premises to hard conclusions:
With bitter corrosives her joyes are seasoned,
Her highest benefits are but illusions.   20

Her waies, a laberinth of wandring passages:
Fooles common pilgrimage, to cursed deities:
Whose fond devotion and idle menages
Are wagde with wearinesse in frutlesse drudgeries.

Blinde in her favorites foolish election,   25
Chaunce is her arbiter in geving dignitie:
Her choyse of visious shewes most discretion,
Sith welth the vertuous might wrest from pietie.

Fortunes Falsehoode. Ca; S, VC, A, H; F compiler
  2 fortunes subtilties] fortune covereth *H*   3 Shrowde] Shrouds *S, VC, A*:
False *H*   5 sootheth] *misprinted* soweth *Ca*   7 Then] Than *Ca*   10 bloudie]
blady *S, VC*   26 dignitie *S, VC, H, F compiler*: dignities *Ca, A*   27 visious
MSS., F compiler: visions *Ca*   28 pietie.] pietie, *Ca*

                            F

To humble suppliaunts tyrant most obstinate:
She suters aunswereth with contrarieties: 30
Proude with petition, untaught to mitigate
Rigour with clemencie in hardest cruelties.

Like Tygre fugitive from the ambitious,
Like weeping Crocodile to scornefull enemies:
Suing for amitie where shee is odious,   35
But to her followers forswearing curtesies.

No wind so chaungeable, no sea so wavering,
As giddie fortune in reeling varieties:
Now mad, now mercifull, now fearce, now favoring:
In all things mutable, but mutabilities.   40

From Fortunes reach

LET fickle fortune runne her blindest race:
    I settled have an unremoved mind:
I scorne to be the game of phansies chase,
    Or vaine to shew the chaunge of every winde.
Light giddy humors stinted to no rest,   5
Still chaunge their choyce, yet never choose the best.

My choyse was guided by fore-sightfull heede,
    It was averred with approving will,
It shalbe followed with performing deed:
    And seal'd with vow, till death the chooser kill,   10
Yea death though finall date of vaine desires,
Endes not my choyse, which with no time expires.

To beauties fading blisse I am no thrall:
    I bury not my thoughts in mettall mynes,
I aime not at such fame, as feareth fal,   15
    I seeke and find a light that ever shines:
Whose glorious beames display such heavenly sightes,
As yeeld my soule the summe of all delights.

37 wind *MSS.*, *F compiler*: mind *Ca*   38 varieties] vanities *S(b.c.)*, *A*
From Fortunes reach. Cb; *S*, *VC*, *A*, *H*, *F*
6 choose *S*, *VC*, *A*: chose *Cb*, *H*, *F*   18 the *VC*, *A*: a *Cb*, *H*, *F* (*omitted S*)

My light to love, my love to lyfe doth guyde
  To life that lives by love, and loveth light: 20
By love of one, to whom all loves are ty'de
  By dewest debt, and never equald right.
Eyes light, harts love, soules truest life he is,
Consorting in three joyes, one perfect blisse.

Content and rich

I DWELL in graces courte,
  Enrichde with vertues rights:
Faithe, guides my wit: love, leades my will:
  Hope, all my minde delights.

In lowlie vales I mounte   5
  To pleasures highest pich:
My seely shrowde true honor bringes,
  My poore estate is rich.

My conscience, is my crowne:
  Contented thoughts, my rest: 10
My hart is happie in it selfe:
  My blisse is in my brest.

Enough, I reckon welth:
  A meane, the surest lot,
That lies too high, for base contempt: 15
  Too low, for envies shot.

My wishes are but few,
  All easie to fulfill:
I make the Limites of my power,
  The bondes unto my will.   20

I have no hopes but one,
  Which is of heavenly raigne:
Effects attainde, or not desired,
  All lower hopes refraine.

21 of S, VC, A, H: to Cb, F   22 equald MSS.: equall Cb
Content and rich. Ca; S, VC, A, H
  7 honor bringes] honors bringes S: honours bringe VC   15, 16 too . . . Too]
to . . . To Ca   21 hopes S, VC: hope Ca, S(b.c.), A (H illegible)

I feele no care of coyne,   25
   Weldoing is my welth:
My minde to me an empire is:
   While grace affordeth health.

I clippe high clyming thoughts,
   The winges of swelling pride: 30
Their fall is worst that from the hight
   Of greatest honors slide.

Sith sayles of largest size
   The storme doth soonest teare:
I beare so low and small a sayle,   35
   As freeth me from feare.

I wrastle not with rage
   While furies flame doth burne:
It is in vaine to stop the streme,
   Untill the tide doth turne.   40

But when the flame is out
   And ebbing wrath doth end:
I turne a late enraged foe
   Into a quiet frend.

And taught with often proofe,   45
   A tempered calme I finde
To be most solace, to it selfe:
   Best cure, for angrie minde.

Spare diet, is my fare:
   My clothes, more fit, then fine: 50
I know I feede and cloth a foe
   That pampred, would repine.

I envie not their happe,
   Whome favour doth advance:
I take no pleasure in their paine,   55
   That have lesse happie chaunce.

32 honors *MSS*.: honor *Ca*   40 doth] do *S, VC*   46 finde] finde: *Ca*
51 foe] foe: *Ca*   52 pampred *S, VC, A*: pampered *Ca, H*

To rise by others fall,
    I deeme a loosing gaine:
Al states with others ruines built,
    To ruine runne amaine.   60

No chaunge of fortunes calmes,
    Can cast my comforts downe:
When fortune smiles, I smile to thinke,
    How quickly shee will frowne.

And when in froward moode   65
    Shee proves an angrie foe:
Smale gaine I found to let her come,
    Lesse losse to let her goe.

Scorne not the least

WHERE wards are weake, and foes encountring strong:
Where mightier doe assault, then doe defend:
The feebler part puts up enforced wrong,
And silent sees, that speech could not amend.
Yet higher powers must thinke, though they repine,   5
When sunne is set: the little starres will shine.

While Pike doth range, the silly Tench doth flie
And crouch in privie creekes, with smaller fish:
Yet Pikes are caught when little fish goe bie:
These, fleet aflote; while those, doe fill the dish.   10
There is a time even for the worme to creepe:
And sucke the dew while all her foes doe sleepe.

The Marlyne cannot ever sore on high,
Nor greedie greyhound still pursue the chase:
The tender Larke will find a time to flie,   15
And fearefull Hare to runne a quiet race.
He that high growth on Ceders did bestow:
Gave also lowly mushrumpes leave to grow.

Scorne not the least. Ca; *S, VC, A, H*; *F compiler*
   7 Tench] *misprinted* Teutch *Ca*   11 for *MSS.*: from *Ca*   worme *S, VC*: wormes
Ca, S(b.c.), A, H   12 her *S, VC, A*: their *Ca, S(b.c), H*   18 mushrumpes
MSS., F compiler: mushrumpt *Ca*   to] *misprinted* so *Ca*

In Hamans pompe poore Mardocheus wept;
Yet God did turne his fate upon his foe.   20
The Lazar pinde, while DIVES feast was kept,
Yet he, to heaven; to hell, did Dives goe.
We trample grasse, and prize the flowers of May:
Yet grasse is greene when flowers doe fade away.

19 Hamans] Amans *Ca*

II

POEMS FROM *MŒONIÆ*

The virgin Mary to Christ on the Crosse

WHAT mist hath dimd that glorious face,
    What seas of griefe my sun doth tosse?
The golden raies of heavenly grace
    Lies now ecclipsed on the crosse.

Jesus my love, my sonne, my God,   5
    Behold thy mother washt in teares:
Thy bloody woundes be made a rod,
    To chasten these my latter yeares.

You cruell Jewes come worke your ire,
    Upon this worthlesse flesh of mine: 10
And kindle not eternal fire,
    By wounding him which is divine.

Thou messenger that didst impart,
    His first discent into my womb,
Come helpe me now to cleave my heart,   15
    That there I may my sonne intombe.

You Angels all that present were,
    To shew his birth with harmony,
Why are you not now ready here,
    To make a mourning symphony?   20

The cause I know, you waile alone,
    And shed your teares in secresie,
Least I should moved be to mone,
    By force of heavy company.

The virgin Mary to Christ on the Crosse. Ma; *cf. version in F, p.* 112
20 symphony?] symphony *Ma*

But waile my soule, thy comfort dies,   25
   My wofull wombe lament thy fruit,
My heart give teares unto my eies,
   Let sorrow string my heavy lute.

Man to the wound in Christs side

O PLEASANT port, O place of rest,
   O royall rifte, O worthy wound,
Come harbour me a weary guest,
   That in the world no ease have found.

I lie lamenting at thy gate,   5
   Yet dare I not adventure in:
I beare with me a troublous mate,
   And combred am, with heape of sinne.

Discharge me of this heavy load,
   That easier passage I may finde,   10
Within this bowre to make aboade,
   And in this glorious tombe be shrin'd.

Heere must I live, heere must I die,
   Heere would I utter all my griefe:
Heere would I all those paines descrie,   15
   Which here did meete for my releefe.

Heere would I view that bloudy sore,
   Which dint of spitefull speare did breed,
The bloody woundes laid there in store
   Would force a stony heart to bleede.   20

Heere is the spring of trickling teares,
   The mirror of al mourning wights,
With dolefull tunes, for dumpish eares
   And solemne shewes for sorrowed sights.

Man to the wound in Christs side. Ma; *F*
  3 Come] Now *F*   8 And . . . heape] A combred soule with heapes *F*
9 heavy] loathsome *F*   12 glorious tombe be shrin'd] tombe to be enshrind *F*
13 must . . . must] wold . . . wold *F*   17 that] the *F*   19 bloody woundes]
paineful pangues *F*   20 a] my *F*   23 dolefull] paineful *F*   eares *F*: cares *Ma*
24 sorrowed] doelful *F*

O happy soule that flies so hie,   25
   As to attaine this sacred cave:
Lord send me wings that I may flye,
   And in this harbour quiet have.

Upon the Image of death

BEFORE my face the picture hangs,
   That daily should put me in mind
Of those cold qwalmes, and bitter pangs,
   That shortly I am like to finde:
But yet alas full little I   5
   Doe thinke hereon that I must die.

I often looke upon a face
   Most ugly, grisly, bare, and thinne,
I often view the hollow place,
   Where eies, and nose, had sometimes bin,   10
I see the bones acrosse that lie:
   Yet little thinke that I must die.

I reade the Labell underneath
   That telleth me whereto I must,
I see the sentence eake that saith,   15
   Remember man that thou art dust:
But yet alas but seldome I
   Doe thinke indeede that I must die.

Continually at my beds head,
   A hearse doth hang which doth me tel,   20
That I yer morning may be dead,
   Though now I feele my selfe full wel:
But yet alas, for all this I
   Have little minde that I must die.

25 flies] soares *F*   26 attaine] atchieve *F*   27 me] *misprinted* we *Ma*
Upon the Image of death. Ma; *F*
   3 qwalmes (*changed from* ?names) *F*: names *Ma*   10 bin,] bin *Ma*   16 dust]
misprinted durst *Ma*

The gowne which I do use to weare,　　　　　25
　　The knife wherewith I cut my meate,
And eke that old and ancient chaire,
　　Which is my onely usuall seate:
All those do tell me I must die,
　　And yet my life amend not I.　　　　　30

My ancestors are turnd to clay,
　　And many of my mates are gone,
My yongers dayly drop away,
　　And can I thinke to scape alone?
No, no, I know that I must die,　　　　　35
　　And yet my life amend not I.

Not *Salomon* for all his wit,
　　Nor *Samson* though he were so strong,
No king nor person ever yet
　　Could scape, but death laid him along:　　40
Wherefore I know that I must die,
　　And yet my life amend not I.

Though all the East did quake to heare,
　　Of *Alexanders* dreadfull name,
And all the West did likewise feare,　　　　45
　　To heare of *Julius Cesars* fame,
Yet both by death in dust now lie,
　　Who then can scape but he must die?

If none can scape deaths dreadfull dart,
　　If rich and poore his becke obey,　　　　50
If strong, if wise, if all do smart,
　　Then I to scape shall have no way.
Oh grant me grace O God that I,
　　My life may mend sith I must die.

36 amend] *misprinted* amsnd *Ma*

III

SAINT PETERS COMPLAINT

The Author to the Reader

DEARE eie that daynest to let fall a looke,
On these sad memories of Peters plaintes:
Muse not to see some mud in cleerest brooke,
They once were brittle mould, that now are Saintes.
Their weakenesse is no warrant to offend: 5
Learne by their faultes, what in thine owne to mend.

If equities even-hand the ballance held,
Where *Peters* sinnes and ours were made the weightes:
Ounce, for his Dramme: Pound, for his Ounce we yeeld:
His Ship would groane to feele some sinners freightes. 10
So ripe is vice, so greene is vertues bud:
The world doth waxe in evill, but waine in good.

This makes my mourning muse resolve in teares,
This Theames my heavy penne to plaine in prose.
Christes Thorne is sharpe, no head his Garland weares: 15
Still finest wits are stilling *Venus* Rose.
In Paynim toyes the sweetest vaines are spent:
To Christian workes, few have their tallents lent.

License my single penne to seeke a phere,
You heavenly sparkes of wit, shew native light: 20
Cloude not with mistie loves your Orient cleere,
Sweete flightes you shoote; learne once to levell right.
Favour my wish, well wishing workes no ill:
I moove the Suite, the Graunt restes in your will.

Saint Peters Complaint

LAUNCHE foorth my Soul into a maine of teares,
Full fraught with grief the traffick of thy mind:
Torne sailes will serve, thoughtes rent with guilty feares:
Give care, the sterne: use sighes in lieu of wind:
Remorse, the Pilot: thy misdeede, the Carde: 5
Torment, thy Haven: Shipwracke, thy best reward.

Shun not the shelfe of most deserved shame:
Sticke in the sandes of agonizing dread:
Content thee to be stormes and billowes game:
Divorc'd from grace thy soule to pennance wed: 10
Flie not from forreine evils, flie from thy hart:
Worse then the worst of evils is that thou art.

Give vent unto the vapours of thy brest,
That thicken in the brimmes of cloudy eies:
Where sinne was hatchd, let teares now wash the nest: 15
Where life was lost, recover life with cries.
Thy trespasse foule: let not thy teares be few:
Baptize thy spotted soule in weeping dewe.

Flie mournefull plaintes, the Ecchoes of my ruth,
Whose screeches in my fraighted conscience ring: 20
Sob out my sorrowes, fruites of mine untruth:
Report the smart of sinnes infernall sting.
Tell hartes that languish in the soriest plight,
There is on earth a farre more sorry wight.

A sorry wight, the object of disgrace,   25
The monument of feare, the map of shame,
The mirrour of mishap, the staine of place,
The scorne of time, the infamy of fame:
An excrement of earth, to heaven hatefull:
Injurious to man, to God ungratefull.   30

Saint Peters Complaint. Ca; A, O; F compiler, Cb, Cc

  2 grief] teares *A*: greifes *O, F compiler*   5 the . . . the] thie . . . thie *O, F compiler, Cb*   7 deserved] deservinge *O*   10 to] in *A*   17 Thy] For *O* 18 in] with *O*   19 Flie mournefull] Yee mourning *O*   ruth,] ruth; *Ca* 20 screeches] scretches *Ca*   screeches in my] lowdest skrikes, in *O*   fraighted] frighted *O*

Ambitious heades dreame you of fortunes pride:
Fill volumes with your forged Goddesse praise.
You fancies drudges, plungd in follies tide:
Devote your fabling wits to lovers layes:
Be you O sharpest greeves, that ever wrung, 35
Texte to my thoughtes, Theame to my playning tung.

Sad subject of my sinne hath stoard my mind
With everlasting matter of complaint:
My threnes an endlesse Alphabet do find,
Beyond the panges which *Jeremy* doth paint. 40
That eyes with errours may just measure keepe:
Most teares I wish that have most cause to weepe.

All weeping eies resigne your teares to me:
A sea will scantly rince my ordurde soule:
Huge horrours in high tides must drowned bee: 45
Of every teare my crime exacteth tole.
These staines are deepe: few drops, take out no such:
Even salve with sore: and most, is not too much.

I fear'd with life, to die; by death, to live:
I left my guide, now left, and leaving God. 50
To breath in blisse, I fear'd my breath to geve:
I fear'd for heavenly raigne, an earthly rod.
These feares I fear'd, feares feeling no mishaps:
O fond, o faint, o false, o faultie lapse.

How can I live, that thus my life denied? 55
What can I hope, that lost my hope in feare?
What trust to one, that truth it selfe defied?
What good in him, that did his God forsweare?
O sinne, of sinnes; of evils, the very woorst:
O matchlesse wretch: O caitife most accurst. 60

Vaine in my vauntes, I vow'd if frendes had fail'd,
Alone *Christes* hardest fortunes to abide:
Gyant, in talke: like dwarfe, in triall quail'd:
Excelling none, but in untruth and pride.

---

33 plungd *A, O, F compiler, Cc*: plunge *Ca, Cb*   37 stoard] sturde *A, O*
40 which] that *A*   44 scantly] scarselye *O*   45 horrours] errors *O*
bee:] bee *Ca*   59 evils, the very] evill all the *O*

Such distance is betwene high wordes and deedes: 65
In proofe the greatest vaunter seldome speedes.

Ah rashnesse: hastie ryce to murdering leape,
Lavish, in vowing; blind, in seeing what:
Soone sowing shames, that long remorse must reape:
Nurcing with teares, that oversight begat. 70
Scoute of repentance, harbinger of blame:
Treason to wisedome, mother of ill name.

The borne-blind beggar for received sight, Joh. 9
Fast in his faith and love, to *Christ* remain'd:
He stouped to no feare, he fear'd no might: 75
No change, his choyce: no threates his truth distain'd.
One wonder wrought him in his duety sure:
I after thousands, did my Lord abjure.

Could servile feare of rendring natures due,
Which growth in yeares was shortly like to claime, 80
So thrall my love, that I should thus eschue
A vowed death and misse so faire an aime?
Die: Die: disloyall wretch thy life detest:
For saving thine, thou hast forsworne the best.

Ah life, sweete drop, drownd in a sea of sowers, 85
A flying good, posting to doubtfull end:
Still loosing monethes and yeares to gaine new howers:
Faine, time to have, and spare, yet forst to spend.
Thy growth, decrease: a moment, all thou hast:
That gone, ere knowne: the rest: to come or past. 90

Ah life the maze of countlesse straying wayes,
Open to erring steps, and strow'd with baites,
To winde weake senses into endlesse strayes,
Aloofe from vertues rough unbeaten straightes.
A flower, a play, a blast, a shade, a dreame: 95
A living death, a never turning streame.

---

69 shames] shame *A, O*   73 *Sidenotes from Cb; also in A*   79 Could]
Cold *Ca*   81 eschue] eschue, *Ca*   85 sowers *Cc*: showers *Ca, A, O, Cb*
91 straying] straynning *A*   94 rough] right *O*

And could I rate so high a life so base?
Did feare with love cast so uneven accompt:
That for this goale I should runne Judas race,
And Caiphas rage in cruelty surmount?   100
Yet they esteemed thirty pence his price: Mat. 26.
I, worse then both, for nought denied him thrise.

The mother sea from overflowing deepes,
Sendes foorth her issue by divided vaines:
Yet back her ofspring to their mother creepes,   105
To pay their purest streames with added gaines.
But I that dronke the drops of heavenly flood:
Bemyred the giver with returning mud.

Is this the harvest of his sowing toile?
Did *Christ* manure thy hart to breed him bryars?   110
Or doth it neede this unaccustomde soyle
With hellish doung to fertile heavens desires?
No: no: the Marle that perjuries do yeeld,
May spoyle a good, not fat a barraine field.

Was this for best desertes the duest meede?   115
Are highest worthes well wag'de with spitefull hire?
Are stoutest vowes repeal'd in greatest neede?
Should friendship at the first affronte retyre?
Blush craven sott, lurke in eternall night:
Crouche in the darkest caves from loathed light.   120

Ah wretch, why was I nam'd, sonne of a dove,   Mat. 16.
Whose speeches voyded spight, and breathed gall?
No kin I am unto the bird of love:
My stony name much better sutes my fall.
My othes, were stones: my cruell toung the sling: 125
My God, the marke: at which my spight did fling.

Were all the Jewish tyrannies too few,
To glut thy hungry lookes with his disgrace:
That thou more hatefull tyrannies must shew:
And spit thy poyson in thy makers face?   130

98 uneven] unjust *O*   101 esteemed *O, F compiler, Cb*: esteem'd *Ca, A*
106 their] the *O*   107 dronke] dronke, *Ca*   flood *A, O, F compiler, Cb*:
food *Ca*   108 with] by *A, O*   109 his] this *O*   110 Christ] Christ, *Ca*
112 heavens] heavenly *A*   124 much better sutes] doth better suite *A*
127 too] to *Ca*

Didst thou to spare his foes put up thy sword:
To brandish now thy toung against thy Lord?   John 18.

Ah toung, that didst his praise and Godhead sound,
How wert thou stain'd with such detesting wordes,
That every word was to his hart a wound,   135
And launst him deeper then a thousand swordes?
What rage of man, yea what infernall sprite,
Could have disgorg'd more loathsome dregs of spite?

Why did the yeelding sea like marble way
Support a wretch more wavering then the waves?   140
Whome doubt did plunge, why did the water stay,   Math. 14.
Unkind, in kindnesse; murthering, while it saves?
O that this toung had then bene fishes food,
And I devour'd before this cursing moode.

There surges, depthes, and seas unfirme by kinde,   145
Rough gustes, and distance both from ship and shoare,
Were titles to excuse my staggering minde,
Stout feete might falter on that liquid floare.
But here, no seas, no blastes, nor billowes were,
A puffe of womans wind bred all my feare.   150

O coward troupes far better arm'd then harted,
Whom angry words, whom blowes could not provoke, Joh. 18.
Whome though I taught how sore my weapon smarted,
Yet none repaide me with a wounding stroake.
O no: that stroke could but one moitie kill,   155
I was reserv'd both halves at once to spill.

Ah, whither was forgotten love exilde?
Where did the trueth of pledged promise sleepe?
What in my thoughtes begat this ougly childe,
That could through rented soule thus fiercely creepe?   160
O viper feare, their death by whome thou livest,
All good thy ruynes wrecke, all evels thou givest.

---

132 *Sidenote A (at* 131): John 16. *Cb*   134 wert] art *O*   141 water]
waters *A*   145 There] Their *A, O, Cc*   146 gustes] golfes *O*   149 nor] no *A*
151 coward] cowardes *A*   152 *Sidenote*] Joh. 15. *Cb, A*   154 repaide] paid *A*
161 viper feare,] viper, feare *Ca*

Threates threw me not, tormentes I none assayde:
My fray, with shades: conceites, did make me yeeld,
Wounding my thoughtes with feares: selfely dismayde 165
I neither fought, nor lost, I gave the field.
Infamous foyle: a maidens easie breath
Did blow me down, and blast my soule to death.

Titles I make untruthes: am I a rocke? Math. 16.
That with so soft a gayle was overthrowne? 170
Am I fit pastor for the faithfull flocke, Joh. 21.
To guide their soules that murdred thus mine owne?
A rocke, of ruine; not a rest, to stay:
A pastor, not to feede: but to betray.

Fidelitie was flowne, when feare was hatched, 175
Incompatible brood in vertues nest:
Courage can lesse with cowardise be matched,
Prowisse nor love lodgde in devided brest.
O Adams child cast by a silly Eve,
Heire to thy fathers foyles, and borne to greeve. 180

In Thabors joyes I egre was to dwell, Math. 17.
An earnest friend while pleasures light did shine: Mar. 9.
But when eclipsed glory prostrate fell, Math. 16.
These zealous heates to sleepe I did resigne.
And now my mouth hath thrise his name defil'd, 185
That cryed so loud three dwellings there to build.

When *Christ* attending the distressefull hower
With his surcharged brest did blisse the ground,
Prostrate in panges, rayning a bleeding shower,
Me, like my selfe, a drowsy friend he found. 190
Thrise in his care sleepe closde my carelesse eye:
Presage, how him my tong should thrise deny.

Parted from *Christ* my fainting force declin'd,
With lingring foote I followed him aloofe.
Base feare out of my hart his love unshrinde, Mark. 14.
Huge, in high wordes: but impotent, in proofe. Luc. 22. 195

166 neither] never *A, O, F compiler*   171 Am *A, O, F compiler, Cb*: And *Ca*
pastor] pastor, *Ca*   *Sidenote A: omitted Cb*   172 thus] this *A*   173 ruine]
ruinge *A*   178 lodgde] lodge *A, F compiler*   180 thy] the *O*   181 Thabors]
Thabor *A*   182 *Sidenote* Mar. 9.] Joh. 21. *Cb*   192 Presage] presagd *O*
193 Parted *A, O, F compiler*: Parting *Ca*

My vauntes did seeme hatcht under *Sampsons* lockes,
Yet womans wordes did give me murdring knockes.

So fare luke-warme desires in crasie love,
Farre off in neede with feeble foote they traine: 200
In tydes, they swimme: low ebbes they scorne to prove,
They seeke their friendes delightes, but shun their paine.
Hire of a hireling minde is earned shame:
Take now thy due: beare thy begotten blame.

Ah, coole remisnes, vertues quartane fever,   205
Pyning of love, consumption of grace:
Old in the cradle, languor dying ever,
Soules willfull famine, sinnes soft stealing pace,
The undermyning evill of zealous thought,
Seeming to bring no harmes till all be brought.   210

O portresse of the doore of my disgrace,
Whose toung, unlockt the trueth of vowed minde;
Whose wordes, from cowardes hart did courage chase,   John. 18.
And let in death-full feares my soule to blinde.
O, hadst thou bene the portresse to my tombe: 215
When thou wert portresse to that cursed roome.

Yet love, was loath to part; feare, loath to die:
Stay, daunger, life, did counterplead their causes:
I favouring stay, and life, bad daunger flie:
But daunger did except against these clauses.   220
Yet stay, and live, I would, and daunger shunne:
And lost my selfe, while I my verdict wonne.

I stayed, yet did my staying farthest part:
I liv'd; but so, that saving life, I lost it:
Daunger I shund, but to my sorer smart: 225
I gayned nought, but deeper domage crost it.
What daunger, distance, death is worse then this:
That runnes from God, and spoyles his soule of blisse?

---

198 womans] womens *O*   201 scorne *O, F compiler, Cb*: scornd *Ca, A*
205 remisnes *A, O, F compiler, Cb*: remisses *Ca*   215 to] of *A, O*   216 cursed]
wicked *O*   223 farthest] furthest *O*   224 liv'd] lyve *O*

O *John* my guide into this earthly hell,   John 18. 16.
Too well acquainted in so ill a court,   230
Where rayling mouthes with blasphemies did swell,
With taynted breath infecting all resort.
Why didst thou lead me to this hell of evils:
To shew my selfe a feind among the divels?

Evill president, the tyde that wafts to vice,   235
Dumme Orator, that woes with silent deedes,
Writing in workes lessons of evill advise,
The doing tale that eye in practize reades:
Taster of joyes to unacquainted hunger:
With leaven of the old seasoning the yonger.   240

It seemes no fault to doe that all have done:
The nomber of offenders hides the sinne:
Coatch drawne with many horse doth easely runne.
Soone followeth one where multitudes begin.
O, had I in that court much stronger bene: 245
Or not so strong as first to enter in.

Sharpe was the weather in that stormy place,   Joh. 18.
Best suting hearts benumbd with hellish frost,
Whose crusted malice could admit no grace,
Where coales were kindled to the warmers cost.   250
Where feare, my thoughtes canded with ysie colde:
Heate, did my tounge to perjuries unfold.

O hatefull fire (ah that I ever saw it)
Too hard my hart was frozen for thy force,
Farre hotter flames it did require to thawe it,   255
Thy hell resembling heate did frize it worse.
O that I rather had congeal'de to yse:
Then bought thy warm'th at such a damning price.

O wakefull bird, proclaymer of the day,
Whose piersing note doth daunt the Lyons rage: Mat. 26 260
Thy crowing did my selfe to me bewray,   Mar. 14.
My frightes, and brutish heates it did asswage.

235–330 *Transposed to follow* 714 *in* Ca, A, O, Cb   235 wafts *F compiler,* Cb:
waft Ca: wastes A, O   239 joyes] joyes: Ca   247 *Sidenote*] *misprinted*
Job. 18. Cb   251 canded] congeald O   253 I ever] ever I A   254 thy]
the A   257 that I rather] rather that I A   258 damning] *misprinted* dauncing Ca

But O, in this alone unhappy cocke:
That thou to count my foyles wert made the clocke.

O bird, the just rebuker of my crime,   265
The faithfull waker of my sleeping feares:
Be now the dayly clocke to strike the time,
When stinted eyes shall pay their taske of teares.
Upbraide mine eares with thine accusing crow:
To make me rue that first it made me know.   270

O milde revenger of aspiring pride,
Thou canst dismount high thoughtes to low effectes:
Thou madst a cocke me for my fault to chide,
My lofty boastes this lowly bird correctes.
Well might a cocke correct me with a crow: 275
Whome hennish cackling first did overthrow.

Weake weapons did *Golias* fumes abate,   I. Reg. 17.
Whose storming rage did thunder threates in vaine:
His body huge harnest with massie plate,
Yet *Davids* stone brought death into his braine.   280
With staffe and sling as to a dog he came:
And with contempt did boasting fury tame.

Yet *David* had with Beare and Lyon fought,
His skillfull might excusde *Golias* foyle:
The death is easde that worthy hand hath wrought,   285
Some honor lives in honorable spoyle.
But I on whome all infamies must light:
Was hisde to death with wordes of womans spite.

Small gnats enforst th'Egyptian king to stoupe,   Exod. 8.
Yet they in swarmes and arm'd with piercing stings: 290
Smart, noyse, annoyance, made his courage droupe,
No small incombrance such small vermine brings:
I quayld at wordes that neither bit nor stonge,
And those delivered from a womans tounge.

---

273 madst *A, O, Cb*: madest *Ca*   278 storming *A, Cb*: scortching *Ca*: scorn-
inge *O, F compiler*   287 But] But, *Ca*   288 womans *A, O*: womens *Ca*
289 th'Egyptian] the giptian *A, O*

Ah feare, abortive ympe of drouping mind: 295
Selfe overthrow: false friend: roote of remorse:
Sighted, in seeing evils: in shunning, blind:
Foyld without field: by fansy, not by force:
Ague of valor: phrensie of the wise:
True honors staine: loves frost: the minte of lies.   300

Can vertue, wisedome, strength by woemen spild
In *Davids*, *Salomons*, and *Sampsons* fals,   2. Reg. 11.
With semblance of excuse my errour guild,   3. Reg. 11.
Or lend a marble glose to muddy walles?   Jud. 16.
O no their fault had show of some pretence.   305
No vayle can hide the shame of my offence.

The blaze of beauties beames allured their lookes,
Their lookes, by seeing oft, conceived love:
Love, by affecting, swallowed pleasures hookes:
Thus beauty, love, and pleasure them did moove.   310
These Syrens sugred tunes rockt them asleepe:
Enough, to damme, yet not to damme so deepe.

But gratious features dasled not mine eies,
Two homely droyles were authors of my death:
Not love, but feare, my sences did surprize: 315
Not feare of force, but feare of womans breath.
And those unarm'd, ill grac'd, despisde, unknowne:
So base a blast my truthe hath overthrowne.

O women, woe to men: traps for their falls,
Still actors in all tragicall mischaunces: 320
Earthes necessarie evils, captiving thralles,
Now murdring with your tongs, now with your glances,
Parents of life, and love: spoylers of both,
The theefes of Harts: false do you love or loth.

In time, O Lord, thine eyes with mine did meet,   325
In them I read the ruines of my fall: Luk. 22.
Their chearing raies that made misfortune sweet,
Into my guilty thoughts powrde flouds of gall,
Their heavenly lookes that blist where they beheld,
Darts of disdaine, and angry checks did yeeld.   330

296 overthrow] overthrowne *A*   319 women] woman *A*, *Cb*   327 misfor-
tune] misfortunes *A*

O sacred eyes, the springs of living light,
The earthly heavens, where Angels joy to dwell:
How could you deigne to view my deathfull plight,
Or let your heavenly beames looke on my hell?
But those unspotted eyes encountred mine,   335
As spotlesse Sunne doth on the dounghill shine.

Sweet volumes stoarde with learning fit for Saints,
Where blisfull quires imparadize their minds,
Wherein eternall studie never faints,
Still finding all, yet seeking all it findes.   340
How endlesse is your labyrinth of blisse,
Where to be lost the sweetest finding is?

Ah wretch how oft have I sweet lessons read,
In those deare eies the registers of truth?
How oft have I my hungrie wishes fed,   345
And in their happy joyes redress'd my ruth?
Ah that they now are Heralds of disdaine:
That erst were ever pittyers of my paine.

You flames devine that sparkle out your heats,
And kindle pleasing fires in mortall hearts: 350
You nectared Aumbryes of soule feeding meats,
You graceful quivers of loves dearest darts:
You did vouchsafe to warme, to wound, to feast:
My cold, my stony, my now famishde breast.

The matchles eies matchd onely each by other,   355
Were pleasd on my ill matched eyes to glaunce:
The eye of liquid pearle, the purest mother,
Brochte tears in mine to weepe for my mischaunce.
The cabinets of grace unlockt their treasure,
And did to my misdeed their mercies measure.   360

These blasing comets, lightning flames of love,
Made me their warming influence to know:
My frozen hart their sacred force did prove,
Which at their lookes did yeeld like melting snow.
They did not joyes in former plentie carve,   365
Yet sweet are crums where pined thoughts do starve.

349 You] Yet *A*: Yee *O*   351 Aumbryes *Cb*: Ambrose *Ca, A*   355 The]
Thei *A*: Thes *F compiler*   361 lightning] lightinge *A*: lighteninge *O*

O living mirrours, seeing whom you shew,
Which equall shaddows worthes with shadowed things:
Ye make thinges nobler then in native hew,
By being shap'd in those life giving springs.　　　　370
Much more my image in those eyes was grac'd,
Then in my selfe whom sinne and shame defac'd.

All seeing eyes more worth then all you see,
Of which one is the others onely price:
I worthles am, direct your beames on me,　　　　375
With quickning vertue cure my killing vice.
By seeing things, you make things worth the sight,
You seeing, salve, and being seene, delight.

O Pooles of *Hesebon*, the bathes of grace,　　Can. 7. 3.
Where happy spirits dyve in sweet desires:　　　　380
Where Saints rejoyce to glasse their glorious face,
Whose banks make Eccho to the Angels quires:
An Eccho sweeter in the sole rebound,
Then Angels musick in the fullest sound.

O eies, whose glaunces are a silent speech,　　　　385
In cyphred words, high misteries disclosing:
Which with a looke all sciences can teach,
Whose textes to faithfull heartes need little glosing:
Witnes unworthy I, who in a looke,
Learnd more by rote, then all the scribes by booke.　　390

Though malice still possessd their hardened minds,
I, though too hard, learnd softnes in thine eye,
Which iron knots of stubborne will unbindes,
Offring them love, that love with love wil buy.
This did I learne, yet they could not discerne it,　　395
But wo, that I had now such need to learne it.

O Sunnes, all but your selves in light excelling,
Whose presence, day, whose absence causeth night,
Whose neighbour course brings Sommer, cold expelling,
Whose distant periods frieze away delight.　　　　400

369 Ye] Yea *A, Cc*　　381 their] thy *A*　　390 scribes] clarkes *O*　　391 Though]
Tough *Cc*　　still] full *O*　　possessd *A, O, F compiler, Cb*: possesse *Ca*　　399 course]
course, *Ca*　　brings *A, O, F compiler, Cb*: bring *Ca*

Ah, that I lost your bright and fostring beames,
To plundge my soule in these congealed streames.

O gracious spheres, where love the Center is,
A native place for our selfe-loaden soules:
The compasse, love, a cope that none can mis: 405
The motion, love that round about us rowles.
O Spheres of love, whose Center, cope and motion,
Is love of us, love that invites devotion.

O little worldes, the summes of all the best,
Where glory, heaven, God, sunne: all vertues, starres: 410
Where fire, a love that next to heaven doth rest,
Ayre, light of life, that no distemper marres:
The water, grace, whose seas, whose springs, whose showers,
Cloth natures earth, with everlasting flowers.

What mixtures these sweet elements do yeeld,   415
Let happy worldlings of those worlds expound,
But simples are by compounds farre exceld,
Both sute a place, where all best things abound.
And if a banishd wretch gesse not amisse:
All but one compound framde of perfect blisse.   420

I outcast from these worlds exiled rome,
Poore saint, from heaven, from fire, cold Salamander:
Lost fish, from those sweet waters kindly home,
From lande of life, strayed pilgrim still I wander:
I know the cause: these worldes had never a hell   425
In which my faults have best deservde to dwell.

O Bethelem cisternes, *Davids* most desire,   2. Reg. 23.
From which my sinnes like fierce Philistims keepe,
To fetch your drops what champion should I hire,
That I therein my withered heart may steepe.   430
I would not shed them like that holy king,
His were but tipes, these are the figured thing.

409 summes] some *O*   410 God] godes *O*   sunne] soone *Ca*   420 compound framde] compounde, frames *O*: compound frame *Cb*   423 those] theis *O*
425 never a hell *A, O, F compiler*: never hell *Ca*   426 have] had *O*   428 Philis-
tims] Phillistians *O*   429 champion] champions *A, Cb*   should] could *O*
430 withered] wretched *O*   may] might *O*

O Turtle twins all bath'd in virgins milke,   Can. 5. 11.
Upon the margin of full flowing bankes: 12.
Whose gracefull plume surmounts the finest silke,   435
Whose sight enamoreth heavens most happy rankes,
Could I forsweare this heavenly paire of doves,
That cag'd in care for me were groning loves.

Twice *Moyses* wand did strike the Horebb rocke,
Ere stony veynes would yeeld their christall blood: Exod. 17. 440
Thy eyes, one looke servd as an onely knocke,   verse 6.
To make my heart gush out a weeping floode,
Wherein my sinnes as fishes spawne their frye,
To shew their inward shames, and then to dye.

But O, how long demurre I on his eies,   445
Whose looke did pearce my heart with healing wound:
Launching impostumde sore of perjurde lies,
Which these two issues of mine eyes hath found:
Where runne it must, till death the issues stop,
And penall life hath purgde the finall drop.   450

Like solest Swan that swimmes in silent deepe,
And never sings but obsequies of death,
Sigh out thy plaints, and sole in secreat weepe,
In suing pardon, spend thy perjurde breath.
Attire thy soule in sorrowes mourning weede: 455
And at thine eies let guilty conscience bleede.

Still in the limbeck of thy dolefull breast,
These bitter fruites that from thy sinnes do grow:
For fuel, selfe accusing thoughtes be best,
Use feare, as fire, the coales let penance blow.   460
And seeke none other quintessence but teares,
That eyes may shed what entred at thine eares.

Come sorrowing teares, the ofspring of my griefe,
Scant not your parent of a needfull aide:
In you I rest, the hope of wishde relief,   465
By you my sinfull debts must be defraide.

---

433 twins] doves *O*   435 finest] fayrest *O*   439 wand] rod *O*   Horebb *A*,
O: stubborne *Ca*   442 floode] floode. *Ca*   447 Launching] Launcinge *O, Cb*
461 none] noe *O*   463 teares,] teares *Ca*

Your power prevailes, your sacrifice is gratefull,
By love obtayning life, to men most hatefull.

Come good effectes of ill deserving cause;
Ill gotten impes, yet vertuously brought forth: 470
Selfe-blaming probates of infringed lawes.
Yet blamed faults redeeming with your worth:
The signes of shame in you ech eie may reade,
Yet while you guiltie prove, you pitty pleade.

O beames of mercy beat on sorrowes cloude,   475
Poure suppling showers upon my parched ground:
Bring forth the fruite to your due service vowde,
Let good desires with like deserts be crownde.
Water young bloming vertues tender flower,
Sinne did all grace of riper groth devour.   480

Weep Balme and mirrhe you sweet Arabian trees,
With purest gummes perfume and pearle your ryne:
Shed on your hony drops you busie bees,
I barraine plant must weep unpleasant bryne,
Hornets I hyve, salt drops their labour plies,   485
Suckt out of sinne, and shed by showring eies.

Yf *David* night by night did bath his bed,   Psal. 6. 7.
Esteeming longest daies too short to moane:
Inconsolable teares if *Anna* shed,
Who in her sonne her solace had forgone,   Tob. 10. 490
Then I to daies, and weekes, to monthes and yeares,
Do owe the howrely rent of stintlesse teares.

If love, if losse, if fault, if spotted fame,
If daunger, death, if wrath or wrecke of weale,
Entitle eyes true heires to earned blame,   495
That due remorse in such events conceale;
Then want of teares might well enroll my name,
As cheefest Saint in Calender of shame.

---

468 life,] life *Ca*   471 probates] probates, *Ca*   472 redeeming] redeemed *O*
476 Poure] Powre *Ca*   477 vowde] *misprinted* vovde *Ca*   482 ryne A, *F*
compiler, Cb: misprinted ryve *Ca*: eyne *O*   484 plant *A, O*: plaint *Ca*   bryne]
misprinted bryve *Ca*   487 *Sidenote*] at 489 *Cb*   490 forgone,] forgone. *Ca*

Love, where I lov'de, was due, and best deservde,
No love could aime at more love-worthie marke,   500
No love more lov'de then mine of him I servde,
Large use he gave, a flame for every sparke.
This love I lost, this losse a life must rue,
Yea life is short to pay the ruth is due.

I lost all that I had, and had the most,   505
The most that will can wish, or wit devise:
I least performd, that did most vainely boast,
I stainde my fame in most infamous wise.
What daunger then, death, wrath, or wreck can move
More pregnant cause of teares then this I prove?   510

If Adam sought a veyle to scarfe his sinne,   Gen: 3. 7.
Taught by his fall to feare a scourging hand:
If men shall wish that hils should wrap them in,
When crymes in finall doome come to be scand:
What mount, what cave, what center can conceale   515
My monstrous fact, which even the birds reveale?

Come shame, the lincea of offending mind,
The ougly shroud, that overshadoweth blame:
The mulct, at which fowle faults are justly fynde,
The dampe of sinne, the common sluce of fame,   520
By which impostumde tongues their humors purge,
Light shame on me, I best deserve thy scourge.

Caines murdring hand imbrude in brothers blood,
More mercy, then my impious toung may crave: Gen. 4.
He kild a ryvall with pretence of good,   525
In hope Gods doubled love alone to have.
But feare so spoild my vanquisht thoughts of love:
That perjurde oathes my spightfull hate did prove.

---

501 No *A, O, Cb*: Nor *Ca*   509 then,] then *Ca*   move] move, *Ca*   513 should]
would *A, O*   517 shame,] shame *Ca*   lincea *A, O*: livery *Ca*   518 over-
shadoweth] overshadeth *O*   520 sinne,] sinne *Ca*   fame,] fame. *Ca*   522 deserve
thy *A*: deserv'd the *Ca, O*   scourge.] scourge, *Ca*   527 thoughts] thought *O*
528 hate] harte *O*

Poore *Agar* from her phere enforc'd to flye,   Gen. 21.
Wandring in Barsabeian wildes alone: 530
Doubting her child throgh helples drought would die,
Laid it aloofe and set her downe to moane.
The heavens with praiers: her lap with teares she fild,
A mothers love in losse is hardly stild.

But *Agar* now bequeath thy teares to me,   535
Feares, not effects, did set aflote thine eies:
But wretch I feele more then was feard of thee,
Ah, not my sonne: my soule it is that dies.
It dies for drought yet had a spring in sight,
Worthie to die, that would not live and might.   540

Faire *Absolons* fowle faults compar'de with mine, 2 Reg. 15.
Are brightest sands, to mud of Sodome lakes.
High aymes, yong spirits, birth of royall lyne,
Made him play false, where kingdoms were the stakes.
He gazde on golden hopes, whose lustre winnes   545
Sometime the gravest wittes to grievous sinnes.

But I whose crime cuts off the least excuse,
A kingdome lost, but hopd no mite of gaine:
My highest marke, was but the worthles use
Of some few lingring howres of longer paine.   550
Ungratefull child, his parent he pursude:
I gyants warre with God himselfe renude.

Joy infant Saints, whom in the tender flower   Mat. 2.
A happy storme did free from feare of Sinne:
Long is their life, that die in blisfull hower,   555
Joyfull such ends as endles joyes beginne.
Too long they live, that live till they be nought:
Life sav'd by sinne, base purchase, dearely bought,

---

529 *Sidenote*] Gen. 22 *Cb* (*at* 535), *A*   532 set] satt *O*   533 praiers] plaintes *O*
540 live] love *O*   541 faults] fault *O*   542 of] in *A*   Sodome] Sodomes *O*
545 lustre] lustrey *Ca*   546 Sometime] Sometymes *A, O*   wittes]
heades *O*   547 cuts] cutt *O*   548 hopd *A, F compiler, Cb*: hope *Ca, O*
549 use] use, *Ca*   551 parent *A, O, Cb*: parents *Ca*   552 gyants] Gyaunt *A*
553 flower] flower, *Ca*   555 blisfull] blessed *O*   556 joyes] joye *O*

This lot was mine, your fate was not so fearce,
Whom spotlesse death in cradle rockt asleepe: 560
Sweet Roses mixt with Lillies strowd your hearce,
Death virgin white in martirs red did steepe:
Your downy heads both pearles and rubies crownde,
My hoary locks did femall feares confound.

You bleating ewes that waile this wolvish spoile 565
Of sucking lambs new bought with bitter throwes,
To balme your babes your eies distill their oile,
Ech hart to tombe her child wide rupture showes.
Rue not their death whom death did but revive:
Yeld ruth to me that lived to die alive. 570

With easie losse sharpe wreakes did he eschew,
That Sindonles aside did naked slip:
Once naked grace no outward garment knew,
Rich are his robes whom sinne did never strip.
I that in vaunts displaide prides fairest flagges, 575
Disrobde of grace am wrapt in *Adams* ragges.

When traitor to the sonne in mothers eies,
I shall present my humble suit for grace:
What blush can paint the shame that will arise;
Or write my inward feeling in my face? 580
Might she the sorrow with the sinner see:
Though I dispisde: my griefe might pittyed bee.

But ah, how can her eares my speech endure,
Or sent, my breath still reeking hellish steeme:
Can mother like what did the sonne abjure, 585
Or hart deflowrde a virgins love redeeme?
The mother nothing loves that sonne doth loth,
Ah lothsome wretch detested of them both.

O sister Nymphes the sweet renowmed paire,
That blisse *Bethania* bounds with your aboade: 590
Shall I infect that sanctified aire,
Or staine those steps where *Jesus* breathd and trode?

561 strowd] strewd *A, O*   565 spoile] spoile, *Ca*   567 balme] blame *A:*
bath *O*   580 feeling] feelinges *A, O*   583 eares] eare *A, O*   585 what]
whoe *O*   590 bounds] bonds *Ca*

No: let your praiers perfume that sweetned place:
Turne me with Tygers to the wildest chase.

Could I revived *Lazarus* behold,   John. 11. 595
The third of that sweet Trinitie of Saints,
Would not astonish't dread my sences holde?
Ah yes, my heart even with his naming faints.
I seeme to see a messenger from hell,
That my prepared torments comes to tell.   600

O *John*, O *James*, we made a triple corde,   Mat. 17.
Of three most loving and best loved friends: Luke 8.
My rotten twist was broken with a worde,
Fit now to fuell fire among the fiends.
It is not ever true, though often spoken: 605
That triple twisted corde is hardly broken.   Eccles. 4. 12.

The dispossessed divels that out I threw,
In *Jesus* name, now impiously forsworne:
Triumph to see me caged in their mew,
Trampling my ruins with contempt and scorne.   610
My perjury was musicke to their daunce:
And now they heap disdaines on my mischance.

Our rocke (say they) is riven, O welcome hower,
Our Eagles wings are clipt, that wrought so hie:
Our thundring Clowde made noise but cast no shower,   615
He prostrate lies, that would have scal'de the sky.
In womans tongue our runner found a rub,
Our *Cedar* now is shrunke into a shrub.

These scornefull wordes upbraide my inward thought,
Proofes of their damned prompters neighbour voice: 620
Such ugly guests still wait upon the nought,
Fiends swarm to soules that swarve from vertues choise.
For breach of plighted truth, this true I trie:
Ah, that my deed thus gave my word the lie.

---

596 Saints,] Saints? *Ca*   606 triple *A, O, Cb*: tripld *Ca*   Sidenote] *at* 607 *Cb*:
omitted *A*   611 perjury was] perjuries was *A*: perjuries were *O, Cb*   614 wrought]
sord *O*: rought *F compiler*   615 thundring *A, O*: thundering *Ca*   620 neigh-
bour] neighbours *O*   621 guests] gesse *Ca*

Once, and but once, too deare a once to twice it,   625
A heaven, in earth, Saints, nere my selfe I saw:
Sweet was the sight, but sweeter loves did spice it,
Both sightes and loves did my misdeed withdraw.
From heaven and Saints to hell and Divels enstranged,
Those sights to frights, those loves, to hates are changed. 630

Christ, as my God, was templed in my thought,
As man, he lent mine eies their dearest light:
But sinne, his temple hath to ruine brought:
And now, he lightneth terrour from his sight,
Now of my lay unconsecrate desires,   635
Prophaned wretch I tast the earned hires.

Ah sinne, the nothing that doth all things file:
Outcast from heaven, earthes curse, the cause of hell:
Parent of death, authour of our exile,
The wrecke of soules, the ware that fiends do sell,   640
That men to monsters: Angels turnes to Divells:
Wrong, of all rightes: selfe ruine: root of evils.

A thing most done, yet more then God can doe,
Dayly new done, yet ever done amisse:
Friended of all yet unto all a foe,   645
Seeming a heaven, yet banishing from blisse,
Served with toyle, yet paying nought but paine:
Mans deepest losse, though false esteemed gaine.

Shot, without noyse: wound without present smart:
First, seeming light, proving in fyne a load,   650
Entring with ease, not easily wonne to parte,
Far in effects from that the showes abode,
Endorc'd with hope, subscribed with dispaire:
Ugly in death, though life did faine it faire.

---

625 too] to *Ca*   627 loves] love *O*   628 Both] But *Cb*   sightes]
sight *O*   misdeed *A, O, Cb*: misdeeds *Ca*   629 enstranged] estraunged *A, O, Cb*
631 templed] tempted *Ca* (*F*)   635 lay] late *O*   638 cause *A, O, Cc*: course
Ca, Cb   640 soules,] soules *Ca*   ware *A, O, F compiler*: wares *Ca*   sell,]
sell. *Ca*   646 blisse,] blisse. *Ca*   647 yet paying] repayinge *O*   648 deepest]
greatest *O*   650 light,] light; *Ca*   652 the] that *O*   abode] abroade *O*   abode,]
abode. *Ca*

O forfeyture of heaven: eternall debt,   655
A moments joy: ending in endles fires:
Our natures skumme: the worlds entangling Net:
Night of our thoughts: death of all good desires.
Worse then all this: worse then all tongues can say,
Which man could owe, but onely God defray.   660

This fawning viper, dumme till it had wounded,
With many mouthes doth now upbraide my harmes:
My sight was vaild till I my selfe confounded,
Then did I see the dissenchanted charmes.
Then could I cut th'anotomy of sinne,   665
And search with *Linxes* eyes what lay within.

Bewitching evill, that hides death in deceites,
Still borrowing lying shapes to maske thy face,
Now know I the deciphring of thy sleightes,
A cunning dearely bought with losse of grace.   670
Thy sugred poyson now hath wrought so well:
That thou hast made me to my selfe a hell.

My eye, reades mournefull lessons to my hart,
My hart, doth to my thought the griefes expound,
My thought, the same doth to my tounge impart,   675
My tounge, the message in the eares doth sound.
My eares, backe to my hart their sorrowes send:
Thus circkling griefes runne round without an end.

My guilty eye still seemes to see my sinne,
All thinges Characters are to spell my fall,   680
What eye doth read without, hart rues within,
What hart doth rue, to pensive thought is gall,
Which when the thought would by the tounge disgest:
The eare convayes it back into the brest.

659 tongues] *misprinted* tongue *Ca*   661 it] he *Cb*   664 the] those *O*
665 th'anotomy] then notomy *A*: the Anatomye *O, Cb*   669 deciphring *Cb*: deciphering *Ca, A, O*   670 cunning] cunning, *Ca*   671 Thy *A, O, F compiler,*
Cb: A *Ca*   674 griefes *A, O, Cb*: griefe *Ca*   676 in the] to my *O*
677 sorrowes] sorrow *A*   682 gall,] gall. *Ca*

Thus gripes in all my partes do never fayle,   685
Whose onely league is now in bartring paines:
What I, in grosse: they trafficke by retayle:
Making each others miseries their gaines.
All bound for ever prentizes to care:
While I in shop of shame trade sorrowes ware.   690

Pleasd with displeasing lot I seeke no change,
I wealthiest am when richest in remorce:
To fetch my ware no seas nor lands I range,
For customers to buy I nothing force.
My home-bred goods at home are bought and sold,   695
And still in me the interest I hold.

My comfort now is comfortlesse to live,
In Orphian seate devoted to mishap:
Rent from the roote, that sweetest fruit did give,
I scorne to graffe in stock of meaner sap.   700
No juice can joy me but of *Jesse* flower,
Whose heavenly roote hath true reviving power.

At sorrowes dore I knockt, they crav'de my name;
I aunswered one, unworthy to be knowne:
What one? say they, one worthiest of blame.   705
But who? a wretch, not Gods, nor yet his owne.
A man? O no, a beast? much worse, what creature?
A rocke: how cald? the rocke of scandale, Peter.

From whence? from *Caiphas* howse, ah dwell you there?
Sinnes farme I rented, there, but now would leave it: 710
What rent? my soule: what gaine? unrest, and feare,
Deare purchase. Ah too deare. Will you receive it?
What shall we give? fit teares, and time, to plaine me,
Come in, say they; thus griefes did entertaine me.

With them I rest true prisoner to their jaile,   715
Chain'd in the yron linkes of basest thrall,
Till grace vouchsafing captive soule to bayle,
In wonted see degraded loves enstal.

698 Orphian] Orphan *A, O, F compiler*, **Cb**   seate] state *O, F compiler*, **Cc**
700 scorne *A, O*: scorn'd *Ca*   705 one? say they,] one, say they? *Ca*
707 beast?] beast: *Ca*   709 you *A, O*, **Cb**: thou *Ca*   there?] there, *Ca*
712 Ah] Oath *Ca (F)*, **Cb**   too] to *Ca*   713 time *A, F compiler*: times *Ca*: tunes *O*
715 jaile] *misprinted* yaile *Ca*   718 see] sea *Ca*

Dayes, passe in plaintes: the nightes without repose:
I wake, to weepe: I sleepe in waking woes.   720

Sleepe, deathes allye: oblivion of teares:
Silence of passions: balme of angry sore:
Suspence of loves: securitie of feares:
Wrathes lenitive: hartes ease: stormes calmest shore:
Senses and soules reprivall from all cumbers: 725
Benumming sence of ill, with quiet slumbers.

Not such my sleepe: but whisperer of dreames:
Creating straunge chymeraes: fayning frightes:
Of day discourses giving fansie theames,
To make dumme shewes with worlds of anticke sightes: 730
Casting true griefes in fansies forging mold:
Brokenly telling tales rightly foretold.

This sleepe most fitly suteth sorrowes bed,
Sorrow the smart of evill, Sinnes eldest child:
Best, when unkind in killing who it bred,   735
A racke, for guilty thoughtes: a bit, for wild.
The scourge, that whips: the salve that cures offence:
Sorrow, my bed, and home, while life hath sence.

Heere solitary muses nurse my griefes,
In silent lonenesse burying worldly noyse,   740
Attentive to rebukes, deafe to reliefes,
Pensive to foster cares, carelesse of joyes:
Ruing lifes losse under deathes dreary roofes,
Solemnizing my funerall behoofes.

A selfe contempt, the shroud: my soule, the corse: 745
The beere, an humble hope: the hersecloth, feare:
The mourners, thoughtes, in blackes of deepe remorse:
The herse, grace, pittie, love, and mercy beare.
My teares, my dole: the priest, a zealous will:
Pennance, the tombe: and dolefull sighes, the knill.   750

Christ, health of feverd soule, heaven of the minde,
Force of the feeble, nurse of Infant loves,
Guide to the wandring foote, light of the blind,
Whome weeping winnes, repentant sorrow moves,

    735 who] whom A, O   748 mercy] misprinted merry Ca   751 soule] soules O
753 foote] soules O   of] to O   754 moves,] moves. Ca

Father in care, mother in tender hart: 755
Revive and save me slaine with sinnefull dart.

If king *Manasses* sunke in depth of sinne,
With plaintes and teares recovered grace and crowne:
A worthlesse worme some milde regard may winne,
And lowly creepe, where flying threw it downe. 760
A poore desire I have to mend my ill:
I should, I would, I dare not say, I will.

I dare not say, I will; but wish, I may:
My pride is checkt, high wordes the speaker spilt:
My good, O Lord, thy gift; thy strength my stay: 765
Give what thou bidst, and then bid what thou wilt.
Worke with me what thou of me doest request:
Then will I dare the most, and vow the best.

Prone looke, crost armes, bent knee, and contrite hart,
Deepe sighes, thicke sobs, dewd eyes and prostrate prayers,
Most humbly beg reliefe of earned smart, 771
And saving shroud in mercies sweete repaires.
If justice should my wrongs with rigor wage:
Feares, would dispaires: ruth, breed a hopelesse rage.

Lazar at pitties gate I ulcered lie, 775
Craving the reffues crummes of childrens plate:
My sores, I lay in view to mercies eye,
My rags, beare witnesse of my poore estate.
The wormes of conscience that within me swarme:
Prove that my plaintes are lesse then is my harme. 780

With mildenesse, *Jesu*, measure my offence:
Let true remorse thy due revenge abate:
Let teares appease when trespasse doth incense:
Let pittie temper thy deserved hate.
Let grace forgive, let love forget my fall: 785
With feare I crave, with hope I humbly call.

757 depth] deepe *O*   769 looke] lookes *O*   knee] knees *O*   770 dewd]
misprinted deepe *Ca*   771 reliefe] release *O*   777 to] of *O*   780 harme.]
harme, *Ca*

Redeeme my lapse with raunsome of thy love,
Traverse th'inditement, rigors dome suspend:
Let frailtie favour, sorrow succour move:
Be thou thy selfe, though chaungling I offend.   790
Tender my suite, clense this defiled denne,
Cancell my debtes, sweete *Jesu*, say Amen.

The ende of Saint Peters Complaint.

788 rigors *A, O, Cb*: rigorous *Ca*   789 sorrow *A, O*: sorrowes *Ca*

IV

POEMS FROM PROSE WORKS

Epitaph on Lady Margaret Sackville

Of *Howards* stemme a glorious branch is dead,
　Sweet lights eclipsed were in her decease:
In *Buckehurst* line she gracious issue spread,
　She heven with two, with four did earth increase:
Fame, honour, grace, gave aire unto her breath,　　　　5
　Rest, glorie, joyes were sequeles of her death.

Death aymed too high, he hit too choise a wight,
　Renowned for birth, for life, for lovely partes,
He killd her cares, he brought her woorths to light,
　He robd our eyes, but hath enricht our hearts:　　　10
He let out of the Arke a *Noyes* dove,
　But many hearts are Arkes unto her love.

Grace, Nature, Fortune did in her conspire
　To shew a proofe of their united skill:
Slie Fortune ever false did soone retire,　　　　　　15
　But doubled Grace supplied false Fortunes ill:
And though she raught not to her fortunes pitch,
　In grace and nature few were found so rich.

Heaven of this heavenly Pearle is now possest,
　Whose luster was the blaze of honors light:　　　　20
Whose substance pure of every good the best,
　Whose price the crowne of vertues hiest right,

Epitaph on Lady Margaret Sackville. *1595*; S, VC, A
　Title] An other Epitaphe upon the deathe of the Lady Buckehurst *VC*: *no title sup-*
plied in other MSS. or editions　　3 *Buckehurst*] Buckehurstes *VC*　　4 increase:]
increase *1595*　　8 lovely S, *VC*: lively *1595*: lowly *A*　　11 He *MSS.*: *Lot 1595*
the *MSS.*: her *1595*　　12 are *MSS.*: were *1595*　　16 doubled *MSS.*: double
1595　　17 raught] wrought *MSS.*　　18 nature *MSS.*: vertue *1595*

Whose praise to be her selfe, whose greatest blisse
To live, to love, to be where now she is.

Lines from a hymn of Prudentius

THE tounsmen flock to the imbrued sands
There makinge sute with voyce, with vowe, with gifte.
Men also come from farre and forreine landes,
To everye coast fore-ranne the fame so swifte
That heere the patrons of the worlde did lye,   5
By whose good prayers eche wighte might seeke supplye.

24 love,] love *1595*

Lines from a hymn of Prudentius. EC
4 swifte] swifte. *EC*

APPENDIX I

[The] Peeter Playnt

       peer
That sturdy peter   an   did boaste
The champion stout which did with othe auowe
Amyds a thousand pyckes and blody blades
At his deare masters syde to yeld the ghoast
Perceyuyng that he conquered of two mades
            his credit   distayne
Euen at the pinch from promiss did [d] retyre   5
              angry smart
The shame the pitye and the grypyng griefe
          his
Both of his falt and of masters paynes
[A Thousand daggers stabbed in his hart]
       puniardes [pushes] stabbe
A thousand [woundes prickyns pearce] his harte

The bowes which [shott the sa] leueld at his dolful brest
The sharpest arows and most deadly flyghts   10
Were theis of Chryste when they on him did rest
These eyes were bowes there lookes lyke arowes lyght
Which not content to hurt his heauy hart
glanced to the soule
[Euen pea lanced the soule] and Wounded in such wyse
    he was fayne   till
That al his dayes while lyf did quyte departe   15
   to   still
He oynted it with liquor of his eies

          once to a minion bold   face
Thre seuerall tymes [twy]se by two handmades voyce
next [once] to a man last to that reuyl rout
[and last by meanes of that accursed crue]
    vought   [adheren]
He sed and swore [that he nere folower was]
       adherents   neuer
of Chrysts whome he [denyed that he] knew   20
[to folowe Chryst a man he neuer knew]

But when
∧ The cocke had blazed out this [stubborne] brall
     in   as   thing
and brought [the] day for witnes of the cryme
                            stubborn
[When as] the [whe] wretch scarse markyng yet his fall
Did with his eies meete theies of Christ his king

In What distresse pore peeter did remayne   25
at this encountrynge ech with others eies
Let no man vant that he cann mak it playne
[It is for man to great an enterpryse]
No tunge can reache the truthe scarce mynde surmyse
It seemd that Chryst amids that iuysh crew
forlorne of [his] frends these speaches did reherce   30

[fol. 50ᵛ] Behold that Which I sayed is now to trewe
O frende disloyall o discyple fierce

No youthful dame her [f] beaut[e]uouse face in glasse
of Christall bryghtnes did so well discrye easely prie
As this old sely [se] wret did in this passe   35
                 foul de
In th'eies of Chryst his fylthye falt espye
Nor egre eare though couetous to heare
                      preache
and without pause attent to teachers speache
could learne so much in twyse tw hundred yeres
               in a turne
as with one looke he did in moment reach   40

               it
lyke as sometyme (though vnworthy be
to lyken sacred matters with profane)
by lookes a louer secret thoughts can se
             e
asc and searche th[at] hart thoughe it no words do frame
Let amorous knyghts traynd vp in cupids schoole   45
teache those which are vnskilful in this art,
        openyng mouth
how Without vsynge tong or wrytynge toole
by lookes the louers know ech others hart
the eies may serue for to display the hart

Ech   a   did seem
[Thus euery] eie of Chryst [seemd] run*n*yng tunge   50
   [tu*n*g] peters   ech lyk a listnyng
and p [euery] eis so many eagre ∧ eare[s]
prest to receyue the voyce and it esteame
accordyng to that sense that it should beare
more fierce he seemd to say ar thy eies
                          crosse
then the impious hands which shall naile me on the   55
Nether feele I any blow which do so annoy me
       gylty
of so many w*hi*ch this ∧ rable doth on me lay
as that blow which came out of thy mouth

None [faytf] faythful fou*n*d I none courteous
           ch
of so many that I haue vousa[f]ued to be myne   60
but thow in whome my was more kyndled
Art faythless and and vngratefull aboue all other
All other with there (cowardly) flyght did onely offend me
                  my
But thow hast denyed and now w*i*th the other (foes) ghilty
standest feedynd thy eies with my damage (and sorows)   65
As though part of this pleasur belonged vnto the

Who by one and one could count
The wordes of wrath and of loue full
Which peter seemed to se imprinted
In the holy gyre (compasse) [o .] those two calme   70
                  can
eies, it wold make him brast that could vndersta*n*d (*p*erceiue) the*m*
for if from mortall eie often cometh
               (this)
virtue, which hath force in vs, He which p*r*oueth let him gesse
what an eie diuyne (or of God) is able to worke in ma*n*s senses

As a feld of snow which frosen   75
The winter in close valew hiddyn laye
At the sprynge[.]tyde of the son heated
doth quyte melt and resolue in to water
          entered was
So the feare which [entred] ∧ in the frosen hart
Of peter then when the truth he conceled   80

When toward him his eies he turned
did quyte thow and into teares was resolued

He teres or weepyng were not as riuer or torrent
Which at the scorchyng hot season could euer dry vpp
for though Chryst kyng of heauen immayntenant   85
did retorne him the grace which he had lost
yet all the [he] remnant of his lyf
There was neuer nyght but therin he did wake
Herynge the cock tell him how vnfayful he had ben
and geu[y]ynge new teares to his old falt   90

        his chere
[fol. 51ᵛ] That face which litle before had ben
Attyred with the coloure of death
By reason of the blood which was retyred to the harte
leuyng th'other parts cold and pale
Of the beames of those holy eies warmed   95
        as red as fyre
Waxed flame and by the same dores
that feare entred it vanished away
and in his due place shame appeared

   ——

Vewynge the wrech how diuerse
from his former state he founde him self   100
       him
His hart not suffysyng to stand there presente
before his offended lord that so had loued him
Without taryance for [fo] the fierce or mercyful
sentence which the hard tribunal seat did giue on him
from that odious [house] hated house that then he was in   105
weepyng bitterly he went forth

   ——

And desyrous to encounter some that iust penance (& payn
would geue [for] him for his greuous error

Notes

    4 *In the outer margin*: when dasht with dread
                     & cowardyce he
                     fades
                     and at the pinch his
                             fayth
                     loyalty doth stayne

8 *In the inner margin*: did with
16 *In the outer margin*: to oynt the wounde to bath yᵉ sores
19 *In the outer margin*: he was not of the fold
                          [made his choise]

                                              holy
42 *In the outer margin*: profaned thyngs in [sacred] talke [to]
                          to name
51 *In the outer margin*: eche ey of peter lyke a
                          [runnyng] listnynge eare
98, 106 *Short lines below the first few letters of these lines (as here reproduced)* **mark stanza divisions**

APPENDIX II

POEMS IN *F* OF DOUBTFUL AUTHORSHIP

Conceptio B. Virginis sub porta aurea

A GOLDEN gate was her conceaving place,
That was the gate unto the golden age;
The mine, the mint, the treasurie of grace;
Our gold to coyne, and for to kepe in gage,
    Wherewith the raunsome of our sinnes was paid,   5
    Our pardon gotte, and al our debtes defraid.

To sacred seate this gate the entrie was,
Wherein the Arkes and Temples glorie shin'd;
Due roume to her, through whom he was to passe,
That by those former figures was design'd: 10
    Eve was the gate that lette in all our paine,
    This Babe the gate that lette it out again.

Foure onely folkes bredde without fault are nam'd,
And all the rest conceaved are in sinne;
Without both man and wife was Adam fram'd;   15
Of man, but not of wife did Eve begin;
    Of Virgin pure our Lord conceaved was;
    Of man and wife this Babe was born in grace.

Præsentatio B. Virginis

A GLORIOUS temple wrought with secret art,
Where God, where Angels, where al graces shine,
To earthly temple brought with lowly hart,
Truth to the type, thing figur'd to the signe:
    But earthly roumes surrendered up their grace,   5
    When hevenly woorkes so glorious were in place.

She dove-house is for Christ to build his nest;
She dove of Noë, that bringes the bough of Peace;
She onely dove of undefiled brest;
Whose younglinges bloud must cure our foule disease: 10
    How fitting for her was the bird of Love,
    Who bare that Bird, that was our Turtle-dove.

Præsentatio B. Virginis.   11 fitting] sitting *F*

In her the Holy Ghost, in her the Sonne,
Both sign'd by doves, she in and of them both:
Hers is the Father, by her vertues wonne   15
To be her Spouse, and plighted her his trouthe:
   Thus are the Father, Sonne, and Holy Ghost,
   Her doves, she theires, devoted to them most.

Ubi est Deus meus?

   ALAS I live without my life,
     I see without my sight;
   I fede without my chiefe repast,
     I joy without delight.
   I am a wheat-sheafe without corne,   5
     A clowde without a showre;
   I am a shippe without a saile,
     A field without a floure.
   Who wold not deme my life a death?
     And blindnes judge my sight?   10
   My feding hunger? and my joy
     Fitte for a mourning wight?
   Who wold not deme my sheafe a clodde?
     My cloude a blast of aire?
   My shippe a shelf? my flourelesse field   15
     A desert of despaire?
   My life is dead, my light is dim'd,
     Consum'd my chiefe repast,
   Dasht my delight, thresht is my sheafe,
     My clowde no rain wil cast.   20
   My shippe is sunke in seas of grefe,
     My field is barrain ground;
   And all my comfort is in care,
     My mirth in mourning drownd.
   For CHRIST my life, my light, my fode,   25
     My joy, my showre, my corne,
   My saile, my flowre, and al my weale,
     Hath left me here forlorne.

Optima Deo

BEHOLD how first the modest Rose doth prie
Out of her somer coate in virgins hew,
One half in sight, half hidden from the eie;
The lesser sene, the fairer to the view.

But in her pride her leaves she doth display,⁣ 5
And fades in fine, and semeth not the same;
It semes not she that was a dainty praye
For ev'ry am'rous youth and galant Dame.

So with the passing of a sliding day
Of mortal life the floure and leafe doth passe; 10
Ne with the new returne of flouring May
Doth it renew the bounteous wonted glasse.

Then croppe the morening Rose, while it is faire;
Our day is short, the evening makes it die;
Yeld God the prime of youth, eare it empaire; 15
Least he the dregges of crooked age denie.

Unworthy receaving

I FREEZE in fire, I thirst amiddest the crystal streames;
I live in darke environed with glistering beames;
In mirth I moane, in joy it self I pine away,
I raunge and roave, and with a guide I goe astray;
In life I die, in freedome sit a servile slave; 5
In wealth I want, in perfect wisedome do I rave;
In love I loathe, in health I feele a deadly fitte;
In blisse I paire, in heven I find a hellish pitte;
Christ shrined hath him self within my mortal chest,
And shoured his vermilion bloud within my brest; 10
Which though it yeldeth freedome, life, love, wealth, and blesse,
Yet live I stil in darknes thral and depe distresse.
When sinne doth stoppe the springes of grace this hevenly fode
Heapes wrath on the receavers head, and doth no good.
Receave we may this Angels meate, and nothing winne, 15
Unlesse we clense our soules from spottes of filthy sinne.

Beatus vir qui non abiit etc.

O HAPPIE wight that hath not raun'gd astray,
Though by the cursed crew of wicked prest;
Nor setled standing fote in sinners way,
Nor made the chaire of pestilence his rest:
But by Gods sov'reign lawe his wil did guide, 5
And day and night his thoughtes therto appli'ed.

As stately plant that growes by crystal streames,
Whose braunches bend with loades of timely fruicte;
Whose leafe endures unparcht with Phœbus beames;
So shal he prosper stil in his pursuite: 10
Farre other fortune shal the wicked find,
Whose hap shal flie like dust before the wind.

And at the dismal day of final dome,
Though rise they shal, they shal not rise to joyes;
With troupes of Saintes they shall possesse no roume,   15
Who heaven have lost for gayning præsent toyes:
God knowes that just mens paths to glorie tendes,
But Hel and Death are sinners journeyes endes.

S. Peters complaint

How can I life, that have forsaken life,
And dasht with dreade denied my sovereigne Lord?
What can I loke for but debate and strife,
Who to forsweare the truthe could oathes affoord?
   One threatning word my courage did so daunte,   5
And qwailed so the fervour of my hart,
That though with hautie termes I earst did vaunt,
That no event shold me from Christ depart:
   Yet did I yeld with breach of plighted trouth
To disavow my wordes and inward thought;   10
And while that love and life did wrastle boathe,
Life wanne the field, and Love was set at nought.
   O fatal fray, o foule and filthy foile!
When soch a Love did yeeld to soch a life;
And at the push that champion did recoyle,   15
Whose boasting bragges before were heard so rife.
   And could the feare of rendring natures due,
Which tract of yeres was shortly like to claime,
So bind my wittes, that I for to eschue
A little brunt my soule so sore wold maime?   20
   Was life so dere, and Christ become so base?
Was God now waxed of so smal account,
That Peter nedes must folow Judas race,
And al the Jewes in crueltie surmount?

S. Peters complaint.   7 did] dit *F*

Where was the hart, that earst did nothing feare   25
The armed troupe with al their bloudie blades?
Where was the sword that stroke of Malchus eare?
How were thou now subduëd by two maides?

Or was there none on whom to wreake thine ire,
But onely Christ, and this thy seely soule?   30
Ahlas, did he deserve no better hire,
Then Perjury and Treacherie so foule?

What mistie clowde could dazel so thine eies?
What charme could so bewitch thy carelesse mind?
What franticke frensie did thy hart surprise?   35
What develish drift could so thy senses blind?

As both to kil thy soule, and to forsweare
Thy onely God with soch blasphemous wordes;
That ev'ry one was to his heart a speare,
And launc'd him deeper then a thousand swordes?   40

What grisely Beare, what ramping Lions pawe,
What Boarish tuske, what Dragons deadly sting,
What tearing tooth, what rage of rav'ning jawe,
Could have committed a more crewel thing?

Our Ladie to Christ upon the Crosse

WHAT mist hath dimd that glorious face?
    What seas of grefe my Sonne so tosse?
    That golden rayes of hevenly grace
    Are now eclipsed on the Crosse.
Jesu my sonne, my life, and God,   5
    Behold thy Mother washt in teares;
    Thy bloudie death is made a rodde
    To chasten these her later yeres.
You raging Jewes come wreake your ire
    Upon this woorthlesse flesh of mine,   10
    And kindle not æternal fire
    With wounding him that is divine.
Thou messenger that did'st imparte
    His first descent into my wombe,
    Come help me now to cleve my hart   15
    That here I may my Sonne entombe.
You Angels al that present were
    To shew his birth with harmonie,
    Why are you not now redie here
    To make a mourning symphonie?   20

The cause I know; you waile alone,
   And shede your teares in secrecie;
   Least I shold moved be to moane
   By force of heavie companie.
But waile my soule, thy comfort dies,   25
   My woful wombe lament thy frute,
   My hart geve teares unto mine eies,
   Let Sorow string my doleful lute.

Christes answere

WITHDRAW thy tender eies a while
   From this my bloudie Passion;
   Abstract the griefe of this exile,
   Expect a hevenly vision.
This Crowne of thornes that is so sharp   5
   Shalbe a glorious crowne of joy;
   David shal play upon his harp
   The historie of this annoy.
The bloud I shede shalbe a price
   To raunsome many a soule from sinne;   10
   These woundes wide open shal entice
   Some stonie hartes to enter in.
Your crystal eies shalbe a floude,
   That runnes amidst Hierusalem;
   And ev'ry sigh for this my bloude   15
   Within your hart shalbe a gemme.

Christ upon the Crosse to man

BEHOLD I fainte and fade away,
For them that least my case do rew,
For to repaire their deepe decay,
Who in my bloud their handes imbrue.
   Alas I see the soare uncur'd,   5
For whose redresse my bloud is shed;
I see them stil in sinne inur'd,
Whose sinnes these paines of mine have bred.
   Loke up (o Man) unto the Crosse,
Take view of my distressed case;   10
Cast of the care of earthly drosse,
Folow nomore thy wicked race.

The stones relent, the hevens do waile
Al this depe deluge of distresse;
Even with the dead my paines prevaile,   15
Soch are the griefes which me oppresse.
   Yet will not men unlose the knotte,
That knitteth fast their hartes in sinne;
Their soules they still defile and spotte,
And stil lie trapt in Satans ginne.   20

The Complaint of the B. Virgin having lost her Sonne in Hierusalem

Quæsivi quem diligit anima mea;
Quæsivi, et non inveni.

How may I live, since that my life is gone?
How can I see, since that I lacke my light?
How can I draw my ling'ring daies alone,
Since that my joy doth not appere in sight?
What may be found to slake my bitter grefe,   5
Since I have lost (alas) my sole relefe?

If wives lament the absence of their feeres;
If children do their parentes death bewaile;
Or infantes losse procure the parentes teares;
If some be sad, when faithful frendes do faile: 10
If some complaine for goodes that go to wracke;
And some for wonted joyes that now they lacke:

Wel may I mourne, that misse my Turtle-dove,
My bounteous parent, and my child most dere,
My wealth, my whole delite, mine onely love,   15
My sunne that wonted was to shine ful cleare:
What shold I say? my Lord, my God, and al;
The greatest losse (ay me) that could befal.

My pleasures past are cause of greater woe,
When I bethinke in this unhappie howre   20
What Gabriel ones fore-told me long agoe
Of my swete child, that great shold be his power,
And how that Davids seate he shold obteine,
In Jacobs house for evermore to raigne.

When I bethinke me on the joyes I felt   25
In Nazareth, whil'st that both God and Man
Nine moneths and more ful swetely with me dwelt;
His majestie was so contented than
Within the closure of my wombe to lie,
Whose onely hand enclos'd both earth and skie.   30

When I bethinke what comfort did abound,
Whil'st at the greeting of my frendly voice
The babe unborn in mothers wombe was found
In presence of his Saviour to rejoice:
Wherfore in signe of grateful mind I song   35
Magnificat with chereful hart and tongue.

O happie Bethlem with thy sacred Stall,
Thrise blessed farre above each princely Towre;
Where first in flesh thy Lord that ruleth al
As bridegrome issued from his closed bowre;   40
Whose glorious garde was heard that night to sing
Glorie on high unto the Hevenly King.

Then Shepheardes came their Pastor to adore,
Then Kinges made haste their Lord and King to see;
Gold, Frankencense, and pretious Myrrhe great stoare,   45
Eachone presentes these roial giftes all three;
And al admire to see him luld a slepe,
Whose eies stil wake his chosen flocke to kepe.

There Angels Bread I might refresh with milke;
His qwiv'ring corps there might I wrappe and fold   50
In homely cloutes, and not in costly silke,
Who claddes and shroudes each creature from the cold;
There might I taste with many a tender kisse
That well most clere of endlesse weale and blisse.

But now I see that Simeon said ful true   55
Of this my luckelesse lotte and bitter smart,
That time shold come when soare my soule shold rue,
When sorowes sword shold pearce my tender hart:
But I ne thought my time had bene so nere,
So sone to lacke my Lord and love most dere.   60

Yet from that day my joyes were never pure,
For sone my Spouse from heven is warn'd by night;
A werie way nedes must we both indure,
To save and kepe our blessed barne by flight;
Whil'st for his sake the guiltlesse Lambes be slaine,   65
And woful Ewes in piteous wise complaine.

To Ægypt when we reache with feare and toile,
Their Idoles al come tombling down apace;
Five yeres and more unknown in forrein soile
With faithlesse folkes we dwelt in moch disgrace;   70
And hardly there we plied our handes to paine,
With daylie worke our daylie bread to gaine.

Meane while my Babe by course of growing age
Could crepe about, and after speake, and goe;
Whose sober chere, whose wordes ful sadde and sage,   75
Whose lovely lookes did move and pearce me so;
Whose gestures al remaine so firmely set
Within my brest, I can them not forget.

The Wolfe ones dead, came summones out of hand,
To native soile we must return againe;   80
No soner are we entred in the land,
But newes were brought of Archelaus raigne:
From Jurie must we flitte therfore in haste,
In Nazareth to plant our selves at last.

In Nazareth a dere and happie place,   85
For there my blisse began to spring anew;
There might I joy to see the comely grace
That dayly gan ful clere to shine and shew,
In good behaviour of my blessed child,
With maners swete obedient meke and milde.   90

His face to view was comfort to my sight,
His hevenly voice was musicke to my eare,
My chiefe repose to see him rest by night,
My best repast to fede my Lord most dere:
My labour light, and pleasaunt was the paine,   95
That was imploy'd my Saviour to sustaine.

But now my joyes obscured are with woes,
Since I ne see those glist'ring eies most bright,
That semely mouth with lippes more red then rose,
That fore-head faire wherein I toke delight;   100
Those alabastre handes and sacred feete,
And to be short I lacke my Saviour swete.

And art thou slaine (swete Lord) with cruël death
Through wretched spite and bloudie Tyrannes hand?
Or dost thou live (dere child) and draw thy breath   105
Yet hap'ly hidde in unacquainted land?
If thou be dead, then farewel life for me,
And if thou live, why live I not with thee?

And if thou live, how could'st thou leave in woe
Thy mother dere, that brought thee first to light?   110
How could'st thou leave thy mourneful parent so
That for thy weale takes care both day and night?
How could'st thou goe some other where to dwell,
And make no stay to bid her once farewell?

The Annuntiation altered from that before

SPEL Eva backe, and Ave shall you find,
The first began, the last reverst our woe;
By Eve an Angel foiled first mankind,
By Ave now an Angel foiles our foe:
   Soch Agentes as were cause of our annoy   5
   Are now made Agents to repaire our joy.

With hawtie mind to Godhead man aspir'd,
And was by pride from place of pleasure cast;
With lowly mind our manhood God desir'd,
And us therby in greater pleasure pla'ste: 10
   Man by aspiring did procure our fall,
   God by descending freëd us from thrall.

O Virgin blest, the hevens to thee incline,
In thee their joy and Sovereign they agnize;
Their glorie is too base to match with thine,   15
Whose chast receipt God more then heven did prize:
   Haile fairest heven that heven and earth dost grace,
   And bar'st the sunne whose light the night doth chase.

COMMENTARY

I. POEMS IN MANUSCRIPTS

The Author to his loving Cosen (page 1)

MSS.: *S, H*.

The compiler of *F* made changes in ink in the printed text of the copy of *Ca* with which *F* is bound.

The poem was almost certainly originally in *A*, and perhaps also in *VC*. (See descriptions of these manuscripts in Textual Introduction, I.)

Printed in *Ca*.

Running-title: *The Epistle Dedicatory*.

Title. No authority is known for the extended title of the St. Omer editions, 'To my worthy good cosen Maister W.S.' (see Textual Introduction, III. VI, p. lxix).

l. 6. *by his Apostle*. See Eph. v. 19; Col. iii. 16; 1 Cor. xiv. 26.

l. 9. *Heathens*. No example of the plural form is supplied in *O.E.D.* before 1630. It occurs in *The Rosarie of our Ladie* (Antwerp, 1600), sig. D3, when the Sibyls are described as 'Prophetisses of God among the Heathens'. The reference here, as in the *Rosarie*, appears to be to the Greeks and Romans.

l. 33. *censures*. Southwell elsewhere uses *censure* in the general sense of 'judgement', as in 'To the Reader', l. 2, and also in 'At home in Heaven', l. 35; the particular connotation of 'adverse judgement' is not contained in its meaning.

To the Reader (page 2)

MSS.: *S, A, H; B*.

The compiler of *F* made changes in the printed text of *Ca* (*F*).

The poem was probably formerly in *VC*.

Printed in *Ca*.

l. 11. *courser*: more ordinary, usual; see *O.E.D.* 'coarse'.

ll. 17-18. The work of grace upon nature is also the theme of the first of the poems in the Sequence that follows this introductory poem in the manuscripts (except in *B*). In the Letter to his Father Southwell writes: 'Nature by Grace is not abolished, but perfected; not murdered, but manured; neither are her impressions quite razed or annulled, but suited to the colours of faith and virtue' (ed. Trotman, p. 38).

THE SEQUENCE ON THE VIRGIN MARY AND CHRIST (page 3)

MSS.: *S, VC, A, H, F; B.*
 There are slight variations in the titles as given in the MSS.

Ten of the poems printed in *Ma*; two others, 'The Nativitie of Christ' and 'Christs Childhoode', previously published in *Ca*; last two poems remained unpublished until Turnbull's edition, 1856. (See Textual Introduction, V, p. xciv.) In *Ma* the poems are printed without stanza divisions.

Southwell's devotion to the Virgin is demonstrated by his membership in the Sodality of the Blessed Virgin, in which he was Prefect in 1585 at the English College, Rome. See Devlin, p. 66; Janelle, pp. 19, 26–27.

i. *The Virgine Maries conception* (page 3)

Another version of the poem, entitled '*Conceptio B. Virginis sub porta aurea*', is in *F.* (See Appendix II, p. 108.)

l. 3. Elias *little cloude.* 1 Kings xviii. 44. The phrase recalls one of the titles of the Virgin, *Nubes Domini levis.* The traditional method of regarding events of the O.T. as foreshadowing events of the N.T. is most marked in the poems of the Sequence.

l. 4. *distill.* Images of distillation occur frequently throughout Southwell's work, with variation according to the application of the image in the general sense of moisture falling in drops, as here, or to the whole cycle by which a substance is vaporized and subsequently returned to a liquid of greater concentration or purity. Here the image is applied to the action of the grace of God; other occurrences relate the process of distillation specifically to the grace made available in the sacrament of penance, when tears of contrition are seen as the quintessence.

l. 6. *the good. our good* in *Ma* and *A* was presumably an early error, the result of transference from the parallel phrase *our ill* in the same line.

l. 9. Cf. *MMFT*, sig. K2ᵛ: 'Whatsoever thou hadst done to obtaine him [Christ], had beene but a mite for a million.'

l. 17. This line sustains the repetition of the linking words *man* and *wife* in the final four lines, in contrast to the reading in the '*Conceptio*'.

ii. *Her Nativity* (page 3)

l. 1. *Orient starre*: the morning star, actually the planet Venus, visible in the eastern sky before sunrise. The transference of aspects of the classical devotion to Venus gives particular significance to the Virgin's title, *Stella matutina.* Sixteenth-century writers did not ordinarily distinguish between planets and stars.

l. 5. *Load-starre*: usually, the North Star, as a point from which measurements could be taken at sea, recalling the Virgin's title, *Stella maris.* See *O.E.D.* 'lodestar'.

l. 6. *card*: sea-chart, or the graduated card (called also the *flie*) that is set in the compass to indicate the thirty-two directive points.

l. 17. Isa. xi. 1. 'And there shall come forth a rod out of the root of Jesse, and a flower shall rise up out of his root' (Douay). The pun *virga/virgo* is lost in the English translation, and the translation of the A.V., which gives *branch* for *flower*, changes the image contained in the Vulgate, and here adapted by Southwell.

iii. *Her Spousals* (page 4)

l. 3. *fatall lie*: the contradiction of what has been decreed by fate.

l. 17–18. The misreading in *Ma* or an earlier copy of *she* as *the*, l. 17, led to the subsequent change of *her* to *their* in an attempt to impose some sense on the lines.

iv. *The Virgins salutation* (page 5)

For a version of this poem entitled 'The Annuntiation altered from that before' see Appendix II, p. 117.

l. 3. The omission of this line in the printed editions is indicative of the lack of revision not only in *Ma*, when some haste in printing may be supposed, but in *1620*. The line is supplied here from *S*.

l. 7. *breast*: the Virgin's womb, as frequently.

l. 8. *agnize*: acknowledge, recognize. Cf. the holograph sermon on Mary Magdalen, fol. 62: 'Thynckest thow that she can agnise the so longe as thow concealest thy selfe.'

l. 10. *receit*: place of reception.

l. 11. *dost*. A singular verb is required; the plural form *doe* of the printed editions is an error deriving from the inversion of the clause.

l. 12. *sunne of justice*. The phrase translates the Vulgate *sol justitiæ* (Mal. iv. 2). It also occurs in *MMFT* (sig. K4ᵛ).

v. *The Visitation* (page 5)

ll. 11–12. The reference is to Elizabeth's greeting with the words incorporated into the *Ave Maria*: 'Blessed art thou among women, and blessed is the fruit of thy womb' (Luke i. 42). The compressed syntax may be expanded: She (Mary) brings the inspiration for the words expressed and the song sung by Elizabeth, whose voice expresses the words and sings the song that is particularly hers (Mary's).

vi. *The Nativitie of Christ* (page 6)

The compiler of *F* included this poem and 'Christs Childhoode' in his transcription of the Sequence, although in doing so he was disregarding his usual practice of omitting the printed poems in the volume with which his manuscript is bound, *Ca* (*F*). He made some changes in the version he transcribed, but he did not make them also in the printed text.

l. 8. *dasled*. The verb generally has a bad connotation, suggesting faulty evaluation and misjudgement; here the implication is that sinful man is unable to see clearly.

l. 13. Cf. St. Bernard: 'Quid enim melius seipso poterat dare vel ipse?' (ed. Migne, *Operum Tomus Secundus: Tractatus morales. Lib. de diligendo Deo.* Cap. 1, col. 975.) The argument in the stanza recalls St. Bernard's exposition of God's gifts to man: 'In primo opere me mihi dedit; in secundo, se; et ubi se dedit, me mihi reddidit. Datus ego, et redditus, me pro me debeo, et bis debeo.'

ll. 19–24. The imagery recalls imagery in the Psalms, as in Ps. civ. 14, when the work of the Creator in feeding beasts and men is described; Ps. xxxvii. 2 and Ps. xc. 5–6, when man's life is seen to be as transitory as grass.

l. 22. *brutest*. The superlative form is found in the sixteenth and seventeenth centuries; the commoner *brutish* occurs in *An Humble Supplication* (ed. Bald), p. 32.

ll. 23–24. Cf. Bellarmine, *An Ample Declaration of the Christian Doctrine*, trans. Richard Hadock (Rouen, n.d.; *S.T.C.* 1834): 'The unspotted wombe of the B. Virgin MARIE, without companie of man, at the only commandement of God, by the worke of the Holy Ghost, brought foorth that precious corne, of the living bodie, of the Sonne of God' (sig. B5ᵛ).

vii. *His circumcision* (page 7)

l. 2. *angring*. This is a rare form, now obsolete (*O.E.D.* 'angry', *v.*). *angry* was commonly applied in the sixteenth century, as now, to an inflamed sore.

l. 3. *sonne*. *Ma* has *soone*, a rare spelling, indicating contemporary pronunciation. The form occurs in *S* in 'Saint Peters Complaynte', l. 45; it is also in *Ca* in the 'Complaint', l. 410, when mod. E. *sun* is intended.

l. 5. *cast*: defeated in a legal action (*O.E.D. v.* 14).

l. 7. *vein*. *vine* in *Ma* is apparently an error rather than a spelling variant.

l. 10. The syntax is excessively distorted: 'Which showers bring a harvest of joy to heaven.' This is an early expression of the notion of showers of tears falling upward.

l. 12. *nectared cup*: a vessel for nectar, the drink of the gods. Here the mixture of the blood and water foreshadows the blood and water running from the side of Christ, and hence, the sacrament of the Eucharist.

viii. *The Epiphanie* (page 8)

l. 1. *blaze*: announce. Cf. 'Peeter Playnt', l. 21 (Appendix I, p. 104).

l. 5. *pace*. In the sixteenth century *pace* and *pass* coincided in meaning and spelling; the forms *pase* (*S*, *F*), and *passe* (*A*, *H*)—altered from *paste* in *A* and *F*—occur in the manuscripts.

l. 6. *Whose*. The antecedent is the *nobler starre*, Mary (*Stella maris*), the reference introducing the familiar *sun/son* pun.

ll. 7–9. *these plannets . . . their raies . . . their light*. The reference throughout is to Mary and Joseph; the light that shines from them (*their raies*) is at first obscured by their poverty-stricken surroundings, and is only gradually revealed to the Wise Men who, seeing the light reflected from Mary and Joseph (*their light*), recognize its divine source. Cf. *MMFT*, sig. D6–6ᵛ: 'But alas, in what cloud hast thou hidden the light of our waie?'

ix. *The Presentation* (page 9)

l. 2. Lev. xii. 8.

l. 7. *cheape penny worth*: a good bargain, good value for little money. Cf. *MMFT*, sig. K2ᵛ, when Mary is rebuked: 'Whatsoever thou hadst done to obtaine him, had beene but a mite for a million, and too slender a price for so soveraigne a peniworth.' Southwell addresses the Queen in similar terms in *An Humble Supplication* (ed. Bald), p. 4: 'And if our due Care of our Cuntry be such, . . . we are contented to pay our lives for the ransome [of a soul]: how much better should we thinke them bestowed, if soe high a pennyworth as your gratious self, or the whole Realme might be the gayne of our deare purchase?'

x. *The flight into Egypt* (page 9)

l. 4. *hath*. The line is an adjectival clause dependent on *wight* (Herod), and not on *nature*, as implied by the reading *hast* in *Ma* and *VC*. *his*, l. 5, and its dependent clause, l. 6, similarly refer to Herod.

l. 6. *graceth*: is a source of heavenly grace to; in this sense, now obsolete, the earliest example cited in *O.E.D.* is dated 1634.

l. 7. *starres*. The reference is to the Holy Innocents. *leese*: lose.

ll. 13–14. The Innocents are called *flores Martyrum* in the hymn of Prudentius inserted in the Breviary on the Feast Day, 28 December.

l. 14. *frame*: compose, form.

xi. *Christs returne out of Egypt* (page 10)

l. 4. *all the infantes spoile*: the destruction of all the Innocents.

l. 9. A marginal gloss in *S* and *VC* (where it has been cut in binding) reads: *nazareth signifieth a flower*. The reference is to the etymology of Nazareth suggested by St. Jerome (*Epist. xlvi: Ad Marcellam*). The name does not occur in the O.T., and there is some doubt concerning its Hebrew origin.

l. 11. *flower he is*: flower of the tree of Jesse (Isa. xi. 1 [Vulgate]). *and in a flower he bred*. The reference is to one of the titles of the Virgin, *Rosa mystica*.

xii. *Christs Childhoode* (page 11)

l. 7. Cf. Southwell's reference to his youthfulness in the Letter to his Father: 'Hoary senses are often couched under green locks.' In the argument that follows, in which Southwell recalls scriptural examples of young men who achieved the work of their elders, he cites the account of Christ teaching in the Temple when he was twelve (ed. Trotman, p. 40).

l. 8. *semblant*. The reading of the manuscripts (except *F*), with its simple reference to outward appearance, has been adopted, although the meaning of *semblance*, outward appearance as different from the inward reality, is more apt here.

xiii. *The death of our Ladie* (page 11)

l. 2. *summ*. *sunne* in *VC* and *H* may be indicative of ambiguity resulting from the use of a contracted form. The correct text cannot now be assumed with any confidence, but the use of imagery of the sun at the end of the poem, ll. 17–18, suggests that it should be adopted here also as part of a pattern of imagery of the kind seen in 'Her Spousals' and 'The Presentation'.

l. 10. *of whose*: for us whose. The reference in the line is to Mary as intercessor before God.

l. 11. *praise*. *prize* (variant spelling, *prise*) may be intended here; cf. 'The Assumption of our Lady', ll. 17–18.

xiv. *The Assumption of our Lady* (page 12)

ll. 7–10. Cf. *MMFT*, sig. L8–8ᵛ: 'He is nowe too bright a sunne for so weake a sight: your looks are limited to meaner light, you [have] the eies of a bat, and not of an Eagle.'

l. 10. *loftye glades*: beams of the clear light of heaven. For *glades* see *O.E.D. sb.²* 3 (obs.), where the earliest use quoted is from Phaer's translation of the *Aeneid*, 1555–8: 'Down from heaven by shade A streaming star descends, and long with great light makes a glade' (*Ae.* ii. 693–4). The origin of the word is unknown; in this sense it is associated with the light of the tails of comets, and flashes of lightning. *Glodes*, with similar meaning, is found in *Pearl*, l. 79.

A childe my Choyce (page 13)

MSS.: *S, VC, A, H*; *B*.

Printed in *Ca*.

The poem, in fourteeners, is transcribed in *S, VC*, and *A*, and printed in four four-lined stanzas; it is transcribed in *H* in short lines in eight four-lined stanzas.

l. 14. *spring*. The reference to the season of the renewing of natural life implies at the same time the celebration at Easter of the Christian restoration of life.

l. 16. Cf. the final lines of *A Short Rule* (1596–7; Allison and Rogers, no. 787): 'O Lorde, erect my former weaknesse, correct my present sinfulnesse, direct my future frailty: Direct it (O Lord) from passed evil, in present good, to future reward, sweete Jesus, Amen.'

New heaven, new warre (page 13)

MSS.: *S, VC, A, H, F.*

Printed in 1602.

Title. The single title was apparently given in error to two separate poems linked only by metrical form and subject. There is a distinct change in theme, tone, and imagery in the last four stanzas of the poem, ll. 25–48. (See Textual Introduction, V, p. xciv, and n. 2.)

ll. 13–14. The imagery here represents Gabriel as the servant sent ahead to engage a lodging for his master. *Take up* in this sense, to engage or hire (a lodging), is cited in *O.E.D.* (90, v. [b]) in use in 1602.

l. 17. *Graces*: Virtues, one of the nine orders of angelic beings.

l. 44. *pight*: pitched; this reading is preferable to that of the printed editions, *dight*, decked out, arrayed—already archaic by the end of the sixteenth century, and with a suggestion of rich decoration out of harmony with the remainder of the imagery.

The burning Babe (page 15)

MSS.: *S, VC, A, H, F; B.*

    A has an unusual number of errors in the poem; two hands, slightly later than the original scribe's, have attempted to make emendations.

Printed in *1602*.

    VC, H, and *B* transcribed the poem in eight four-lined stanzas; in *F* it has been copied in short lines, but without stanza divisions. *S* and *A* have transcribed it in sixteen long lines (fourteeners), also reproduced in *1602*, where, however, the setting in small italic fount at the end of sig. L suggests the necessity for compression rather than respect for literary tradition.

ll. 9–12. The imagery parodies the love poetry of the Petrarchan tradition. See also *MMFT*, sig. B1ᵛ: 'The fire of her true affection enflamed her heart, and her enflamed heart resolved into uncessant teares so that burning and bathing betweene love and griefe, shee led a life ever dying, and felt a death never ending.'

l. 12. *fed*. In this connotation of feeding a fire, this is an earlier use of the verb than the first cited in *O.E.D.* Its adoption here is preferable to the reading of the printed text, *bred*, since it is not suggested that the fire was first engendered by tears, but that mysteriously the tears increased the flames.

l. 14. *frie*: burn with strong passion.

l. 24. *are*. The plural verb is influenced by the complement more than by the singular subject.

l. 31. *S*, which has extremely rare points of punctuation, has a semicolon at the end of this line, as if to indicate the dramatic effect of the final words.

New Prince, new pompe (page 16)

MSS.: *S, VC, A, H, F; B.*

Printed in *1602*.

The poem was transcribed and printed as seven four-lined stanzas, without stanza divisions except in *VC, H*, and *B*. The lack of stanza divisions in *1602* may be the result of compression in the last leaf of sig. L.

Sinnes heavie loade (page 17)

MSS.: *S, VC, A, H, F.*

Printed in *1602*.

l. 7. *one*. In the course of transcription *one* was interpreted as an alternative spelling of *owne*, the variant appearing in *VC* and *F*. The image here is based on that of the classical figure of Atlas, who upheld the earth with shoulders and hands, and with it is linked (l. 8) the image of Ps. xcv. 4 ('Quia in manu eius sunt fines terrae' [Vulgate, Ps. xciv. 4]). Cf. 'The Complaint of the B. Virgin', l. 30 (Appendix II, p. 115).

l. 23. *thy foe*: sinful man, perhaps with particular reference to the soldiers about to arrest Christ.

l. 28. *thou seal'st a peace with bleeding kisse*. The peace secured by the passion of Christ is affirmed in the Mass, specifically in the *Pax Domini*, spoken by the priest directly preceding the *Agnus Dei* and the Communion. It is more precisely enacted in the ceremonies of the *Depositio Crucis* on Good Friday, when priest and congregation in turn prostrate themselves before a crucifix (the *Pax*), and kiss it—actions attributed in these lines to Christ at the time the bond of peace between God and nature was re-established.

l. 32. *yeeld thy soule a way*. The action of physical nature (Earth) is represented as offering the soul of Christ the way to hell; the phrase *yeeld away*, as in *VC* and in *1602*, has no recorded precedent in *O.E.D.* Cf. variations in the meaning of *yeeld* based on the notion of giving—at l. 35 with the sense 'make submission for', and at l. 41 in the sense 'submit, agree'. The verb appears with similar sense variations in the prose writings, as in the Letter to his Father, when Southwell begs him: 'yield your soul a happy captive to God's merciful inspirations' (ed. Trotman, p. 62).

l. 34. *them*. The reference is to *blood . . . soule . . . corse* of the previous lines.

l. 35. *Now then*. The text is apparently corrupt here; *For them* may be the correct reading, the error arising in part from the misinterpretation of a contracted form, *thē*.

Christs bloody sweat (page 18)

MSS.: *S, VC, A, H, F*; *B*.

Lines 1–12 printed in *Ma*, without stanza division; lines 13–24, unpublished in early editions, first printed from *A* by Turnbull (1856), and from *S* by Grosart (1872).

F has for sub-title: '*Et factus est sudor eius quasi guttæ sanguinis.*' Twelve additional lines not in other manuscripts are inserted after l. 6, as follows:

> And if (quoth he) the bath must be of bloud,
> To wash away the leprocie of sinne;
> Then hart and veines gush out a bloudie floud,
> That al the world may wash and bathe therin:
> Yea let my bodie be a clowde of bloud,
> To powre down shoures for mans eternal good.
>
> For this so bloudie homage ful of smart
> The Mount was Church, the Priest Gods heavy Ire,
> Obedience was the Knife, the Hoast his Hart,
> The Altars humble Will, and Love the Fire:
> But Lord how could this fire endure unqwench't,
> That in the middes of bloudie streames was drencht?

These lines were printed in McDonald, p. 46. Their authenticity is discussed in the Textual Introduction, IV. III, p. lxxxiv.

l. 2. *pours. powers* in *Ma* is a common variant.

l. 5. *shedding. sheeding* in *Ma* is a dialect form. *shed* is to let fall in drops (*O.E.D. v.* 8).

ll. 13–24. Punctuation supplied in these lines follows generally the system in the previous lines as printed in *Ma*.

l. 13. See 1 Kings xix. 17–40. *powre.* The spelling in *S, poure*, is misleading for the modern reader; the revision to *powre* here, and in 'Of the Blessed Sacrament', l. 53, and 'I dye without desert', l. 27, preserves the monosyllabic form of the word.

Christs sleeping friends (page 19)

MSS.: *S, VC, A, H, F*; *B*.

Printed in *Ma*, without stanza divisions.

l. 4. The phrase 'watch and pray', the words of Christ to the disciples in Gethsemane (Matt. xxvi. 41, Mark xiv. 38) is reversed in the manuscripts, giving a reading that is preferable for the distribution of the alliterative *p. vaine* in *Ma* is obviously an error.

l. 13. The figure of Jonah, traditionally a type of Christ, is used in this poem as symbol of the disciples who, unaware, slept while Christ suffered and danger threatened. Christ is prefigured in the ship tossed in the storm (ll. 17, 22) and the ivy (Vulgate *hedera*; A.V. *gourd*) devoured by the worm (ll. 26, 31).

l. 17. *gaine*: booty, prey, spoil (*O.E.D. sb.*² 1); an archaism by the end of the sixteenth century. It is perhaps preferable in this context to *game*, the reading of *Ma* and less responsible manuscripts, including *B*. However, the phrase *billowes game* occurs in the 'Complaint', l. 9.

l. 37. *Ye*. If Southwell had any preference for one of the alternative forms of the vocative, it has been obscured by copyists and compositors. *You* occurs in the 'Complaint', ll. 349, 351, 352, 481, and 483. *Yee* is preserved in the manuscript poem 'I dye without desert', l. 19. *You* is used in 'The virgin Mary to Christ on the Crosse' (*Ma* and *F*), ll. 9 and 17.

l. 41. Zacheus. Luke xix. 1–10. A reference also occurs in *TD*, sig. E2ᵛ, when Southwell writes of Lady Margaret Sackville's death: 'Forsaking the earth with *Zacheus*, she climed up into the tree of life.'

Josephs Amazement (page 21)

MSS.: *S, VC, A, H, F*.

Printed in *1602*.

l. 1. *desent*: a spelling variant of *descent*.

l. 2. *receit*: place of reception. *brest*: womb, as frequently.

l. 7. *sence*. In a number of the poems the senses are considered as the source of faulty judgement.

l. 9. *in doome of* : in judgement on, in the process of judging (now archaic; see *O.E.D.* 'doom').

l. 14. *undeserved*: suffered without good cause.

l. 18. *gaulish*: like gall. The normal order of the line requires *doth prove bitter to taste*.

l. 22. *casts*: deliberates upon, plans.

l. 23. *frame*: make ready, prepare; here, bring to the point of action. This sense was already archaic by the sixteenth century (see *O.E.D. v*. 3, 4).

l. 27. *ruing*. The reading in the manuscripts, reasserting *griefe* of l. 25, is preferred before *raging* in the printed editions. The error may have its origin in a misreading of a manuscript reproducing Southwell's habitual spelling of the present participial suffix, -*yng(e)*.

l. 32. *misesteemed shame*: what is mistakenly judged as shameful.

ll. 37–54. In this section of self-examination Joseph is aware of doubts assailing him concerning love (ll. 37-42), faith (ll. 43-48), and hope (ll. 49-54).

l. 49. *hope a pledge of grace*. Hope represents trust in the effective grace of God (Rom. iv. 13), revealed to Joseph in Mary's virtue.

l. 57. *Though fortune mine* . . . : though fortune is my foe; the line echoes the contemporary song.

l. 67. *stocked*: stunted in growth. This use is earlier than that cited in *O.E.D.* (Markham, 1607).

l. 68. *perisht*. The past participle implies a past state extending into the future: fruit on a dying tree is destined to be spoilt.

l. 76. *Sicke* . . . *vaine*: If sorrowful hearts cannot avoid suffering, any more than sick persons can avoid the severities of their illness, moving from place to place makes no difference. *shift* has first the sense of 'avoid', 'elude', and secondly, that of 'change'.

A holy Hymme (page 23)

MSS.: *S, VC, A, H, F.*

The poem is entitled in the manuscripts: 'Saint Thomas of Aquines Hymne. read on corpus christy daye. Lauda Sion Salvatorem.' (*VC* omits Latin title.)

In *S, VC*, and *H*, the poem is transcribed in six-lined stanzas, corresponding to the traditional arrangement of the Latin lines to the point of metrical variation (l. 55); this stanzaic form has been adopted in this edition.

Printed in *Ma*, without stanza divisions.

The poem is doubtfully attributed to Southwell. See Textual Introduction, IV. i, p. lxxviii, and V, p. xcvi.

The poem is also found appended to Luca Pinelli's *Breife Meditations of the Most Holy Sacrament* (printed secretly in England, 1595–1600; *S.T.C.* 19937, Allison and Rogers, no. 648). In the volume the Latin version of the hymn is followed by the translation, sig. ¶6ᵛ–8ᵛ, headed: '*The same in English translated by the Rev. Fa. R.S.*' The text of the translation was set up either from *Ma* or *Mb*—numerous punctuation and spelling variants prevent certain identification. The only significant textual change is the correction of the manifest error *lou'd* for *loud* (l. 13.) A further error is introduced at l. 43.

The Latin text of the hymn is given here from the *Meditations* (copy in the Folger Shakespeare Library). (Printing errors at ll. 48 and 60 have been corrected.)

The sequence after the Epistle of the Masse

> LAUDA Sion Salvatorem,
>   Lauda ducem & pastorem,
>   In hymnis, & canticis.
> Quantum potes, tantum aude,
>   Quia maior omni laude,   5
>   Nec laudare sufficis.
> Laudis thema specialis,
>   Panis vivus, & vitalis,
>   Hodie proponitur.
> Quem in sacræ mensa cenæ,   10

Turbæ fratrum duodenæ,
Datum non ambigitur.
Sit laus plena, sit sonora,
Sit iucunda, sit decora,
Mentis iubilatio.   15
Dies enim solemnis agitur;
In qua mensæ prima recolitur
Huius institutio,
In hac mensa novi regis,
Novum Pascha novæ legis,   20
Phase vetus terminat.
Vetustatem novitas,
Umbram fugat veritas,
Noctem lux eliminat.
Quod in cena Christus gessit,   25
Faciendum hoc expressit,
In sui memoriam.
Docti sacris institutis,
Panem vinum in salutis,
Consecramus hostiam.   30
Dogma datur Christianis,
Quod in carnem transit panis
Et vinum in sanguinem.
Quod non capis, quod non vides,
Animosa firmat fides,   35
Præter rerum ordinem,
Sub diversis speciebus;
Signis tantum, & non rebus,
Latent res eximiæ.
Caro cibus sanguis potus,   40
Manet Christus tamen totus,
Sub utraque specie.
A sumente non concisus,
Non confractus, non divisus,
Integer accipitur.   45
Sumit unus, sumunt mille,
Quantum isti, tantum ille:
Nec sumptus consumitur.
Sumunt boni, sumunt mali,
Sorte tamen inæquali,   50
Vitæ, vel interitus.
Mors est malis vita bonis.
Vide paris sumptionis,
Quam sit dispar exitus.
Fracto demum Sacramento,   55
Ne vacilles, sed memento,
Tantum esse sub fragmento,
Quantum toto tegitur.
Nulla rei sit scissura,
Signi tantum fit fractura   60
Qua nec status, nec statura,
Signati minuitur.

K

Ecce panis Angelorum,
    Factus cibus viatorum:
    Vere panis filiorum,   65
    Non mittendus canibus.
In figuris præsignatur,
    Cum Isaac immolatur:
    Agnus Pascha deputatur,
    Datur manna patribus.   70
Bone pastor panis vere,
    Iesu nostri miserere:
    Tu nos pasce, nos tuere:
    Tu nos bona fac videre,
    In terra viventium.   75
Tu qui cuncta scis, & vales,
    Qui nos pascis hic mortales,
    Tuos ibi commensales,
    Cohæredes, & sodales,
    Fac sanctorum civium. Amen.   80

l. 5. *His worthes*. The manuscript reading avoids the limitation of the sense to *workes*, as in *Ma*.

l. 15. *mindes and voices*. The forms are probably both singular.

l. 18. *prime use*. The error in *Ma*, which has *privy* for *prime*, is typical of faulty reading of manuscript.

l. 20. *Of new Law, new pascall order*. The syntax is clear in the Latin: *Novum Pascha novæ legis*.

l. 22. *annulled*. *annilld* in *Ma* would appear to have no authority, but it represents an attempt to establish a rime with *fulfilld* (l. 23). The feminine endings of *annulled* and *fulfilled* rime in accordance with the practice followed generally throughout the translation; a double rime occurs only in this stanza (ll. 21, 24), and in six other instances. *Annilld* is a form of *annihil* (mod. E. *annihilate*). The Latin text is of no help in establishing the text at this point.

l. 23. *in trueths*. The singular *trueth* of *Ma* and *VC* actually reproduces the Latin *veritas*, but the translation seems to require the plural form.

l. 36. *effects*. The reading of the manuscripts is more acceptable than *affects* of *Ma*. *Effects* refers to the external manifestation (Lat. *Præter rerum ordinem*), as in 'Of Blessed Sacrament of the Aulter', l. 83, *affects* to the inward desire, concerning which faith cannot be said to be *not curious*. But cf. l. 50, and the 'Complaint', l. 652, where *effect(e)s* is used of unseen results, contrasted with what is outwardly to be seen.

ll. 37–60. These lines, embodying the Roman Catholic doctrine of transubstantiation, are omitted in *1620* and later editions. Nine lines are substituted, as follows (*1620*, sig. H11ᵛ–12; misprints have been corrected):

    As staffe of bread thy heart sustaines,
    And chearefull wine thy strength regaines.

By power and vertue naturall:
So doth this consecrated food,
The symbole of Christ flesh and bloud,
By vertue supernaturall,

The ruines of thy soule repaire,
Banish sinne, horrour, and despaire,
And feed faith, by faith received:

The poem is then completed with the last twelve lines of 'A holy Hymme'
(ll. 61–72).

l. 39. *Lie.* The reading of the manuscripts (for Lat. *Latent*) is preferable.

l. 55. The metrical form of the Latin hymn changes at this point; the translation is completed without change.

ll. 64–66. Gen. xxii. 1–14; Exod. xii. 3–28, xvi. 11–36.

l. 71. *Fellow heires.* The reading of *Ma* and *VC* has been adopted as a clear
translation of *Cohæredes*; in this version *sodales*, fellows, is ignored. Once again
the distortions in the word order are best elucidated by means of the Latin text.

Of the Blessed Sacrament of the Aulter (page 26)

MSS.: *S, VC, A, H, F.*
Printed in *SOa*, with the title 'The Christians Manna'.
    The poem was later printed in Walter (1817) and Turnbull (1856) from *A*,
and in Grosart (1872) from *S*.

    The textual authority of the manuscripts is clearly greater than that of the first
printed edition, and the version in *S* has been adopted as copy-text. Light
punctuation has been added. In *SOa* so many editorial changes were made that
a defective copy may be suspected; one stanza, ll. 31–36, is omitted, and the first
part of l. 78 is redrafted without any gain in clarity or rhythmic smoothness.
At other points the substitution of words, as *sowered* for *fevered* (l. 44), *glasses*
for *mirrhors* (l. 74), indicates careless copying. Reference to the text of *SOa*
in the collational apparatus is made only when it lends support to variants in
the manuscripts.

ll. 1–6. These lines are based on '*Lauda Sion*'; see 'A holy Hymme', ll. 19–27. At
many points in the poem there are textual echoes and sometimes close paraphrase
of the Latin hymn.

l. 3. *glymses*: glimpses. This form without *p* was regular until the sixteenth
century.

l. 27. *eagrest*: keenest. *Eager* occurs with special reference to hunger, perhaps
originally as a technical term in falconry. (See *O.E.D.* 7.)

ll. 31–40. The meditative pattern of the Ignatian Exercises appears here, in
which the application of the senses is prelude to the application of the understanding (*witt*), affections (*will*), and memory.

ll. 47–48. 'Those who receive the Body of Christ unworthily are condemned to death; what assures the believer of Heaven destines the wicked to Hell.' (Cf. 'A holy Hymme', l. 52.)

l. 55. *endew'd*: endowed, invested.

l. 63. *rifled hell*. The reference may be to the apocryphal account of the Harrowing of Hell. See also Eph. iv. 8.

l. 76. *defynes*: discerns accurately; the meaning is adapted from the use of the verb to denote limitation, i.e. to determine, or to state precisely. No example of its application to sight is quoted in *O.E.D.* until its use in passive forms in the eighteenth and nineteenth centuries.

l. 77. *frame*: construct.

l. 83. *effects of bodyes*. The reference is to the manifestation to human sense of angels in the form of men.

l. 90. John ii. 1–11; Exod. iv. 2–4.   Moyses. *S* has the name in Italian hand.

Saint Peters Complaynte (page 29)

MSS.: *S, VC, A, H, F.*
   In *F* the poem is transcribed on the final blank leaf (sig. H4) of *Ca* (*F*) with which the manuscript is bound; it lacks title and the first four lines, originally transcribed at the bottom of sig. H3ᵛ, now missing. (See Textual Introduction, I. v, p. xlviii.)

Printed in McDonald, Appendix A, pp. 141–3.

The punctuation is based on that of related passages in the 'Complaint', for which *Ca* is copy-text. The compositor uses a colon interchangeably with a comma for the lightest mark of punctuation.

For a discussion of the relationship of this poem and other versions, see Textual Introduction, IV. iv, p. lxxxvi.

l. 15. *pretence*: assertion of right; the word retains the sense of Lat. *prætendere*, from which it is ultimately derived.

l. 33. *Judas race*: the tribe of Judas (but here applied loosely to treacherous friends); in the 'Complaint', l. 99, the phrase has the totally different reference to a contest (in running). Judas was the keeper of the accounts, and the play on meanings in the stanza is developed in the imagery of money and value.

l. 44. Peter's plea for mercy here and in ll. 67–72 does not occur in the four-lined stanza version in *F*. (See Appendix II, p. 111.)

l. 62. *detestinge*: using words of execration while calling God to witness; see also the 'Complaint', l. 134. The four-lined stanza version in *F* has *blasphemous* in this context (l. 38). See Matt. xxvi. 74; Mark xiv. 71.

l. 70. *thy deserved hate*: thy hate which I have merited; this awkwardly compressed phrase occurs also in the 'Complaint', l. 784.

S. Peters afflicted minde (page 31)

MSS.: *S, VC, A, H, F; B.*

Manuscripts show no stanza divisions except *VC*, in which the poem is transcribed in eight-lined stanzas, and *B*, where it is transcribed in six four-lined stanzas, as here.

Printed in *Ma*, without stanza divisions.

Title. The reference to Peter is doubtfully authentic; the poem makes no direct allusion to his sufferings after his denial of Christ.

l. 10. *languor*: mental suffering; the term had this connotation from the fourteenth to the seventeenth centuries.

l. 12. *pinde*: imprisoned (see *O.E.D.* 'pin', *v.*¹ II. 10, used specifically of animals in a pound). In *An Humble Supplication* (ed. Bald, p. 39), Southwell writes of 'venerable Prælates and other Priests and gentlemen . . . pined in *Wisbiche*'.

l. 13. *kinne*. The reading of the manuscripts is preferred to that of the printed texts; the variant *kinde* (now archaic, for *kin*) was probably influenced by *pinde* in the previous line.

l. 15. *Forlorne*. The reading of *Forborne* in *S* is possible, in the sense of 'bereft' or 'shunned'. Cf. *MMFT*, sig. D2: 'If they can forbeare him, surely they do not knowe him.'

l. 19. *mishaps*. The sense of accidental misfortune or bad luck is attached to the word (see *O.E.D.*), although in this context it implies the results of sinful actions.

l. 22. *dislikes*: what arouses most repugnance. This use of the plural in this sense is slightly earlier than the first instance cited in *O.E.D.* (1597).

Mary Magdalens blush (page 32)

MSS.: *S, VC, A, H.*

In *VC* this poem and the following, 'S. Peters remorse', are in reverse order, probably as the result of a simple error in transcription.

Printed in *Ca*.

l. 2. *raving*: delirious, as in a fever (which brings a high colour to the face, as in blushing); therefore, acting and speaking without reason.

ll. 9–12. Knowledge of sin gained through the process of remorse is expressed by St. Gregory, as quoted in *EC*, sig. G2ᵛ-3:

> *Sæpe quod torpentes latuit, fletibus innotescit, et afflicta mens certius invenit malum, quod fecerat, et reatum suum cuius secura non meminit, hunc in se commota depræhendit.* Oftentimes that which we knowe not through our sloth, we learne by teares, and an afflicted mind more certainly findeth a committed fault, and the guilt which in securitie it remembred not, being troubled it espyeth.

l. 15. *flights*. The term is used specifically of the trajectory of arrows. The reference here and in the following lines is to the arrows shot by Cupid as symbol of profane love.

l. 17. *Woe worth.* . . . With frequent reiteration the common phrase did not retain the strength of the curse that is literally called down.

l. 18. *drave.* The variants in *A* and *H*—forms of the verb *draw*—indicate an early manuscript error rather than the result of spelling ambiguity, such as is found in the text of 'Marie Magdalens complaint', l. 41, where the two verbs *drive* and *draw* have been confused.

l. 30. The number of variants in the manuscripts and *Ca* here have obscured the original reading; Southwell uses the singular *hap* more frequently, generally in the sense of 'good fortune'. The play on *hap* and *hope* is found in 'Davids Peccavi', l. 4.

S. Peters remorse (page 33)

MSS.: *S, VC, A, H, F.*

Manuscripts have no stanza divisions, except *VC*, in which the poem is transcribed in eight-lined stanzas. (See note on the order of 'Mary Magdalens blush' and this poem in *VC*, p. 133, above.)

Printed in *Ma*, without stanza divisions.

l. 3. *hoast*: sacrifice.

ll. 33–34. *Did mercy spin* . . .: 'If mercy did spin. . . .' The conditional construction was lost by inaccurate punctuation in *Ma*, which placed a question mark at the end of l. 34.

ll. 40, 42. *A* agrees with the text of *Ma* at these points, while an independent version is preserved in other manuscripts. The use of the subjunctive *be* (l. 40) in the manuscripts is preferred to *am* for its recurrence in similar constructions, as in 'Christs bloody sweat', l. 21.

l. 43. *dust of dead supplies*: useless memories of former resources now lost.

Davids Peccavi (page 35)

MSS.: *S, VC, A, H, F.*

Printed in *1602*.

Title. The title in *SOa*, 'Saint Peters Peccavi', attempts to group the poem with others in this section concerned with various aspects of Peter's remorse, but the reference to the power of *fancies toyes*, ll. 18, 25–30, is more suitably applied to David.

ll. 1–12. The imagery draws upon a number of the images used to express the agony of the troubled spirit in Ps. cii, the fifth penitential psalm. The theme of the poem, emphasizing the change in the sinner's relationship with God, is contained in verse 10: 'For thou hast lifted me up and cast me down.'

l. 19. *over-wrought*: won over, overpowered (*O.E.D.* 'overwork', *v.* I. 2, now obsolete).

ll. 22, 24. *doome*: the faculty of judging, discernment (*O.E.D. sb.* 3b.).

A Phansie turned to a sinners complaint (page 36)

MSS.: *S, VC, A, H, F.*

The poem is entitled in the manuscripts: 'Dyers (Maister diers *A*) phancy turned to (into *VC*) a Sinners Complainte.' It is transcribed without stanza divisions, except in *VC*, where it is arranged in eight-lined stanzas.

Printed in *1602*, in four-lined stanzas, as reproduced here.

The poem is a line-by-line parody of a poem of Sir Edward Dyer's, entitled 'A Fancy' on the evidence afforded by the title of this poem of Southwell's. The text of Dyer's poem is given here as printed from MS. Ashmole 781 by Ralph M. Sargent in *At the Court of Queen Elizabeth: the Life and Lyrics of Sir Edward Dyer* (O.U.P., 1935), pp. 184–7. For ease of comparison, the stanzas are set out in four short lines, as are those of Southwell's poem, instead of the two long lines preferred by Sargent.

A FANCY

H EE that his mirth hath loste,
Whose comfort is dismaid,
Whose hope is vaine, whose faith is scornd,
Whose trust is all betraid;

If hee have held them deare, 5
And cannot cease to moane,
Come, let him take his place by mee:
He shall not rue alone.

But if the smalest sweete
Be mixt with all his sowre, 10
If in the day, the moneth, the yeare,
He feele one lightening howre,

Then rest hee by himself,
He is noe mate for mee,
Whose feare is falen, whose succor voyde, 15
Whose hurt his death must be;

Yet not the wished death,
That hath noe plainte nor lacke,
Which making free the better parte,
Is onely natures wracke; 20

Oh noe, that were too well:
My death is of the mind,
Which alwaies yeelds extreamest paines,
Yet keepes the most behind:

As one that lives in shewe, 25
But inwardlye doth dye,
Whose knowledge is a bloody feild,
Wheare all help slaine doth lie;

Whose harte the Aulter is,
Whose spirit the sacrifize   30
Unto the Powers, whome to appease
Noe sorrowes can suffize:

My fancies are like thornes,
On which I goe by night,
Mine arguments are like an hoste,   35
That force hath put to flight:

My sense my passions spie,
My thoughts like ruins old
Of famous Carthage or the town
That Sinon bought and sold,   40

Which still before my face
My mortall foe doth lay,
Whome love and fortune once advaunced
And now hath cast away.

O thoughtes, noe thoughts, but woundes,   45
Sometimes the seate of Joy,
Sometymes the chaire of quiet rest,
But now of all Annoy!

I sewed the soyle of peace,
My blisse was in the springe,   50
And day by day I ate the fruits,
That my Lives tree did bring.

To nettells now my Corne,
My feild is turnd to flint,
Where, sittinge in the Cipros shade,   55
I reade the Hiacint.

The peace, the rest, the life,
That I enjoyed of yore,
Came to my lot, that by my losse,
My smarte might smarte the more.   60

Thus to unhappie man,
The best frames to the worste,
O tyme, o place, o woordes, o lookes
Deere then, but nowe accurst:

In *was* stands my delight,   65
In *is* and *shall* my woe;
My horror hastnd in the *yea*,
My hopes hangs in the *noe*.

I looke for noe releefe,
Releefe will come too late,   70
Too late I finde, I finde too well,
Too well stoode my estate.

Behold, suche is the end,
And nothing heere is sure:
Oh, nothinge ells but plaints and cares,   75
Doth to the world enduer.

Forsaken first was I,
Then utterly foregotten,
And he that came not to my faith,
Lo, my reward hath gotten.   80

Then love, where is thy sauce,
That makes thy torments sweete:
Wher is the cause, that some have thought
Their death through thee but meet?

The stately chaste disdaine,   85
The secret thanckfulness,
The grace reserved, the common Light
That shines in worthines?

O that it were not soe,
Or that I could excuse,   90
O that the wrath of Jelousie
My Judgment might abuse!

O fraile unconstant kynd,
And safe in trust to noe man!
Noe woomen angels be,   95
And loe, my mystris is a woeman;

Yet hate I but the falte,
And not the faultie one,
Nor can I rid me of the bands
Wherein I lye alone.   100

Alone I lye, whose like
By love was never yet,
Nor rich, nor poore, nor younge, nor old,
Nor fond, nor full of witt.

Hers still remaine must I,   105
By wronge, by death, by shame:
I cannot blot out of my minde
That love wrought in her name:

I cannot set at nought
That I have held soe deare: 110
I cannot make it seeme soe farre,
That is indeede soe neare.

Not that I meane henceforth
This strange will to professe:
I never will betray such trust   115
And buyld on fickelnesse;

Nor shall it ever faile
That my word have in hand:
I gave my worde, my worde gave me;
Both worde and guift shall stand.   120

Syth then it must be thus,
And this is all to ill,
I yeelde me Captive to my curse,
My harde fate to fulfill.

The sollitarie woodes   125
My Cittie shall become:
The darkest den shalbe my lodge,
Whereto noe light shall come:

Of heban blacke my boorde,
The wormes my feast shalbe,   130
Wherewith my Carcasse shalbe fed,
Till they doe feede on mee:

My wine of Niobe,
My bedd the cragie rocke,
The serpents hysse my harmony,   135
The scritchinge owle my clock:

Mine Exercise naught ells
But raginge agonies,
My bookes of spightfull fortunes foiles
And drerye tragedies: 140

My walkes the pathes of plaint,
My prospect into Hell,
With Sisiphus and all his pheres
In endles paines to dwell.

And though I seeme to use   145
The Poets fained stile,
To figure forth my wofull plight,
My fall, and my Exile;

Yet is my greefe not faind,
Wherein I strive and pine: 150
Whoe feeleth most, shall finde it least,
Comparinge his with mine.

My song, if anie aske
Whose greivous Case is such,
Dy er thou let his name be knowne: 155
His folly shewes to much,

But best were thee to hide,
And never come to light,
For in the world can none but thee
These accents sound aright.   160

And soe an end, my Tale is tould:
His life is but disdaind,
Whose sorrowes present paine him soe,
His pleasures are full faind.

l. 3. *cras'de*: unsound, broken. (See *O.E.D.* 'craze', *v.* Lit., broken in pieces.)

l. 15. *race*: course of life (recalling Heb. xii. 1).

l. 30. *hoast*: sacrifice (the word occurring in Dyer's poem at this point). *hoast* in the sense of 'army' recurs at l. 35, an awkward repetition avoided by Dyer.

l. 37. *passions spie*: an agent reporting suffering.

l. 51. *eate*: (a past tense) ate.

l. 62. *frames*: deteriorates, falls off. Cf. *O.E.D. v.* 2, where the verb is cited with generally more favourable connotation in the sense of 'follows', 'succeeds'. The word has been adopted from Dyer's poem; Southwell does not normally use *frame* in this sense.

l. 68. *hangd*. The existing texts of Dyer's poem, giving both *hang'd* and *hangs*, do not help in determining Southwell's text here.

l. 87. *rayes*. The reading is supported by Dyer's poem, l. 87, which has *light* here.

l. 106. *By*. The notion of time is contained in these phrases, in which *by* is equivalent to *through*.

l. 108. *wrought*. The spelling variants *wrote* (*S*, *VC*, *H*), *wrotte* (*F*), and *wrought* (*A*) are forms of the past participle of *work*; this interpretation is supported in Dyer's poem. Although the context suggests the past tense of *write*, as in *1602* (*writ*), it is probably incorrect here.

l. 122. An awkwardly compressed construction: 'no scourge is unjustly severe'.

l. 127. *dennes*. *denne* in *VC* reproduces the form in Dyer's poem, and may be correct here.

l. 151. *feeleth*. The reading in the manuscripts (excluding *F*) is supported by Dyer's poem.

A vale of teares (page 41)

MSS.: *S*, *VC*, *A*, *H*, *F*.
  The poem is transcribed in four-lined stanzas.

Printed in *Ma*, without stanza divisions.

l. 3. *dumpish*: melancholy, depressing (to an observer).

l. 7. The description of the mountain torrent has many of the features of a passage in *EC*, sig. P6ᵛ:

  We see the fludd, that riseth in the top of a Mountayne, to fall and roule downe with a continuall noyse: It gusheth out with a holowe and horse sound, then it runneth roaring down, over craggye and rough clyffes, and is continuallye crushed and broaken with divers encounters, til at the foote of the hill, it entereth into the Sea. And so fareth it with mans lyfe. . . .

frie: turbulence; no example of a noun with this meaning is cited in *O.E.D.*, although as a verb, now obsolete, it is found with reference to water, meaning 'to be agitated', 'boil', 'seethe'.

l. 8. *thow'd*. The same form, used in a figurative sense, occurs in the 'Peeter Playnt', l. 82 (Appendix I, p. 105).

l. 24. *framde*: contrived.

l. 26. *strait*: difficult to traverse.

l. 33. *mated minds*: minds matched in mood with the place. *mated* includes also the meaning of 'amazed', 'confounded' (*O.E.D.* 'mate', *v.*¹).

l. 34. *sooth*: affirm, demonstrate.

l. 44. The interpretation of the poem in terms of spiritual experience is here made fully explicit. The reference to hope clarifies the significance of the previous lines of the stanza, in which green, the colour of hope, is found in the dark and screening pines, suggesting the evergreens of graveyards, and in the green plain, overshadowed by threatening cliffs.

l. 45. *tickle*: insecure, precarious; cf. its use in a figurative sense in *EC*, sig. F7ᵛ: 'Hope of felicitye hangeth, on so tickle and slipperye termes', and sig. P5ᵛ: 'Lyfe, it selfe is so frayle, and tickle a thinge.'

l. 48. *Beset*: surrounded with.

l. 49. *christall springs*: here, the source of divine grace, from which the sinner is cut off. *vaine*: a narrow channel. (See *O.E.D.* 'vein', *sb.* II. 6.) It was believed that fresh water was returned from the deepest part of the ocean through unknown channels in the earth to springs and well-heads.

l. 52. *thunder wracke*: the threat of destruction in the sound of thunder.

l. 54. *motives*: that which stirs the emotions. The sense here, with reference to emotions aroused in the contrite heart of the sinner, does not seem to include the later sense of what moves the will to act. *suitly to*: in accordance with, agreeing with.

l. 60. The response of nature to the mourner's mood is also explicit in a passage in *MMFT*, sig. F1–1ᵛ, which closely resembles this section of the poem:

> Thy eies seeme to tell thee that every thing inviteth thee to weep, carrying such outward shewe, as though all that thou seest were attyred in sorrow to solemnize with general consent the funeral of thy maister. Thy eares perswade thee, that all soundes and voyces are tuned to mourning notes, and that the Eccho of thy own wailings, is the cry of the verie stones and trees, as though (the cause of thy teares being so unusuall) God to the rockes and woodes, had inspired a feeling of thine and their common losse.

l. 61. The reading of the manuscripts is preferable; the verb is not *Sit* but *Set . . . afloate*, bring to full tide, or, as here, overflow with (tears). (Cf. *O.E.D.* 'afloat', 3.)

l. 64. *That . . . amount*: so that sorrow for sin may be more fully experienced in thy songs. *amount*: mount up, increase (see *O.E.D. v.* 4). The dedication of a poet's talents to the expression of penitential grief was one of the manifestations of the Counter-Reformation.

l. 65. *plainfull*. This reading from *S* and *H* has been preferred to *painfull*, where the emphasis lies upon personal suffering rather than on remorse for sin.

l. 68. *latter day*: the Day of Judgement.

l. 70. *Limbecke*: alembic, the vessel used in the process of distillation.

l. 74. *burdon*: (*bourdon*) the low accompaniment to a melody; the confusion with *burden* (*VC, A, F*) or *burthen* (*Ma*) dates from its earliest recorded use in English. The most usual construction is with *to*, as in *Ma*.

The prodigall childs soule wracke (page 43)

MSS.: *S, VC, A, H, F; B*.

The poem is transcribed in four-lined stanzas, as here. In *S* it has been copied by the second scribe, who has elsewhere limited his work to correction.

Printed in *Ma*, in sixteen-syllabled lines without stanza divisions.

The punctuation in *Ma* has been retained, although in the sixteen-syllabled lines in which the poem is set it is probable that mid-line commas denote metrical breaks otherwise obscured by the setting; with the adoption of the four-lined stanza of the manuscripts, these commas now appear in superabundance at the end of the first and third lines in each stanza. The same difficulty arises in the text of other poems printed in long lines in *Ma*: 'Mans civill warre' (p. 49), 'Seeke flowers of heaven' (p. 52), and 'The virgin Mary to Christ on the Crosse' (p. 71). (See comment on page layout in *Ma* in Textual Introduction, III. VII, p. lxxiii.)

The example of the Prodigal Son as repentant sinner appears frequently in Southwell's work. Latin verses entitled *Filii prodigi porcos pascentis ad patrem epistola* are preserved in Stonyhurst College MS. A. v. 4 (printed in Grosart, pp. 199–205; see also Janelle, pp. 131–5). Passages in *EC*, sigs. F4 and R6ᵛ, also use the imagery of the parable.

ll. 1–16. The imagery of the sinner tossed in a stormy sea was used in the *Filii prodigi . . . epistola* and elsewhere in the English verse. Similarly sustained sea imagery, but applied to the changing state of man's body, is used in the Letter to his Father (ed. Trotman, p. 52). The first line of the poem is echoed in *TD*, sig. D1ᵛ: 'Your hopes disanchored from the stormie shore. . . .'

l. 2. *maine*. This reading from the manuscripts sustains the image of the ship going into the open sea, and is preferable to *meane* of *Ma*, which is acceptable only in the rare sense of a middle place (see *O.E.D. sb.*² 3, now obsolete). Cf. the adjectival use of *maine*, 'A vale of teares', l. 61.

l. 10. *hold*. A preterite form is needed to sustain the tense structure of the poem, but it seems preferable to understand *did hold* than to accept the change to *held* in *H* and *F*.

l. 16. *Planets*: the North Star's.

l. 26. The irregularity in the rime in this stanza in *Ma*, and in *S* and *A*, is so rare in Southwell's work that an obvious emendation, as in *H* and *F*, should probably be made. The reading in *H* is barely discernible; *of* is written above the line, suggesting that the copyist was making an independent emendation.

l. 38. *put their wicked proofes in ure*: (evil forces) brought to bear their destructive arguments.

l. 50. Cf. Southwell's Letter to his Father: 'The soft gales of your morning pleasures lulled you in slumbery fits' (ed. Trotman, p. 63).

l. 55. *trained*: drawn on by enchantment, allured (*O.E.D. v.*[1] II. 4, now archaic).

ll. 55–60. Cf. Southwell's Letter to his Brother: 'Bail reason out of senses' prison; that after so long a bondage in sin you may enjoy your former liberty in God's Church' (ed. Trotman, p. 65).

Marie Magdalens complaint at Christs death (page 45)

MSS.: *S, VC, A, H.*

    The compiler of *F* made a single change in the printed text of *Ca* (*F*) at l. 26. Printed in *Ca*; revised in *Cb*.

l. 4. *extortion*: the act of forcibly requiring something from another against his will.

ll. 7–10. The light image combined with that of water, as in these lines, is found in *EC*, sig. Z4ᵛ–5: 'What marvayle when the beame is severed from the Sunne, if it leese the lyght? when the bough is cut of from the tree, if it wither? Or if the brooke being parted from the head springe, drye quite upp?' and in Southwell's Letter to his Father: 'Shall the beams be bright and the sun eclipsed, the brooks clear and the headspring troubled?' (ed. Trotman, p. 62).

ll. 17, 18. Eight-syllabled lines, in contrast to the final seven-syllabled lines of other stanzas.

ll. 25, 27. *nestled . . . wrested*. To establish the rime, *nestled* must be pronounced *nest'led*.

l. 26. *sonne*. The reading of *Ca* is supported by *A* (*sunne*). The occurrence of *somme* in the other manuscripts and in *Cb* indicates that an early error in transcription had been widely copied.

ll. 31–36. The image recurs in *MMFT*, sig. B8: 'Her thoughtes were arrested by everie thred of Christes Sindon, and shee was captive in so many prisons, as the Tombe had memories of her lost maister: Love being her Jailor in them all, and nothing able to ransome her, but the recoverie of her Lord.' Later, sig. D5ᵛ–6, Mary speaks of her soul in the body 'like a repining prisoner in a loathed gaile', and longing to rejoin Christ in the 'Tombe of God and man' she declares that her soul would find there 'in the prison of death, the libertie of a joifull life'. The paradox is applied in *EC*, sig. Y7ᵛ, with reference to the actual imprisonment of Catholics: 'Had you rather be the divels then Gods prisoners? Had you rather lyve caytyves here in earth, then dye to be Sayntes in heaven?'

l. 37. *breakst*. The form is an archaic past tense. The spelling *brakest* in *Ca*, with an intrusive syllable, may be the result of the transference of *e* in setting the type.

l. 40. *Loves and lifes*. These are singular forms, misread in the printed editions.

l. 41. *drav'st*. The spelling *drau'st* of *Ca* is ambiguous; following *S* and *VC* (*dravst*) the verb has been accepted here as the past tense of *drive* rather than the present tense of *draw* (as in *A* and *H*). The events of the Crucifixion are recalled as in the past throughout the stanza.

Decease release. Dum morior orior (page 47)

MS.: *S, VC, A, H, F.*

In *F* this poem and the following poem, 'I dye without desert', are transposed almost to the end of the group of Southwell's lyrics. Neither poem shows any sign of the revision found elsewhere in *F*. (See Textual Introduction, I. v, p. l.)

Unpublished in early editions; first printed in collections of Southwell's poems by Walter (1817) and by Turnbull (1856) from *A*, and by Grosart (1872) from *S*.

Walter entitles the poem 'Decease is Release', omits ll. 5–8, and makes numerous textual changes.

Light punctuation has been supplied in accordance with contemporary printing practice. The copyist of *S* includes no marks of punctuation in his transcription.

The underlying political references in this poem and 'I dye without desert' are discussed in Textual Introduction, IV. i, p. lxxx.

l. 14. *N::* nama, or *name*; this insertion in *S* and *H* leaves the reader to understand the reference intended. *Mary* in *VC* and *A* makes the identification with Mary Queen of Scots, with whom the poem is traditionally associated. *F* has *Anna*, possibly a reference to Anne of Denmark, the queen of James I, who styled herself *Anna*. She was believed to be a convert to Roman Catholicism; she was set aside and neglected by James in her later years. She died on 2 March 1619.

l. 35. *my trapp my stile advaunc'd. trapp* here has reference not only to a snare, as in l. 31, but the meaning is extended to include also a reference to the cloth spread over the saddle or haunches of a horse, more usually *trappings*, bearing the arms indicating the title, or *stile*, of the noble rider. (See *O.E.D.* 'trap', *sb.*)

I dye without desert (page 48)

MSS.: *S, VC, A, H, F.*

For order of poems in *F*, see note on 'Decease release', above.

Unpublished in early editions; printed by Walter (1817) and Turnbull (1856) from *A*, and by Grosart (1872) from *S*.

Punctuation has been supplied to augment that in *S* (see note in collational apparatus).

For discussion of possible contemporary reference in the poem, see Textual Introduction, IV. i, p. lxxx.

Title. In *F* there is a preliminary heading: 'Arthur Earle of Britaine murthered by his uncle King John.' Parallels drawn between Queen Elizabeth and King John, both excommunicated, were commonplaces of Catholic propaganda of the period.

l. 23. *wag'd*: paid wages, recompensed.

l. 26. *proofe*: quality as revealed by examination or test.

l. 33. *pursued*. This example of diæresis, to form the trisyllabic word required by the metrical structure, is rare.

Mans civill warre (page 49)

MSS.: *S, VC, A, H, F; B.*

The poem is transcribed in eight-syllabled lines, with stanza divisions in *VC, F,* and *B* only.

Printed in *Ma*, in sixteen-syllabled lines without stanza divisions.

l. 11. *jesses*: the harness on the legs of the hawk. Southwell uses the term in *EC*, sig. B5ᵛ. *Ma* has *lesses*, for mod. E. *leashes*, attached to the varvels of the jesses.

l. 19. *vertues lore*: moral principles; the phrase is recorded in *O.E.D.* from the fifteenth century.

l. 22. *divers bents*: opposed aims; literally, bending various ways (see *O.E.D.* 'bent', *sb.*² 7).

ll. 25–26. *fighting . . . foe*. The construction of these lines is highly compressed. The image continues that of the previous stanza; the unwilling combatants (*fighting frend* and *favoring foe*) destroy each other in their mutual love, which drives sense to entice reason to worldly pleasures, and reason to reject sense in order to save the soul.

ll. 29–30. The image, also used elsewhere in the poems, may be based on a quotation from Eusebius of Emesa, incorporated into *EC*, sig. C5ᵛ:

Virus amaritudinis obscurat fraude dulcedinis, provocat prius odor poculi sed præfocat infusus sapor in virus, mel est, quod ascendit in labia, venenum et fel, quod descendit in viscera. He shrowdeth his bitter poyson, under a deceiptfull sweetenesse, the pleasant savour of the cupp inviteth, but the sweete taste of the poyson choketh, it is honye that commeth upp to our lippes, but gall and poyson, that goeth downe into our bowels.

Life is but Losse (page 50)

MSS.: *S, VC, A, H, F.*

Printed in *Cb*.

l. 11. This rare example of metrical irregularity suggests lack of revision.

l. 20. *dint*: force, strength. Elsewhere Southwell uses *dint* for the stroke itself.

l. 21. *prest*: ready, prepared. The meaning was already becoming obsolete early in the seventeenth century. Cf. 'Peeter Playnt', l. 52 (Appendix I, p. 105).

l. 25. 1 Sam. xxxi. 4.

l. 26. *as ethe to put in ure*: as easy to carry out.

l. 27. Sampsons *leave*: the answer to Sampson's prayer that he might die when he destroyed the house where Dagon was worshipped. Judges xvi. 30.

l. 28. Gen. iv. 8.

Seeke flowers of heaven (page 52)

MSS.: *S*, *VC*, *A*, *H*, *F*; *B*.

The poem is transcribed in six four-lined stanzas.

Printed in *Ma*, in twelve fourteen-syllabled lines, without stanza divisions.

The latter part of the poem, ll. 9–24, without any indication of its source, was first printed in *Ca*, appended in error to the section of 'Loves servile lot' (ll. 1–48) which concludes the poems in the volume. 'Seeke flowers' was printed in four-lined stanzas, as in the manuscripts. (See Textual Introduction, III. 1, p. lvii.)

l. 4. *strait*: constricted. *strickt* in *Ma* and *A* represents a new formation from Lat. *strictus*.

l. 10. *blazed*: emblazoned. *their*. The reference is to *beauties*, l. 9, a plural possessive form.

l. 12. *limbde*. This is an obsolete variant of *limned*, painted.

l. 19. *glebe*: soil.

I dye alive (page 52)

MSS.: *S*, *VC*, *A*, *H*, *F*.

The poem is entitled 'I dye to live' in *H*.

Printed in *Cb*.

Title. Peter uses the phrase in speaking of the effects of his sin in the 'Complaint' l. 570. It expresses the theme of many of the lyrics in this group.

l. 11. Cf. the exposition of the work of grace on nature in the introductory poem, 'To the Reader', ll. 17–18 (and see note).

What joy to live? (page 53)

MSS.: *S*, *VC*, *A*, *H*, *F*.

Printed in *Cb*.

The poem is based on Petrarch's sonnet 'Pace non trovo e non ho da far guerra' (*Rime* 134). Of the various translations and versions made during the period of Petrarch's popularity in England a translation by Thomas Watson, Passion XL in *Hekatompathia, or the Passionate Centurie of Love* (1582), bears closest linguistic resemblance to Southwell's sacred parody.

l. 3. *prostrate in annoy*: subjected to unhappiness.

l. 9. *wracke*: cause of ruin (see *O.E.D. sb.*[1] II. 4b, now obsolete); the temptations are listed in the following stanzas. This meaning, found in the work of Southwell's contemporaries, may be affected in this context by the earlier sense of a disastrous change in condition, a meaning found from the fifteenth century, and occurring elsewhere in Southwell's work.

Lifes death loves life (page 54)

MSS.: *S*, *VC*, *A*, *H*, *F*; *B*.

The poem is transcribed without stanza divisions, except in *VC* and *B*.
Printed in *Cb*.

Title. In *Cb* (*HEH*) the poem is erroneously entitled 'What joy to live'. In the
TC copy a press correction has supplied the correct title.

l. 13. *Where*: in that case when . . .; not a reference to place, as in ll. 15 and 17.

At home in Heaven (page 55)

MSS.: *S*, *VC*, *A*, *H*, *F*.
Printed in *Cb*.

ll. 7–8. The image of force is based on a text (Matt. xi. 12) which had particular
significance for Southwell: *Regnum cælorum vim patitur, et violenti rapiunt illud.*
It appears with its translation, 'The Kingdome of heaven suffereth violence, and
the violent beare it awaye', on the title-page of *EC*. A personal note on the need
of violent force to overcome passion and all other obstacles to perfection is contained in the *Spiritual Exercises and Devotions* (ed. J. M. de Buck, S.J.), para. 20,
section 4.

l. 37. Esther ii. 7.

l. 38. *bare the vaunt*: was praised excessively (lit. was boasted of); cf. Judith
xi. 19.

Looke home (page 57)

MSS.: *S*, *VC*, *A*, *H*.
Printed in *Ca*.

ll. 1–18. These three stanzas are also found in MS. Harl. 6910, fol. 126. There
are no variants in this version, which was probably made from a printed text.

Times goe by turnes (page 57)

MSS.: *S*, *VC*, *A*, *H*.
Printed in *Ca*.

The poem is also transcribed in MS. Harl. 6910, fol. 124, apparently from
one of the printed texts, *Cb–1599*. In Add. MS. 22601, fol. 71ᵛ, ll. 7–12 are
added as a concluding stanza to the first three stanzas of 'Scorne not the least'.

l. 1. *lopped*. There is no support for *lypped* of *Ca*, although such a form, now
obsolete, is recorded in *O.E.D.* ('lip', *v.*²). *Lopped* and *loppinge* occur in 'Decease
release', ll. 4. and 8.

Losse in delaies (page 58)

MSS.: *S*, *VC*, *A*, *H*; *B*.
Printed in *Ca*.

l. 1. *Shun delaies*. The following note is added to this phrase in *B*:

> That is to say, kill sinne in the very thought
> preventing the Evill, ere it bee wrought,
> he tha[t] so Doth, shall never bee caught
> by the world, the flesh, nor the Divill
>   Christ is that rock, against which we must
> Dash all our envy, Pryde and lust,
> And by true sorrow for sin, crave Ayde of him
> to overcome the world, And flesh, which are sattans ginne.

l. 28. *Fligge*: fledged. (See *O.E.D.* 'fledge', *a*.)

l. 39. *prease*: trouble, difficulty. (See *O.E.D.* 'press', *sb.*^{1} 3).

l. 40. *Grought*. This variant of *growth* in *Ca* is cited in *O.E.D.* with an example of its use in Chapman's *Odyssey* (1615), x. 101, where the rime-word is *thought*. Here the spelling may have been in the printer's copy; *A* has the same spelling, and it may be compared with *strengt* in *H* at l. 34.

l. 42. *Bable*: Babylonian; the reference is to Ps. cxxxvii. 8, 9, It is perhaps intended here that the reference should be applied to the contemporary situation in England, when in Catholic eyes the Queen appeared as the 'daughter of Babylon' (v. 8), and her *babes* the anti-Catholic edicts.

Loves servile lot (page 60)

MSS.: *S*, *VC*, *A*, *H*.

The poem is transcribed without stanza divisions, except in *VC*.

The first part of the poem, ll. 1–48, printed in *Ca*, with ll. 9–24 of 'Seeke flowers of heaven' appended in error; these misplaced lines were deleted and the complete poem printed with some revisions in *Cb*. (See Textual Introduction, III. 1, p. lvii.)

The personification of Love in the poem resembles the figure of the woman Temptation in Prov. vii. 5–27. The imagery is also reminiscent of a passage in *EC*, sig. C5–5^v:

> The Devill kisseth where he meaneth to kyll, he giveth us a draught of poyson in a golden cup, and in a sumptuous and statelye shipp wafteth his passengers upon the rockes of eternal ruine: *Dum per voluptates* (sayth *Eusebius Emissenus*) *extrinsecus blanditur, intrinsecus insidiatur: interfecit spiritum dum oblectat affectum.* While with pleasures without he delighteth us, inwardlye he deceyveth us, and killeth our soule, while he flattereth our fancye. For when he moveth us to labour our wittes, and settle our affection in these inferiour things, what doth he perswade us, but with a golden hooke, to fishe in a filthye puddle, and sincke, where nothing can be gotten but venemous and unsavorye vermin. With *Sirens* sweete notes he woeth us into the salte sea of perdition, with *Crocodyles* teares, he endevoreth to intrapp us. . . .

l. 7. *rine*: rind (in use from the fifteenth to the eighteenth centuries).

l. 10. *good in ill*. The reading in *Ca*, *much good will*, is unsupported in the manuscripts, but it deserves consideration in view of the superiority of the text at ll. 15 and 27.

ll. 19–20. 'Even as she rejects her wooer, she offers some fleeting encouragement that leads to greater unhappiness.' *gliding*: fleeting, momentary, with the connotation suggested by the movement of a snake. The language here and at ll. 31 and 62 recalls Southwell's question in the Letter to his Father: 'Who could rely eternal affairs upon the gliding slipperiness and running stream of our uncertain life?' (ed. Trotman, p. 51).

l. 22. *shee*. The line is of regular length with this omission in *A* and unrevised *S*; in this stanza, however, the second and fourth lines are intentionally lengthened. Other lines of seven syllables (with an unaccented final syllable) occur at ll. 54 and 56.

l. 27. *some*. The reading of *Ca* is supported by *A*. Spelling variants in this line create ambiguities in the other texts: *S*, *VC*, and *H* have *To sweete to soure*; *Cb* has *Too sweete to sowre*.

l. 30. *Flees*: flies; *fleas* and *flies* are sixteenth-century homophones.

l. 31. *settes afloote*: brings to full tide, or to an overflowing state; cf. *O.E.D.* 'afloat', 3.

l. 57. *Moodes*: fits of anger.

l. 72. *up-shot*: conclusion; literally, the final shot in a match at archery. (See *O.E.D.* 3.) Here, 'the sense of despair puts an end to the influence of profane love'.

Lewd Love is Losse (page 62)

MSS.: *S, VC, A, H, F.*
    In *F* the compiler has made extensive changes in the text of the poem; words erased or written over are almost impossible to decipher owing to ink smeared in making the changes.
Printed in *Cb*.

ll. 1–12. The argument is expressed in similar imagery in *EC*, sig. E3^v–4: 'O unspeakable blyndnesse of mans harte, that so easilye trayneth to senses lure, and is so soone caught with the bewtye of an Image, and hath not grace to remember whome it resembleth.'

l. 21. Cf. 'The prodigall childs soule wracke', l. 50, note (p. 141).

l. 22. The image is from archery, with reference to the flexure of the bowstring (*wit*) as it is made possible by the bending of the bow (*will*).

l. 27. *eager sight*: an eagerly desired view (of the loved one). *semblant.* Cf. 'Christs Childhoode', l. 8, note (p. 123).

ll. 31–36, 29–30. These lines, in this order, appear as a separate item in MS. Harl. 6910, fol. 126^v. There are no variants in the text.

ll. 37–42. These lines comprise a separate item in MS. Harl. 6910, fol. 164.

Loves Garden grief (page 64)

MSS.: *S, VC, A, H, F.*

In *F* the poem has been transposed to the end of the group of lyrics. (See Textual Introduction, I. v, p. l.)

Printed in *Cb.*

In this poem, and in 'Fortunes Falsehoode' which follows, Southwell was apparently experimenting with forms of versification; these two metrical patterns do not recur elsewhere. In 'Loves Garden grief' the form of the longer lines in the stanzas shows considerable variation both in line length and in the manipulation of rime. (See Textual Introduction, IV. i, p. lxxix and n. i.)

l. 19. *corrosives.* In the sixteenth century the stress fell on the first syllable, so that the medial syllable was comparatively obscured, and variously spelled. The word was used by Southwell to denote bitter mental and emotional suffering of a destructive character, as in *EC*, sig. Q1, when dying sinners are said to be 'amazed with the fittes and corrasives of the mynd'. His father's apostasy was described as 'a continual corrosive, and cross unto me' (Letter to his Father, ed. Trotman, p. 39), and spiritual faint-heartedness was seen to open the way to the 'corrosive of sin' (Letter to his Brother, ed. Trotman, p. 66). The same images he used in writing to his father are linked in the strongest emotional language of *An Humble Supplication*, when he writes of the violence of persecution, 'All the Crosses that in this kinde we beare . . . cannot but be most bitter Corrasives' (ed. Bald, p. 41).

Fortunes Falsehoode (page 65)

MSS.: *S, VC, A, H.*

Changes in the printed text of the poem were made by the *F* compiler in *Ca (F).*

Printed in *Ca.*

The metrical form of the poem—twelve-syllabled lines with predominant dactylic patterns—is not found elsewhere in Southwell's verse.

ll. 2–3. The awkward construction led to the attempts at emendation in *H.*

l. 3. *swallowed.* It is necessary to treat this form as three-syllabled, as elsewhere in the poem with past participles in *-ed*, where the metre requires an extra syllable. Similarly, the suffixes *-ion* and *-ious* are regularly two-syllabled.

l. 7. *Then. Than* in *Ca* is a spelling variant, used until the seventeenth century, and in dialect until the nineteenth.

l. 10. *bloudie.* The variant *blady* in *S* and *VC* may have the sense of 'threatening', as with a sword, but no such adjective is recorded in *O.E.D.* It is more likely that the variant arose from a simple error in reading *blady* for *blody* (*bloody*).

l. 21. *laberinth.* The imagery here, with the reference to the *cursed deities* (l. 22), draws a parallel with the human sacrifice demanded by the Cretan Minotaur.

l. 23. *menages*: conduct of affairs. The sense has developed from the *manège* in which a horse is trained (see *O.E.D.* 'manage'). Here the reference is to fools' useless attempts to advance in worldly prosperity by actions calculated to win Fortune's favour. In the Letter to his Father Southwell asks whether a dying man can 'dispatch the whole manage of all eternity' (Trotman, p. 53).

1. 24. *wagde*: paid for, as elsewhere in Southwell's verse; the spelling indicates a monosyllable here, unlike many past participles in the poem.

1. 27. *visious*. This spelling variant of *vicious* was misread as *visions* (*Ca*), an error perpetuated in later editions.

ll. 27–28. The underlying irony in these lines, together with the syntactical inversion, tends to obscure the meaning: 'Since those strongest in virtue might be corrupted by worldly success, Fortune is a force for most good when she shows her favours to those already corrupted.'

1. 40. Cf. Ovid, *Tristia*, V. viii. 18: 'Et tantum constans in levitate sua est', a sentiment that had become a sixteenth-century commonplace.

From Fortunes reach (page 66)

MSS.: *S, VC, A, H, F; B.*

Printed in *Cb*.

1. 4. *vaine*. Manuscripts have *fane*, the northern form of *vane*, now obsolete.

1. 5. *stinted to no rest*: never controlled. The construction with *to* is not recorded in *O.E.D.*

1. 6. *choose*. The variant *chose* may be a present tense, although such a form was already archaic at the end of the sixteenth century.

1. 24. *Consorting*: giving a single harmonious expression to; the image is based on the playing of musical instruments in harmony. Here Christ is said to allow his lover the single vision of heavenly happiness in the *three joyes* in which he is revealed—as light, as love, and as life.

Content and rich (page 67)

MSS.: *S, VC, A, H.*

Printed in *Ca*.

The poem is based on Sir Edward Dyer's 'My Mind to Me a Kingdom Is', reproduced here from MS. Rawlinson Poet. 85, as edited by Ralph M. Sargent in *At the Court of Queen Elizabeth: the Life and Lyrics of Sir Edward Dyer* (O.U.P., 1935), pp. 200–1. For Southwell's development of parody, see Textual Introduction, IV. 1, p. lxxix.

> My mynde to me a kyngdome is,
> Suche perfect joy therin I fynde,
> That it excells all other blisse
> That worlde afords or growes by kynde:
> Though muche I wante which moste would have,   5
> Yet still my mynde forbides to crave.

No princely pompe, no wealthy store,
No force to wine the victorye,
No wilye witt to salve a sore,
No shape to feade a lovinge eye;   10
    To none of these I yealde as thrall:
    For why? my minde dothe serve for all.

I see how plenty suffers ofte,
And hasty clymers sone do fall:
I see that those whiche are alofte   15
Myshapp dothe threaten moste of all:
    They get with toylle, they keepe with feare;
    Such cares my mynde coulde never beare.

Contente I live, this is my staye:
I seek no more than maye suffyse,   20
I presse to beare no haughtie swaye;
Look, what I lack my mynde suppliese:
    Lo, thus I tryumphe lyke a kynge,
    Content with that my mynde doth bringe.

Some have to muche, yet still do crave,   25
I little have, and seeke no more:
They are but poore, though muche they have,
And I am ryche with lytle store:
    They poore, I ryche; they begg, I geve:
    They lacke, I leave; they pyne, I lyve.   30

I laugh not at an others loss,
I grudge not at an others gaine:
No worldly waves my mynde can toss,
My state at one dothe still remayne:
    I feare no foe, I fawne no freende,   35
    I lothe not lyfe, nor dread no ende.

Some waye theyre pleasure by theyre luste,
Their wisdom by theyre rage of will:
Theire treasure is theire only truste,
A cloked crafte theyre store of skyll: 40
    But all the pleasure that I fynde
    Is to mayntayne a quiet mynde.

My wealth is healthe and perfecte ease,
My conscience cleere my chiefe defense:
I neither seeke by brybes to please,   45
Nor by deserte to breede offence:
    Thus do I lyve, thus will I dye;
    Would all did so, as well as I.

    Some striking parallels, at some points closer to Southwell's version than to
Dyer's poem, may be found in a lyric attributed to John Lyly by R. Warwick
Bond, and printed from Add. MS. 22601, fol. 60, in his edition of Lyly's *Works*
(Oxford: Clarendon Press, 1902), iii, p. 452:

    Soare I will not, in flighte the grounde ile see
    The careless mind scornes fortunes angrie frowne,
    Either life or death indifferent is to mee,
    Preferr I do content before a crowne:

High thoughts I clipp, no stoutenes throwes me downe   5
Even loftiest lookes in small regard I burie
Not feare their force, nor force not of their furie.

Riche in content, my Wealth is health and ease
A conscience cleare my chiefe and sure defence,
Disdaine I do by flatt'ringe meanes to please   10
For by deserts I will not give offence.
Only a wronge revenge shall recompence:
Rest Muse, I feare no foe, nor frowne on frend
Dispise not life, nor yet I dreade not end.

l. 7. *seely shrowde*: simple clothing.

l. 20. *bondes*: bounds, which literally indicate a limit in space, as in the 'Complaint', l. 590, where *Ca* has *bonds*; or bonds, shackles, here used figuratively for restraints. A play on both meanings may be intended here.

l. 24. *All . . . refraine*: eliminate worldly ambitions.

l. 45. *taught with often proofe*: as a result of frequent experience.

l. 52. *repine*: complain; the construction is that of a compressed clause of condition: 'That, if it [the body] were pampered, would nevertheless complain.'

Scorne not the least (page 69)

MSS.: *S, VC, A, H*.

The compiler of *F* has made some changes in the printed text of the poem in *Ca* (*F*).

Printed in *Ca*.

The poem is also transcribed in MS. Harl. 6910, fols. 126^v-7, probably from one of the later printed editions. The lines of religious reference, ll. 19-22, are omitted. Add. MS. 22601, fol. 71^v, contains a transcription of ll. 1-18, with the addition of ll. 7-12 of 'Times goe by turnes' as a concluding stanza; it appears to have been made from one of the early editions, *Ca-1602*.

l. 5. *repine*: suffer wrong; *they* refers to *the little starres* (l. 6). *repine* is normally a word of weaker connotation, to feel dissatisfaction or discontent (as in 'Content and rich', l. 52).

l. 10. *fleet aflote*: swim freely. *fleet* is equivalent to 'swim' (see *O.E.D.* 'fleet', *v.*^{1} 4), and *aflote* adds the connotative meaning of 'freely', 'unhampered', 'unrestricted'.

ll. 11-12. The reading of *S*, after correction, and *VC*, is adopted for the responsibility shown in these manuscripts at other points; here their singular forms repeat the singular structure of the first part of the stanza.

l. 13. *Marlyne*: merlin, a species of falcon. The phrase is proverbial.

l. 19. *Hamans*. See Esther iv. 1. The form *Amans* appears in the manuscripts and earliest editions; the change to *Hamans* was made in *1597* in accordance with the spelling in the Bishops' and the Geneva Bibles in use in England.

ll. 21–22. Southwell makes frequent reference to the parable of Dives (Luke xvi. 19–31), as in the 'Complaint', ll. 775–6, and in his Letter to his Father (ed. Trotman, pp. 38, 46).

II. POEMS FROM *MŒONIÆ*

Although no doubt concerning the authenticity of these three poems has previously been expressed, their absence from the manuscript compilation represented in *S, VC, A*, and *H* makes them suspect, and there is not sufficient internal evidence to counterbalance the lack of any reliable ascription of the poems to Southwell. See Textual Introduction, IV. ii, p. lxxxi.

The virgin Mary to Christ on the Crosse (page 71)

MSS.: *F; B.*

The version in *F*, entitled 'Our Ladie to Christ upon the Crosse', has so many variants that it is printed separately in Appendix II, p. 112.

Printed in *Ma* in fourteen sixteen-syllabled lines without stanza divisions.

The line and stanza division followed here is in accordance with the treatment of the poems of similar verse form in the manuscripts.

ll. 2, 4. *doth . . . Lies.* These singular forms are changed in *F* to agree with the plural subjects, according to normal grammatical usage.

l. 9. *worke your ire.* The reading in *F*, *wreake your ire*, is a more usual phrase, and should perhaps be adopted here. *worke* may be the result of an eye-slip, an error originating in the occurrence of the syllable *worth-* in the line following.

Man to the wound in Christs side (page 72)

MSS.: *F; B.*

The poem is entitled in *F* 'To the wound in Christes side'. It is preceded by a companion poem, 'Christ upon the Crosse to man'. (See Appendix II, p. 113.) The poem is transcribed twice in *B*, pp. 15 and 85.

Printed in *Ma* in eight-syllabled lines without stanza divisions, but with alternate lines indented.

l. 7. *troublous mate*: the body.

l. 19. *in store.* The tag introduces the thought of the wound as the continuing source of restitution for sin by means of the sacrament of penance, the concept developed in the following stanza.

ll. 25–26. The reference is to the contemplative achieving a state of union with God.

Upon the Image of death (page 73)

MSS.: *F*; *B*.

Printed in *Ma*.

    The poem was printed at the end of Simon Wastell's *Microbiblion* (for Robert Mylbourne, 1629), sig. z3ᵛ–4.

l. 3. *qwalmes*. The emendation was supplied by the compiler of *F* after he had erased the first word he had written. This is also the reading in the versions in *B* and in Wastell's *Microbiblion*. *qwalmes* does not occur elsewhere in Southwell's poetry; if this was indeed the original reading, it may be supposed that *names* of the printed editions is a misreading of *cuames*, a spelling not recorded in *O.E.D.* It is possible that the word should be *cares*, used by Southwell in a similar context in 'Christs sleeping friends', l. 1.

l. 21. *yer*. This is a variant spelling of *ere*, before.

l. 32. *mates*: fellows, contemporaries. Southwell uses the word contemptuously in *An Humble Supplication* (ed. Bald, p. 15), in the phrase 'a Company of greedy and mannerles mates'.

ll. 37–38. Cf. St. Bernard's hymn, '*Cur mundus militat*': 'Dic ubi Salomon, olim tam nobilis? vel ubi Samson est, dux invincibilis?' (In *The Paradise of Dainty Devices*, ed. Rollins, p. 6.)

l. 39. *person*: parson; the word is not used elsewhere in Southwell's verse.

ll. 45–46. Cf. St. Bernard's hymn: 'Quo Cæsar abiit, celsus imperio, . . .' Although Alexander (ll. 43–44) is not mentioned specifically in the hymn, he has a long-established place in verse in this tradition.

III. *SAINT PETERS COMPLAINT*

MSS.: *A, O*.

    An account of these manuscript copies of the poem is given in Textual Introduction, II, p. lii. Changes made in the printed text of *Ca* (*F*) by the compiler of *F* are noted where these are in agreement with another source.

Printed in *Ca*; revised in *Cb* and *Cc*. (See Textual Introduction, III. ii, p. lxi, and iii, p. lxiii.)

Title. The title of Tansillo's poem, *Le Lagrime di San Pietro*, on which Southwell's version is ultimately based (see Textual Introduction, IV. iv, p. lxxxvi), plays upon the image of water working upon stone. Although this is a favourite image, and although the poem presents the doctrine of contrition which itself contains a similar notion—Latin *contritio*, a breaking of something hardened—Southwell has not attempted to reproduce the play of meanings in his English title.

The Author to the Reader (page 75)

A. The poem is transcribed (fol. 47–47ᵛ) immediately following the last of the poems in the compilation, 'Scorne not the least', and before the transcription of the 'Complaint'. Although the poem is correctly placed, it would appear that the scribe of *A* considered it as the last of the group of lyrics rather than the introduction to the longer poem; the text follows that of 'Scorne not' in mid-page without any significant break, and a space follows the poem before the beginning of the 'Complaint' at the top of fol. 48.

O. The poem precedes (p. 140) the transcription of the 'Complaint'.

Ca. The poem is correctly set immediately before the text of the 'Complaint', but its position, directly following the prose dedication and the poem 'To the Reader' (see pp. 1–2), is somewhat ambiguous, giving the impression that this poem is also an introductory item to the volume as a whole. Structural and verbal parallels in the two introductory poems are over-emphasized by this juxtaposition, and their divergent purposes are obscured, as may be seen in *1620*, when the heading of this poem was changed to *Rursus ad Eundem*.

l. 14. *Theames.* This occurrence is cited in *O.E.D.* as the earliest example of the use of 'theme' as a transitive verb in the sense 'to furnish with a theme or subject'. *in prose*. The reference may be to the style of the hymns of the Church, also called Sequences, distinguished in the Middle Ages from classical quantitative verse in that the *prosa* was regulated by accent and rime. Alternatively Southwell may be referring to his prose work, *Marie Magdalens Funerall Teares*, which in subject and treatment has obvious links with the poem. See Textual Introduction, IV. iv, p. lxxxix.

l. 16. *stilling*: distilling.

Saint Peters Complaint (page 76)

For a comment on the relationship of the poem with earlier versions, see Textual Introduction, IV, iv, p. lxxxvi.

ll. 1–10. The extended sea imagery at the beginning of the poem is particularly apt to Peter as fisherman and as 'fisher of men'. The imagery also suggests the theme of the poem, announced in l. 10 with the reference to *pennance*, the sacrament called by early Fathers 'a second plank after shipwreck', a phrase recalled in the Second Canon concerning Penance issued by the Council of Trent. (References to the Canons and Decrees of the Council of Trent are to the edition of H. J. Schroeder, O.P. [St. Louis, Mo., and London: B. Herder, 1941].)

l. 18. *Baptize.* The reference to baptism in this context again points to the sacrament of penance, called in the Decrees of the Council of Trent (xiv, ch. ii), citing the words of the early Fathers, 'a laborious kind of baptism'.

l. 20. *screeches*. No example of *scretches*, as in *Ca*, is recorded in *O.E.D.*; this form may represent Southwell's tendency to use phonetic spelling.

l. 28. *infamy.* In an ecclesiastical sense this is a strong term used of the public declaration of heretics as guilty and dishonoured, a stigma inherited by the children and grandchildren of an unrepented heretic. Cf. *An Humble Supplication* (ed. Bald, p. 1): 'yet an infamed life being to free mynds more yrkesome then an innocent death . . .', where *infamed* has wider connotation.

l. 30. *ungratefull*: not pleasing; cf. *TD*, sig. D1: '[the world] hath already given you the most ungrateful congee.' Again with reference to God's reception of man's actions, Southwell uses the form *gratefull*, l. 467.

l. 35. *wrung*: caused anguish or distress; this is an unusual absolute use.

l. 38. *matter of complaint*: material for the literary expression of grief. A reference to the *materia* of the sacrament of penance, the actions of the penitent in making confession, experiencing contrition, and offering satisfaction, may also be implicit here.

l. 39. *threnes*: songs of grief; in this plural form the word has specific reference to the Lamentations of Jeremiah (see l. 40). *Alphabet*. In elegiac Hebrew poetry such as the Lamentations, each stanza begins with one of the twenty-two letters of the Hebrew alphabet.

l. 48. The imagery of medicine recurrent throughout the poem reproduces an analogy made in the Decrees of the Council of Trent (XIV, ch. v), when a parallel is drawn between a patient before a doctor and the penitent making confession before a priest. Southwell uses similar imagery in his account of his pastoral mission in the Letter to his Father: 'I have studied and practised these many years spiritual physic, acquainting myself with the beating and temper of every pulse and travailing in the scrutiny of the maladies and medicines incident unto souls' (ed. Trotman, p. 42).

l. 48. The full stop, from *Ca* (*HEH*), appears to be lacking in other copies.

l. 50. *guide*. The reference is to John (see l. 229, and cf. John xviii. 16). *now . . . God*. The line appears to be corrupt, or in an unrevised state; it should perhaps be emended to: *now left in leaving God*.

l. 59. *evils*. As always, the word is monosyllabic, but it was read as two syllables by the scribe who made the emendation that appears in *O*.

l. 67. Mid-line punctuation is removed in *Cb*, suggesting that *rashnesse* was being read as a genitive. Similar exclamations, however, occur frequently in this passage of self-castigation.

l. 70. *oversight*: failure to see the results of an action. The second meaning implicit in the word, that of 'supervision', in which the supervisor has a status superior to others, adds to the bitterness of Peter's self-examination. The images of sight, or the absence of sight, are recurrent in this and the following stanza, and foreshadow the extended image of sight in terms of 'understanding' revealed in the eyes of Christ (ll. 325–444).

l. 72. *Treason*. Since the stanza develops a series of personifications of *rashnesse*, *traitor* is to be expected rather than *treason*, which replaces the person by the act.

l. 73. Sidenotes giving references to the Vulgate are found in *A* and in *Cb*. Although they have their origin early in the textual history of the poem, there is no evidence to point to Southwell as annotator. It would appear that the attempts to annotate were only half-hearted when first made, and were never completed. The sidenotes have been reproduced from *Cb*, corrected where necessary.

l. 76. *distain'd*: defiled, dishonoured. Cf. 'Peeter Playnt', l. 5 (Appendix I, p. 103), where the revised form of the line reads '[Peter] Euen at the pinch his credit did distayne'.

l. 77. *wrought him in his duety sure*: ensured his loyalty.

l. 79. *Could*. *Cold* in *Ca* is a variant spelling.

l. 86. *doubtfull*. Southwell uses *doubt*, noun and verb, in the sense of 'fear', and so here, 'much feared', 'terrifying'. Cf. also ll. 141, 531, and instances in *MMFT*, where the meaning is clarified by the context, as in the description of Mary's love for Christ: 'The more desirous to enjoy, the more doubtfull it is to loose' (sig. F4ᵛ).

l. 93. *strayes*: acts of straying or wandering; see *O.E.D. sb.* 4.

l. 94. *straightes*: narrow paths.

l. 99. *Judas race*. Cf. 'Saint Peters Complaynte', l. 33, note.

l. 101. *his*. The reference is to Christ; the immediate antecedent was lost in rewriting this passage from the 'Complaynte'. See Textual Introduction, IV. iv, p. xc.

ll. 103–4. The image is based on the belief that fresh water originated in the depths of the ocean (*overflowing deepes*) from which it was sent by narrow channels (*divided vaines*) to the sources of streams.

ll. 109–14. The imagery of the cultivation of the soil by the farmer, Christ (ll. 109–10), develops into the theological question whether heaven's design is not achieved by means of what is evil, as the field (*hart*, l. 110) is fertilized by the deliberate introduction of alien elements (*unaccustomde soyle*, l. 111). Peter denies that his perjuries could be used to produce good soil (ll. 113–14). The argument gives point to the irony underlying the study of Peter in the poem.

l. 116. The image recalls Luke x. 7: 'The labourer is worthy of his hire.'

l. 121. *sonne of a dove*. Matt. xvi. 17 calls Peter *Bar-Jonah*, 'son of a dove', but the Greek text may represent the Hebrew incorrectly. In John i. 42 an alternative reading *Bar-Johannan* means 'son of God's grace'. (See Grosart, note p. 48.)

l. 122. *voyded . . . breathed*. Physical imagery is concentrated in verbs in this and the following stanzas to express Peter's violent revulsion against his own actions.

ll. 125–6. The imagery recalls David's defeat of Goliath. Cf. ll. 277–82, when the story is given its traditional interpretation.

l. 128. *lookes*: watching, observation.

l. 132. *John 18*. This is the first sidenote reference to the betrayal, the dramatic situation which initiated both meditation and poem. In the other Gosepls the story is told in Mark xiv and Luke xxii (see l. 195), and Matt. xxvi. Southwell has not entirely avoided the discrepancies in the details of the accounts (see note on l. 288 below).

l. 134. *detesting*: blasphemous; see the 'Complaynte', l. 62, note.

l. 145. *There*. The adverb is antithetical to *here*, l. 149. *Their* in *A* and *O* presumably must be read with reference to *waves*, l. 140. The confusion is traceable to Southwell's holograph, since he did not habitually distinguish between the adverb and the possessive pronoun; *there* for *their* occurs, for instance, in the 'Peeter Playnt' (Appendix I, p. 103), ll. 12 and 63, and in the sermon on Mary Magdalen.

l. 147. *titles*: title-deeds; here, allowable reasons. Cf. the use of the verb *entitle* in a legal image, l. 495.

ll. 150, 167–8. Cf. *EC*, sig. R2: 'It is a shame for a Christian to feare a blaste of mans mouth, that hath such unvincible shores to support him, as that no man nor divell is able to overthrowe them.'

l. 156. *both halves*: body and soul. *spill*: kill.

l. 158. *trueth of pledged promise*. Cf. 'Peeter Playnt' (Appendix I, p. 103), l. 5, where *credit* (good faith) and *promiss* are both translations of Ital. *di fè*.

l. 160. *rented*: torn, with reference to the birth of the young of the viper (see note on l. 161 below); in its position qualifying *soule* the second meaning may be implicit, 'held for a period of use for which payment is made'.

l. 161. The emendation of the punctuation to correspond with that in *O* clarifies the meaning; the *viper feare* is the *ougly childe* (l. 159) which with its destructive force (*ruynes*) destroys *all good* and brings *all evels* in its birth (l. 162). Southwell refers elsewhere to the ancient bestiary lore, as later at l. 735, and in *EC*, sig. 2C1ᵛ, when he speaks of the persecutors as vipers, 'Whose nature as *Eusebius Emissenus* writeth, is such, that when the female conceyveth of the male, she killeth him, and when she groweth bigge with yonge, she also of her owne brood is murdered. For they refusinge to stay the ordinarye course of cominge forthe gnawe them selves passage through the sydes of the dame, and with theyr birth worke her deathe.' The image recurs in the Letters to his Father and to his Brother.

l. 163. *assayde*: opposed myself against; see *O.E.D.* 'assay'. The older and commoner form in this sense is *assail*. The line is awkwardly balanced, involving a change in the personal pronoun from *me* to *I*. Similar changes in the following lines, when Peter speaks of himself alternatively as agent and sufferer, intensify the expression of climactic emotional experience in this part of the poem.

l. 167. *foyle*: disgrace, stigma; *O.E.D.* 'foil', *sb.*² 2b, where this example is quoted as the earlier of two occurrences. See also ll. 180, 264, 284.

l. 171. *Joh. 21*. The sidenote is correctly placed in *A* only. *Cb* confused two references, setting *Joh. 21.* with the sidenotes at l. 182, and setting *Mar. 9.*, which correctly belongs at l. 182, in this stanza at l. 174. The reference here to Christ's charge to Peter, 'Feed my sheep' (John xxi. 17), not delivered until after the Resurrection, is an anomaly in the dramatic setting of the poem.

l. 176. *Incompatible*. The earliest use cited in *O.E.D.* in the sense of 'mutually intolerant', 'incapable of existing together', is from Daniel's *Rosamund*, 1592. The word was unfamiliar to the manuscript copyists: *A* has *Incomptable*, meaningless in this context, and *O* reads *incompitable*, an error which may represent only the careless substitution of vowels.

l. 178. *Prowisse*: fortitude in time of testing. The parallels expressed in these lines are awkwardly compressed, and the resulting ambiguity has led to attempts to emend by changing *lodgde* to *lodge* in *A* and in *Ca* (*F*), where the *F* compiler made a change in the printed text. The meaning appears to be: 'Courage is less effective when cowardice is present also; neither fortitude nor love can be sustained in a heart of divided loyalty.'

l. 179. *cast*: defeated, overthrown. Cf. the use of *cast* in 'His circumcision', l. 5, when the reference is directly to defeat in a legal action.

l. 181. *Thabors*. The mountain Thabor, five miles south-east of Nazareth, was acknowledged from the fourth century as the place of the Transfiguration.

l. 182. *Math. 17. Mar. 9*. These are references to the account of the Transfiguration. *Math. 16*. This is the third reference to this chapter (cf. ll. 121, 169), here presumably to Peter's rash undertaking to protect Christ from the suffering and death he prophesied (v. 22).

l. 190. *Me, like my selfe*. Peter draws the analogy between his actual and figurative drowsiness.

l. 191. *his*. This is an objective genitive; Peter refers to his assignment to watch over Christ in Gethsemane.

l. 193. *Parted*. The reading in *A* and *O*, and in *Ca* (*F*), where a change has been made by the *F* compiler, is preferable to that of the printed text. It avoids the repetition of the *-ing* suffix in the line, which obscures the meaning by the unavoidable suggestion that *parting* and *fainting* both relate to actions taking place at the same time, although *fainting* is used with purely adjectival force of 'inclined to show cowardly weakness', or 'habitually fearful'; the related action is in fact expressed in the verb *declin'd*, in the strong end-of-line position. These verbs, together with *lingring* and *aloofe* in l. 194, emphasize the stages in the deterioration which led to Peter's final betrayal.

l. 197. *hatcht*: shut in securely, as by the hatches of a door (*O.E.D. v.*[3], now obsolete). There is a pun on *Sampsons lockes*.

l. 199. *fare*. *A* and *Cb* have *farre*, possibly a spelling variant; *O.E.D.* reports such a variant in the sixteenth century. Alternatively, an error may have been introduced as a result of a copyist's confusion of *fare* and *farre* (l. 200). *crasie*: unsound, frail.

l. 200. *traine*: trail, drag along.

l. 204. *beare thy begotten blame*. In conjunction with *begotten* in this phrase, *beare* has the implicit second meaning of 'bring forth', 'bring to light'.

l. 205. *remisnes*. *remisses* in *Ca* is reported in *O.E.D.* in the 1589 edition of

Puttenham's *Arte of English Poesie*, sig. F4ᵛ, where the *O.E.D.* suggests that it is an error for *remissnes*. The coincidence of spelling in Field's printing of the *English Poesie* and Windet's of *Ca* points to the existence of a variant form. Here the reference is to sins of omission, and the word, the keyword of the stanza, introduces a series of images conveying a sense of the danger of weak inaction. It would appear to be connected in meaning to the adjective *remiss*, in the sense of 'weak in colour, sound, or taste', and in its medical use, describing urine weakened in colour as a result of the coolness of the body—an association strengthened by the use of the adjective *coole*, and the following images of physical weakness, intensifying the expression of spiritual laxity in the stanza.

l. 207. *languor*: extended illness (*O.E.D. sb.* 1).

l. 211. *portresse*. See note on l. 288. The play on meanings here is similar to that in l. 197 (see note); the *portresse of the doore* is said to have *unlockt the trueth of vowed minde*, that is, opened the way for Peter's betrayal.

l. 220. *except against these clauses*: object to these arguments; the phrase refers to the formal legal procedure by which a defendant makes a plea to bar the plaintiff's action. See *O.E.D.* 'except', *v.* 2, and 'exception', 4.

l. 226. *deeper domage crost it*: greater injury by loss precluded any possible gain. *domage*, an obsolete form of *damage*, occurs in this sense of loss in 'Peeter Playnt', ll. 64–65, when Christ says to Peter, 'thow . . . standest feedynd thy eies with my damage (and sorows)', where *damage* translates Ital. *danno*, loss. It is used similarly in *MMFT*, sig. B4ᵛ: 'So was there not in the whole world . . . anie greater domage possible then his losse.'

l. 227. *this*. Grosart suggests the emendation *his*; as it stands, the text may be read: 'What . . . is worse than this: that a man should run . . .?'

l. 232. *all resort*: all those who came there (cf. *O.E.D.* 'resort', *sb.* 5b, a crowd of people).

ll. 235–330. This passage is transposed to follow l. 714 in *A*, *O*, and in the earliest printed texts, *Ca* and *Cb*. See Textual Introduction, IV. iv, p. xci.

l. 235. *president*: precedent; the word is accented on the first syllable, as in mod. E. *wafts*. In *Ca waft* may be a past tense; *O.E.D.* cites examples of this form from the seventeenth century. The use of *waft* with the sea as subject (here, *tyde*), meaning 'carry', 'transport', is now obsolete.

l. 239. The punctuation of the early editions breaks the line into two parts. With a colon after *joyes*, *unacquainted* must be read as a substantive, and the line may be understood: 'We see a man giving himself up to pleasure; in our inexperience we are eager to follow his example.' Alternatively, with no mid-line break (as in *A* and *O*) *unacquainted* is an adjective, as it is in 'The Complaint of the B. Virgin', l. 106 (Appendix II, p. 117). The line may then be read: 'Those who precede us in experience appear to find the joys in life we long for.' The point made here and in the following line is that as we follow other people in what we see them do, they lead us on to sin, when we imagine they lead us to an enrichment of life. The image of hunger appeased by joys occurs in ll. 345–6.

ll. 247–58. The description of the weather in the courtyard is used to enforce the figure of the hard heart of the sinner which must be broken by contrition and renewed by the action of grace. *crusted* (l. 249) literally refers to a pie covered with a crust in cooking, but here it has the sense of 'made impenetrable', as if covered by a crust of ice. *O.E.D.* cites a use with similar connotation in the description of snow 'crusted by reason of the frost' in Ascham (1545). *canded* (l. 251) is a form of *candied*, used in the sense of 'covered with anything crystalline and glistening'. The earliest use shown in *O.E.D.* is dated 1600. Shakespeare uses the form *candied* (with ice) in *Timon* (iv. iii. 226).

l. 260. The fear shown by a lion for a cock—especially for a white cock—is part of medieval bestiary lore.

l. 268. *stinted*: dried (after tears); *stintlesse* (l. 492) is also used with reference to tears. *taske*: a fixed payment, tax.

l. 270. 'To make me repent what it (*thine accusing crow*) first revealed to me.' In this stanza the cock is represented in the part of a priest.

l. 277. *fumes*: fits of anger (*O.E.D.* 'fume', *sb.* 7); in this sense *fume* usually occurs in the phrase 'in a fume'.

l. 278. *storming. scortching*, the reading in *Ca*, may be defended on grounds of contemporary use in connexion with anger; here it suggests the image of the destructive heat of lightning. There appears to be more authority for *storming*, in *A* and later editions.

l. 284. *foyle*: disgrace.

l. 286. *spoyle*: the arms of a dead knight (taken by the victor); here the booty is said to be *honorable* when seized after a hard contest.

l. 288. *womans*. The variant *womens* in *Ca* points to the apparent discrepancy in Southwell's treatment of the details of Peter's denial. The singular form is consistent with the earlier emphasis laid upon a single figure at ll. 150, 167, 198, and 211, and the later references at ll. 294 and 316. At these points Southwell is following the Gospel accounts of John, who specifically calls the woman a portress (xviii. 17; see l. 211), and Luke (xxii. 56). Her part in the denials made by Peter has an obvious parallel with the actions of the Queen. Since this emphasis upon one woman questioner is not found in the earlier versions of the poem, it is likely that this political analogy was a late addition, and discrepancies in reference here and at ll. 314 and 317 suggest that it was never clearly imposed upon the thematic structure of the poem. (See Textual Introduction, IV. iv, p. lxxxix.)

l. 289. *th'Egyptian*. The variant in *A* and *O*, *giptian*, indicates an apheetic change (cf. *O.E.D.* 'gipsy'), but no instance of this form is recorded. It may represent no more than the faulty transmission of a form in which the definite article was elided, as in *Ca*, and cf. *theis*, *theies* (*the eyes*) in 'Peeter Playnt', ll. 11 and 24 (Appendix I, pp. 103–4). The reference here is to the third plague of Egypt, described as a plague of lice in A.V., but more accurately as a plague of gnat-like insects (Exod. viii. 16).

l. 292. *incombrance*: trouble, molestation.

l. 295. *abortive ympe*: literally, a child born prematurely; here, a swift reaction (in an unsettled mind).

l. 296. *selfe overthrow. O.E.D.* records sixteenth-century uses of *overthrow* as noun, in the sense (I. 1c) 'that which overthrows or brings down', now obsolete; no example is cited of this combination. Cf. *selfe ruine*, l. 642.

l. 298. *field*: battle.

l. 304. *glose*: false show. *glosse* in *O* represents a common confusion of *glose* with *gloss*, a surface brilliance.

l. 309. *affecting*: arousing desire; this absolute use is now obsolete.

l. 314. *droyles*. The earliest recorded use of 'droil', a servant of all work, or drudge (ultimately of Dutch origin), is dated 1579 in *O.E.D.*

l. 319. *women, woe to men*. The pun is accurately reproduced in the spelling *woemen* at l. 301.

l. 321. *captiving thralles*. The phrase embodies the paradox of the Fall, when Eve, herself a captive of sin, was able to capture Adam to share her bondage. *Captive*, in the figurative sense of 'captivate', 'enthrall', was in common use in the sixteenth century.

l. 323. *spoylers*: robbers.

l. 326. *read*. This ambiguous form is best considered a past rather than a present tense as in *Cc* (*reade*). *ruines*: ensuing harm or injury.

l. 338. *imparadize*: place as in a paradise, bring to a state of rapture. Contemporary uses are all slightly later than this occurrence; Southwell may have been familiar with the Italian *imparadisare*.

ll. 343–8. In these lines Peter speaks of the ministry of Christ as it devolved upon himself and the other disciples, from them descending to the priests on the English Mission in the work of teaching (ll. 343–4), in the administration of the sacraments (ll. 345–6), and in judgement in the tribunal of penance (ll. 347–8).

l. 351. *nectared Aumbryes*. An aumbry is a cupboard for sacramental vessels, customarily on the right side of the altar. The word was apparently unknown to an early copyist, whose variant is responsible for *Ambrose* in *Ca* and *A*, presumably a form of *ambrosia*, suggested by the adjective *nectared* (which with its reference to the food of the gods properly qualifies *meats*). *Ambures* in *O* is also meaningless.

l. 355. *The*. The variant *Thei* (written as *Thè*) in *A* is an unusual form; the copyist's normal abbreviation for *Thy* is *ẏ*.

l. 356. *ill matched*: to be compared with what is evil.

l. 357. *mother*: mother-of-pearl.

ll. 363–4. The imagery is based on *Le Lagrime di San Pietro*, Canto 1, st. 60:

> Come falda di neve, che agghiacciata
> In verno in chiusa valle ascosa giaque,
> A primavera poi dal Sol scaldata
> Tutta si sface, e si discioglie in acque:

Così la tema, che entro al cor gelata
Era di Pietro allhor, che 'l vero tacque,
Quando Christo ver lui gli occhi rivolse
Tutta si sfece, e in pianto si risolse.

See 'Peeter Playnt', ll. 75–82 (Appendix I, p. 105).

l. 368. As mirrors, the eyes of Christ make the reflections (*shaddows*) equal in worth to the things reflected. The following lines develop the idea further in the statement that the reflection is not merely equal in worth but is of greater value; the variant *Yea*, in *A* and in *Cc*, emphasizes this sequence of thought.

ll. 373–8. This stanza, which restates the thought-content of the previous lines, was probably intended for deletion. See Textual Introduction, IV. IV, p. xci.

l. 391. *Though*. The repetition of *though* in the next line probably supplied the reason for the change to *Tough* in *Cc*, although the contrast between the immovable minds of the Jewish scribes and the revelation that came to Peter is made more effective by the use of the strong adjective at the beginning of the line. *possessd*. The reading of the manuscripts and *Cb* is preferable to *possesse* of *Ca*, since Peter is now thinking of events in the past. *their* and *they* (l. 395) refer to the *scribes* of l. 390.

ll. 397–420. The imagery of this section of the poem is designed to represent the eyes of Christ in terms of successively lesser objects: suns, spheres, worlds. As worlds the eyes contain the natural elements, which comprise a perfect whole (l. 420).

l. 399. *neighbour*. Although in common use as an adjective in the sixteenth century, *neighbour* does not usually imply motion, as here in the sense of 'coming close'.

l. 401. *fostring*: supplying with food or nourishment; a eucharistic image is suggested in this analogy with the strengthening and life-giving power of the sun.

l. 403. *spheres*: the bodies in the firmament. *Center*: the centre of each sphere (see l. 407).

l. 405. *compasse*: the firmament, containing the circling spheres. *cope*. O.E.D. cites contemporary examples of the reduction of the phrase 'cope of heaven' to 'cope', as here.

l. 410. *sunne*. The variant spelling *soone* is found in *Ca*, *A*, and *Cb* (*TC*). The meaning is compressed; the line should be read as '(the worlds) where the glory of God lights the heaven, and God is recognized as the sun, while all the virtues, reflecting the nature of God, are seen as stars'.

ll. 413–14. The representation of grace as water in various forms is an analogy repeatedly drawn in Southwell's poetry; in this context it recalls the tears of contrition in the sacrament of penance and the Jesuit practice of meditation, which begins with meditation on sin.

l. 415. *elements*: fire, air, water, and earth, as in ll. 411–14.

ll. 417, 420. *compound(s)*. These instances are cited in *O.E.D.* as earliest uses of the adjective as substantive. The statement that compounds excel simples probably refers to the process of making medicines by the combination of various ingredients which by themselves are injurious to health.

l. 418. *Both*. An emendation seems necessary here. The reference is apparently to *simples* and *compounds*, l. 417, but the meaning is clearer if *Both* is emended to *Which*, with reference to *compounds*. The corruption may have originated in a scribal substitution, although *Both*, occurring in Southwell's hand in 'Peeter Playnt' at the beginning of l. 7, is not easily confused with *Which*.

l. 420. *All . . . framde*. *All* refers to *all best things*, l. 418; *framde* has the general meaning of 'fashioned', 'formed' (see *O.E.D.* 'frame', *v.* 5). The line should be read: 'All are formed into a single compound of perfect bliss.'

ll. 422–4. The imagery of the four elements is recalled once more.

l. 425. *never a hell*. *never* is monosyllablic in Southwell's verse; the reading adopted on the authority of *A* and *O*, and supported by the *F* compiler, supplies metrical regularity.

l. 428. *me* is understood in this line as object of *keepe*.

l. 429. *champion*. The reference is to the three captains in the account in 2 Sam. xxiii. 15–16; the singular, as in *Ca* and *O*, is preferred to the plural in *A* and *Cb* as more apt in its reference to Christ's work of redemption.

l. 436. *enamoreth*. This form, without Southwell's habitual compression, introduces an extra unstressed syllable in the line.

l. 439. *Horebb*. The reading of *A* and *O*, giving the name of the rock, is based on the account in Exodus, to which the sidenote refers, l. 440. *stubborne* in *Ca* may possibly represent an editorial change, made by someone familiar with the account in Num. xx. 8–11, where the name of the rock is not given, but where it is said to be struck twice, a detail lacking in the version in Exodus.

l. 445. *demurre*. Cf. the use of this verb as a noun in *MMFT*, sig. D2: 'All their demurres would be tedious and discourses irkesome.'

l. 447. *Launching*. This form derives from ONF. *lancher* (cf. Central OF. *lancier*, mod. E. *lance*). *Launch*, in the sense 'to let out infection by lancing', is cited in *O.E.D.* in illustrations from the fifteenth to the seventeenth centuries.

l. 448. *Which*. The antecedent is the impostume, or purulent matter, here the subject of *hath found*.

l. 450. *penall life*: life spent as punishment; this use of *penall* is earlier than the earliest cited in *O.E.D.*, dated 1600.

l. 457. *Still*: distill. *limbeck*: alembic. The imagery in this stanza is based on the alchemical process used to obtain the quintessence, the property of the celestial bodies, believed to be latent in matter.

ll. 463–74. The sacramental value of the tears of contrition is clearly stated in this passage.

l. 467. *gratefull*: acceptable to God; cf. l. 30, note.

l. 468. *to men most hatefull.* The reference continues to be to *teares,* l. 463. The meaning was obscured in *Ca* by the lack of mid-line punctuation, which has been supplied.

l. 470. *impes:* offspring. Southwell uses the word with a derogatory connotation; cf. l. 295.

l. 471. *probates:* proofs, evidence (of broken laws). Images of the process of jurisdiction, as in this stanza, emphasize the judicial nature of the sacrament of penance.

l. 476. *suppling:* literally, making supple or pliant, and here, softening, which is the action of contrite tears upon the heart. This is an earlier use in a figurative sense than the examples cited in *O.E.D.*

l. 480. In a state of mortal sin the merit attaching to earlier virtuous acts is rendered void. A new justification, by means of the sacrament of penance, is necessary to revive rights to grace and glory. (See Canons and Decrees of the Council of Trent, VI, chs. xiv and xv.)

l. 481. *Balme and mirrhe.* These resinous products of species of balsam trees were used for their healing properties. In English translations of the Bible balm is used specifically of balm of Gilead; it is named together with myrrh as taken by camel from Gilead for sale in Egypt (Gen. xxxvii. 25). The *Arabian trees* are therefore the species of balsamodendrons that produce these resins.

l. 483. *Shed on:* continue to let fall in drops; *on* is an adverb, not a preposition. *hony drops:* the droplets deposited in the cells of the hive by the worker bees. Spenser uses a similar phrase:

> Sweet words, like dropping honny she did shed.
>
> (*F.Q.* II. iii. 24)

l. 485. *their labour plies.* This is an unusual use of *plies,* which normally has the agent for subject (*O.E.D.* 'ply', *v.*²). Here *their labour* is equivalent to the labouring hornets, which work to supply *salt drops* in contrast to the *hony drops* deposited by the bees. The image represents the pangs of conscience as stinging hornets; the salt drops are therefore the bitter tears of repentance.

l. 487. *Psal. 6. 7.* This sidenote reference is in accordance with the enumeration of some editions of the Vulgate and retained in the Douay translation (1609); in other editions of the Vulgate and in other English translations the reference is to verse 6.

l. 492. *stintlesse:* (of tears) shed without pause.

l. 496. *That . . . conceale.* The line comprises a relative clause qualifying *eyes,* l. 495.

l. 502. *use:* interest. In this sense the word is recorded frequently in the seventeenth century, although not earlier than in this instance (see *O.E.D. sb.* 5b.).

l. 504. *is due.* The relative *that* is omitted.

l. 517. *lincea.* This reading in *A* and *O* is the Latin *lintea,* linen clothes, such as the funeral clothes used to wrap the dead body of Christ in the Sepulchre. (The word occurs, for instance, in the *Quem Quæritis* tropes.) The use of the word with this connotation is confirmed here by the image of the *shroud* in l. 518. The word appears in English as *linsey*, usually in the combination *linsey-woolsey* (its only recorded form in *O.E.D.*), a cloth woven of wool and a coarse linen thread. Cf. also OF. *linceul*, a winding-sheet. The variant *livery* in the printed editions, although an acceptable reading, was probably introduced by an early copyist or by the compositor of *Ca*, unfamiliar with *lincea*.

l. 519. *mulct*: properly a fine levied for an offence; here, apparently used for the court imposing the fine.

l. 520. *dampe*: a noxious or stifling vapour, or a mist; its figurative use here is slightly earlier than examples cited in *O.E.D.* *sluce*. Cf. *An Humble Supplication* (ed. Bald, p. 41), concerning false accusations made against Catholics, 'as though none were so fitt sluces as they, to let out of every mans sinke these unsavoury reproaches'.

l. 522. *deserve thy scourge*. The reading of *A* is preferred for its retention of the person and tense structure of the stanza. The phrase recalls the scourging of Christ, in the same way that other references in the poem to the suffering of Peter reflect the events of the Passion enacted at the same time.

l. 523. *imbrude*. The verb is used regularly with reference to blood, as in *EC*, sig. Aa8ᵛ: 'For thoughe you embrue youre bloodye fystes in oure bleedinge woundes. . . .'

l. 526. 'Hoping that when he (Cain) was alone he would have twice the amount of God's love.'

l. 527. *spoild*: robbed.

l. 530. *Barsabeian wildes*: the desert of Beersheba (Gen. xxi. 14). The Vulgate gives the name as Bersabee.

ll. 531, 539. *drought*: lack of moisture (now archaic in this sense).

l. 541. Absolons. Absolom's treachery is related in 2 Sam. xv.

l. 542. *Sodome lakes*. The city of Sodom lay in a well-watered plain before its destruction because of the sinful nature of its inhabitants (Gen. xiii. 10).

l. 545. *lustre*. *lustrey* in *Ca* is presumably a phonetic spelling; no example is recorded in *O.E.D.* *winnes*: persuades, prevails upon.

l. 552. The reference is to the defeat of the giants by Jove, which supposedly took place at Phlegra. See Virgil, *Georgics* I. 280–3.

l. 561. *strowd*. This form was already becoming archaic and dialectal; the common form was *strewd*, as in *A* and *O*.

l. 566. *bought*. The emendation in *W*, *brought*, given birth to, brought forth (*O.E.D.* 'bring', *v.* 7), supplies an interesting reading. *bought*, in the sense of 'purchased with the pains of childbirth (*throwes*)' introduces a discordant image.

l. 567. *To balme*. The verb was becoming archaic in the sixteenth century; it is derived from the substantive, or from OF. *enbasmer*. Its unfamiliarity may account for the variants in the manuscripts. Readings in later editions, *T'inbalme*, *T'imbalm*, represent contemporary forms of the verb.

l. 572. *Sindonles.* See Mark xiv. 51–52, where the A.V. speaks of the young man as clothed in a linen cloth. The Rheims translation (1582) has *sindon*, retaining *sindone* of the Vulgate. The imagery of this stanza is based on the paradox of the nakedness of grace and the clothing of sin.

l. 589. *sister Nymphes*: Martha and Mary.

l. 590. *bounds. bonds* in *Ca* is a spelling variant.

l. 597. *astonish't.* The force of the verb is stronger than in mod. E.; here it implies a state of shock in which the senses seem paralysed.

l. 602. *friends.* This spelling is found in the earlier state of the forme of outer D in *Ca* (*HEH* and *VC*); the 'corrected' state, in *Ca* (*F*), has *frends*.

l. 609. *mew*: a place of confinement, originally a cage for hawks; here the word is used figuratively for the state of sin. The imagery of this stanza emphasizes the work of evil in terms of violent movement and ecstatic joy in success, recalling the action of the scriptural devils 'possessing' the spirit they torture, and perhaps also, with contemporary relevance, the methods of the pursuivants in hunting down priests and their lay helpers and elatedly publishing the news of their success.

l. 610. *Trampling*: stamping on. This transitive use is rare; the earliest instance cited in *O.E.D.* is dated 1595, when the verb has the weaker sense of treading or walking upon. *ruins*: injuries.

l. 611. *perjury was.* As in the references to questioners in the courtyard (see l. 288, note), there is some variation in the description of Peter's sin as singular (ll. 5, 360) and plural (ll. 252, 264); where variants occur, as here and at l. 628, it is impossible to determine the original form with any confidence.

l. 614. *wrought.* In the sixteenth century this past participle of *work* was used interchangeably, though erroneously, with its homophones *rought*, *raught*, the past participle of *reach*, which, in the sense of 'attained to', is preferable here; cf. 'Epitaph on Lady Margaret Sackville', l. 17 (p. 101).

l. 617. *rub*: obstacle, originally used of an obstruction in a bowling alley which might interfere with the course of a bowl.

l. 619. *upbraide*: bring forward in reproach (now obsolete in this sense). Spenser has a phrase of similar connotation: 'Evill men now dead, his deeds upbraid' (*Ruines of Time*, l. 214). Southwell compresses the construction; the meaning of the line is that the devils speak scornfully of Peter's weakness, bringing into the open what is in his own mind. A similar construction with *upbraide* is used at l. 662.

l. 621. *guests. gesse* in *Ca* is a plural form found in the sixteenth and seventeenth centuries. *nought*: the empty place left when virtue is lost; theologically this is an accurate description of the state of sin.

ll. 625, 627; 629, 630. Unusual double rimes, the extra syllables providing feminine endings, add both weight and length to the lines, which at this point are deliberately and ponderously slow, reflecting Peter's extremity of distress.

l. 629. *enstranged*: removed far (from); here the meaning is extended to imply 'and given over (to)'. The commoner form, *estraung(e)d*, appears in the manuscripts and in *Cb*, with similar meaning.

l. 631. *templed*. The reading of the first state of this forme (outer D), now preserved in two copies of *Ca* (*HEH* and *VC*), was changed in course of printing to *tempted*, the reading in *Ca* (*F*) until it was corrected by the *F* compiler. The scriptural reference in these lines is to 1 Cor. iii. 16–17: 'Know ye not that ye are the temple of God, and that the Spirit of God dwelleth in you? If any man defile the temple of God, him shall God destroy.' The Pauline passage has particular application to the doctrine of the necessity of satisfaction, in support of which it was quoted in the Decrees of the Council of Trent, XIV, ch. viii.

l. 634. *lightneth*: causes (fear) to flash out like lightning. *from his sight*: from where he views Peter's sin.

l. 635. *lay*: immoral, and secondarily, unpriestly.   *unconsecrate*: unhallowed; here, opposed to God's will.

l. 636. *wretch*. The misprint *wrethe* occurs in the earlier state of the forme (outer D) in *Ca* (*HEH* and *VC*).   *hires*: wages.

ll. 637–66, 673–8. These lines are transcribed as a separate item in manuscript Harl. 6910, fols. 123–3ᵛ, apparently from one of the printed editions, *Cc–1602*. In l. 643 *God can* is changed to *we should*.

l. 637. *file*: defile.

l. 640. *ware*. The singular form is required in the construction to agree with *turnes*, l. 641.

l. 652. *abode*: (present tense) presage; this use is slightly earlier than the earliest cited in *O.E.D.*

l. 654. *faine it faire*: imagine it beautiful. *faine* (mod. E. *feign*) is now obsolete in this sense. See also *fayning*, l. 728.

l. 662. *doth now upbraide my harmes*: (the knowledge of sin) reproaches me now for the injuries I have inflicted on myself.

l. 665. *th'anotomy*. *notomy* in *A* may be the original form, although *y̅* (*then*) for *the* is clearly an error. *Nottomy* is shown as an E. Anglian form of *anatomy* in Robert Forby's *Vocabulary of East Anglia* (1830), I, Introduction, p. 118.

ll. 673–84, 685–96. Each group of two stanzas is apparently made up of an original and a revised version of a single stanza, both versions accidently retained in the copy made from the holograph. See Textual Introduction, IV. iv, p. xci.

l. 683. *disgest*: disperse (as speech); see *O.E.D.* 'digest', *v.* 1b. The form, though not unusual in the fifteenth to seventeenth centuries, is listed by Forby in his

Vocabulary of East Anglia (1830), I, Introduction, p. 113, as an example of a dialectal change of a first syllable.

l. 687. *in grosse*. This form represents either mod. E. *engross*, in the sense, now obsolete, to buy up wholesale (often with the derogatory connotation of having the intention of selling at monopoly price), or an adverbial phrase, meaning 'in quantity', 'wholesale', balancing *by retayle* in the line. That it was read as two words is suggested by the punctuation in *Ca*; *1597* and later editions spell *ingrosse*.

l. 694. *nothing*: not at all (adverbial). The meaning of the line is: 'For I exert no pressure upon customers to buy.'

l. 696. *interest*: right, claim to possession; see *O.E.D. sb.* 1a, and 'interess'.

l. 698. *Orphian seate*. The relevance of the figure of Orpheus mourning the loss of Eurydice is sufficiently strong reason to retain the reading of *Ca*. The story of Orpheus was represented in the Renaissance as illustrating that perfect love could be achieved only by dying to imperfect things. (See Edgar Wind, *Pagan Mysteries in the Renaissance* [London, 1958], p. 133.) Peter's imperfect love was, like that of Orpheus, realized by a glance, at which moment Peter knew his loss, in the same way that Orpheus watched helplessly the final loss of Eurydice. In his isolation Orpheus spent seven days on the banks of the Styx:

> septem tamen ille diebus
> squalidus in ripa Cereris sine munere sedit;
> cura dolorque animi lacrimæque alimenta fuere.
> *(Metamorphoses* x. 73–75)

There are Ovidian echoes also in later lines in the stanza, but whereas Orpheus, scorning the love of women, sought consolation in young boys,

> citraque iuventam
> ætatis breve ver et primos carpere flores,
> (ll. 84–85)

Peter's mind was fixed on the flower of Jesse.

ll. 699–702. The image of grafting is to be found also in *EC*, sig. Aa6ᵛ: 'Newe slyppes are ever engrafted when the olde bow is cutt of, and the vertue of the roote that the bough leaseth the slypp enjoyeth.' Peter is making the point that the root and the trunk are all-important, not the natural quality of the grafted slip. The image identifies Christ as both scion of the tree of Jesse (Isa. xi. 1, where the Vulgate has *flos de radice eius ascendet*), and Son of God (with *heavenly roote*).

ll. 703–4. These lines are transcribed as the beginning of a separate item in MS. Harl. 6901, fol. 123ᵛ. The lines which should follow on the next page are missing.

ll. 703–14. Cf. Thomas Watson's Sonnet LVI in *Hekatompathia, or the Passionate Centurie of Love* (1582):

> Come gentle Death: who cals? one thats opprest:
> What is thy will? that thou abridge my woe,
> By cutting of my life; cease thy request,
> I cannot kill thee yet: alas, why soe?
> Thou want'st thy Hart. Who stoale the same away?
> *Love*, whom thou serv'st, intreat him if thou may.

The source of Watson's lines, and perhaps also of Southwell's, is one of the *strambotti* of Seraphino Aquilano:

> Morte: che vuoi? te bramo: Eccomi appresso;
> Prendemi: a che? che manchi el mio dolore;
> Non posso: ohime, non puoi? non per adesso;
> Perche? pero che in te non regna il core.

l. 712. *Ah.* The corruption *Oath*, in the press-corrected state of the forme (outer D) in *Ca* (*F*), may only be explained as an attempt to reproduce a manuscript reading in which *Ah* was confused with *Oth*. The spelling *othe* appears in 'Peeter Playnt', l. 1 (Appendix I, p. 103).

l. 718. *see.* The image has particular reference to the Papal See, associated with Peter as first Bishop of Rome.

ll. 721-6. This stanza is found as a separate entry in MS. Harl. 6910, fol. 164.

l. 725. *reprivall*: reprieve, temporary respite; this form is a spelling variant of *reprieval*.

l. 730. The image recalls the use of strange apparitions and semi-human figures in the dumb shows preceding the acts of tragedies or as part of elaborate dances and masques.

l. 735. The imagery again refers to the belief that the young of the viper are responsible for the death of the mother at birth.

l. 744. *behoofes*: duties; here, what properly belongs to funeral rites. Cf. *MMFT*, sig. I8: 'It considereth behoofe, more then benefite, and what in dewtye it shoulde, not what in deede it can.'

l. 748. *herse*: bier, coffin.

l. 749. *dole*: expression of grief.

l. 750. *Pennance.* The sacramental meaning is clear in this context; the penitent who is fully contrite knows himself dead in sin, and calls for the grace of restoration offered by Christ, who alone can revive the sinner. The imagery, based on Rom. vi and vii, recalls that the Crucifixion is taking place at this time of Peter's ordeal.

l. 757. *Manasses.* The account of King Manasseh's idolatry and subsequent repentance is given in 2 Chron. xxxiii. 1-13.

l. 766. *bidst . . . bid.* The verbs play upon two meanings, 'offer (in payment)' and 'command'. The idea that Peter expresses here and in the following line, that Christ offers what he demands in return, is earlier expressed in l. 394.

l. 772. *shroud.* If *shroud* is read as a verb, the meaning is: 'Saving [me], protect [me] by the precious restorative action of mercy.' Grosart, however, takes *shroud* as a noun.

l. 775. *Lazar.* The parable of Dives and Lazarus is told in Luke xvi. 19-31. Southwell makes the addition that the beggar asks for the crumbs from the plates of children, a detail transferred from Mark vii. 28, the story of the Gentile woman who pleaded with Christ to cure her daughter.

l. 776. *reffues*: refuse (used as an adjective from the fifteenth century).

l. 784. *thy deserved hate*: thy hate which I have deserved.

l. 788. *Traverse*: deny, contradict, or take issue upon (an indictment). A similar phrase occurs in *An Humble Supplication* (ed. Bald, p. 41), concerning the unjust treatment of recusants: 'Their adversaries straight leaving the mayne point, pleadeth against them for their Recusancy; and thus traversing their suits, often causeth their persons to be committed.' The legal imagery in the final lines of the poem recalls both the trial of Christ and the judicial nature of the tribunal of penance.

l. 790. *chaungling*: turncoat, renegade.

l. 791. *Tender*: regard favourably. Christ is not addressed as the advocate but as the judge in the tribunal of penance. A similar use of this verb is found in Southwell's Letter to his Father: 'Tender the pitiful state of your poor soul' (ed. Trotman, p. 61). It is found with a personal object in *TD*, sig. D1: 'The more you tender hir, the more temperate should be your griefe.'

IV. POEMS FROM PROSE WORKS

Epitaph on Lady Margaret Sackville (page 101)

From *The Triumphs over Death*.

MSS.: *S*, *VC*, *A*.

Printed in *1595* (*S.T.C.* 22971), sig. E3, and subsequently in two editions in 1596 (*S.T.C.* 22972, 22973); these early editions of the *Triumphs* were all printed by Valentine Sims for John Busby. Later editions are included in the 'collected' works, *1620*, *1630*, and *1636*. It was edited by J. W. Trotman in 1914 from a copy of *S.T.C.* 22972 in the British Museum, collated with *S* and *A*. The *Epitaph* was reprinted in nineteenth-century editions of the prose works, including editions of the *Triumphs* by Sir Egerton Brydges in 1815 (*Archaica*, vol. 1), and by W. Joseph Walter in 1822. It was included in the poems printed by Turnbull in 1856 and by Grosart in 1872.

Margaret Howard, half-sister of Philip, Earl of Arundel, was married to Robert Sackville, later Lord Buckhurst and the second Earl of Dorset. Of her six children, four—Richard, Edward, Cecily and Anne—were living at the time of her death in August 1591, when she was 29. *The Triumphs over Death*, written in the form of a letter addressed to the Earl of Arundel, is dated 30 September 1591.

The English poem is preceded by a Latin epitaph; the following text is based on *1595*, sig. E3:

> *Clara Ducum soboles, superis nova sedibus hospes,*
> *Clausit in offenso tramite pura diem,*
> *Dotibus ornavit, superavit moribus ortum,*
> *Omnibus una prior, par fuit una sibi:*
> *Lux genus ingenio generi lux inclita virtus,*   5
> *Virtutique fuit mens generosa decus.*

Mors minuit properata dies orbamque relinquit,
Prolem matre virum coniuge flore genus.
Occidit ast alium tulit hic occasus in ortum,
Vivit, ad occiduas non reditura vices. 10

6 *Virtutique MSS.: Virtutisque 1595*　　　7 *minuit MSS.: muta at 1595*　*orbamque*
MSS.: orbemque 1595　　　8 *virum MSS.: verum 1595*　　　9 *ast MSS.: a se*
1595　　10 *Vivit MSS.: vivat 1595*

l. 11. The image of Noah's dove is used in *EC*, sig. G7ᵛ-8, but with different application: 'The cleane and chaste dove, abhorring such a lothsome abode, without this arke [of heaven] can not fynde anye rest: but with the wynges of penitent harte, and longing desire, flickereth still at the wyndowe, untill it please our *Noe* to put out his mercifull hand, and receyve it into the Arke of his heavenlye felicitye.' See also '*Praesentatio B. Virginis*', l. 8 (Appendix II, p. 108).

l. 17. *raught*: reached. This form is confused with the homephone *wrought* in the manuscripts.

l. 19. *Pearle*: the margarite; the play on the name of Margaret occurs also in the prose text of *1595*, sig. E2ᵛ: 'The base shell of a mortall body was unfit for so pretious a Margarite, and the Jeweller that came into this world to seeke good pearles, and gave not onely all he had, but himselfe also to buie them, thought now high time to bring her unto his bargaine, finding her growne to a Margarites full perfection.' (A marginal note beside this passage gives the reference: *Matth. 13.*)

l. 22. The construction is compressed and ambiguous. In accordance with the image of the pearl, its price (to the heavenly jeweller) is the crown which is rightfully claimed by the virtuous. Alternatively, *price* may be a variant of *prize*, reward, but with this interpretation the image of the pearl now bought by heaven is weakened. The image of the crown has its origin in St. Paul: 'Henceforth there is laid up for me the crown of righteousness' (2 Tim. iv. 8).

Lines from a hymn of Prudentius (page 102)

From *An Epistle of Comfort.*

Printed in *EC* (*S.T.C.* 22946; Allison and Rogers, no. 781), printed secretly in England, 1587-8 (n.d., false imprint: *Imprinted at Paris*), sig. X6ᵛ. Other editions of the *Epistle*, with which the text has been collated, appeared in 1605 (*S.T.C.* 22947, A. and R., no. 782), printed secretly in England, and in 1616 (*S.T.C.* 22948, A. and R., no. 783), printed at the English College, St. Omer.

A marginal note gives the source of the hymn: 'Prudent. Him no. 1 in Hemiterium & Chelidon mart' (Hymn to the glory of the Martyrs Emeterius and Chelidonius of Calahorra). The two were brothers and Roman soldiers, martyrs for the Faith in Calahorra, which became subsequently a place of pilgrimage.

The Latin text preceding the translation is as follows:

Illitas cruore nunc arenas incolae
Confrequentant obsecrantes voce, votis, munere,

Exteri nec non et orbis huc colonus advenit
Fama nam terras in omnes præcucurrit proditrix
Hic patronos esse mundi quos precantes ambiant.

l. 1. The Latin text in *EC* omits *sancto* in the first line, usually reproduced as two short lines, as follows:

Illitas cruore sancto
Nunc arenas incolæ

(from the edition of the Hymn printed in 1527, *Basileæ, apud And. Cratandrum*). Southwell's translation also omits the word.

APPENDIX I

Peeter Playnt (page 103)

MS.: Stonyhurst College Library, A. v. 4, fols. 50–51ᵛ.

This first draft of a translation of part of Luigi Tansillo's *Le Lagrime di San Pietro* is in Southwell's secretary hand. Professor Mario Praz announced his identification of the source and discussed the relationship between the draft translation and 'Saint Peters Complaint' in his article, 'Robert Southwell's "Saint Peter's Complaint" and its Italian source', in *Modern Language Review*, xix (3), 273–90 (July 1924), where the text of the draft was reproduced together with its Italian original. Father McDonald also published the English text in his *Bibliographical Study*, Appendix B, pp. 144–7. The importance of this draft is in the information it yields concerning Southwell's method of composition and the place of this passage of translation in the development of the long poem, discussed in the Textual Introduction, IV. IV, p. lxxxvi.

As many features of the manuscript as possible have been reproduced. Words between lines of the text are shown where they occur; marginal notes, though of the same character, have had to be relegated to notes below the text. Deletions are indicated by words and letters within square brackets. Occasional caret marks and parenthetical brackets are in the manuscript. Southwell's spelling has been followed exactly, except that normal scribal abbreviations have been expanded, the omitted letters being shown in italics (although a form involving a letter not in the expanded form—*yᵉ* for *the*—has been retained in the single instance of its occurrence in a marginal note).

l. 5. *credit*: trustworthiness, good faith (Ital. *di fè*). *distayne*: dishonour.

l. 16. *oynted*: anointed.

l. 21. *blazed*: announced. The word was misread by Professor Praz (followed by Father McDonald) as *chased*.

l. 44. *asc*. This spelling may have been influenced by Ital. *ascose*.

l. 51. [*tung*]. g was only partly formed before the word was deleted.

l. 52. *prest*: ready.

l. 76. *valew*. This form is presumably an error for *vale* or *valley*.

l. 82. *thow*. This was misread as *thaw* by Professor Praz, whose reading was accepted by Father McDonald.

l. 85. *immayntenant*: (adv.) immediately, at once (Ital. *immantinente*).

APPENDIX II

POEMS IN *F* OF DOUBTFUL AUTHORSHIP

The authorship of these poems is discussed in Textual Introduction, IV. III, p. lxxxii. They were first printed in McDonald, pp. 42–43; 49–58.

Conceptio B. Virginis sub porta aurea (page 108)

Cf. 'The Virgine Maries conception' (p. 3, and notes). The *'Conceptio'* is based on a series of images derived from titles in the Litanies of the Virgin.

ll. 1–2. Cf. 'The Corone of our B. Ladie' in *The Rosarie of our Ladie* (Antwerp, 1600), sig. D3: 'Of this mervelous virgin the Sybilles . . . do thus sing:

> *Now comes the virgin cleare, the golden age drawes nigh:*
> *New Offspring doth appeare, sent from the heavens high,*
> *Which is Gods issue deare.'*

The representation of a gate to a new age is also a classical image, occurring, for instance, in the symbolism associated with initiation into the Mysteries. The image also recalls the titles in the Litanies of the Virgin, *Janua cœli, . . . Porta orientalis clausa*. Here, and in l. 7, the image is applied to her mother's womb; then, l. 2, and later, l. 12, to the Virgin herself. The image does not occur in the 'Conception'.

l 4. *for to kepe in gage*: to hold as pledge.

ll. 7–8. Titles from the Litany of Loretto are recalled here: *Sedes sapientiæ, . . . Fœderis arca*. The Virgin also is called *Templum Domini, Tabernaculum Dei, Arca Testimonii*, titles indicating the symbolism of the Ark and the Temple (*those former figures*, l. 10) as types of the Virgin.

Præsentatio B. Virginis (page 108)

The imagery of the poem, like that of the preceding poem, is based on titles of the Virgin.

l. 11. *fitting*. The error *sitting* for *fitting* is also found in *F* in the revision of 'The Assumption of our Lady', l. 4.

Ubi est Deus meus? (page 109)

The theme of the poem is the renunciation of the world and the desire for heavenly joys, as in several of the poems in the manuscript compilation. The structural organization is also typical of some of Southwell's lyrics, as, for instance, 'S. Peters afflicted minde' (p. 31), where it is shown in its simplest form.

Optima Deo (page 109)

A sacred parody, translating (ll. 1–14) Tasso's *Gerusalemme Liberata*, xiv. 14, 15, a plea to 'Gather ye rosebuds' expressed not only by Herrick but by numerous translators and imitators; see, for instance, Spenser's version in *The Faerie Queene*, II. xii. 74, 75, and others of his near contemporaries cited in the Variorum Edition in the note on this passage, pp. 388–90.

l. 15. *Yeld God*. This phrase reverses the common expression *God yield* (*you*). *empaire*: decay; in the Letter to his Father Southwell reminds him that with age 'your senses impair' (ed. Trotman, p. 44). Southwell uses the verb transitively in *An Humble Supplication* (ed. Bald, p. 40), when he speaks of 'every Libeller repayring his wants with impayring our honors'.

Unworthy receaving (page 110)

Title. The reference is to the taking of Communion in a sinful state, which obstructs the reception of sacramental grace.

l. 3. *pine away*: literally, grow wasted from hunger; here, the verb is used in a general sense.

l. 8. *paire*: grow worse.

l. 10. *vermilion*. The word does not occur elsewhere in Southwell's verse; it is associated with the colour of blood in contemporary and slightly later use. The clumsiness of the rhythmic patterns in ll. 9–11 suggests that if the poem is Southwell's it is unrevised work.

l. 12. The construction is awkwardly inverted; the meaning appears to be: 'Yet I continue to live as a slave in darkness and in great affliction.'

Beatus vir qui non abiit etc. (page 110)

The poem is a version of Ps. i.

l. 2. *crew of wicked*. The form of the phrase, with the omission of the definite article, is not typical of Southwell's writing.

l. 4. *chaire of pestilence*. The phrase, a simple translation of the Vulgate *cathedra pestilentiæ*, occurs in the Douay version (1609) and is found also in Richard Stanyhurst's translation of the Psalm, published with his *First Foure Bookes of Virgil his Æneis*, 1582.

ll. 17, 18. *tendes . . . endes. tend* is expected here; the rime *tend/end* would improve the sound of the verse by removing one of the recurrent plural forms in the last line. In the Vulgate both *path* and *journey* are in singular form: 'Quoniam novit Dominus viam justorum; et iter impiarum peribit.'

S. Peters complaint (page 111)

For a discussion of the relationship of this poem with the twelve-stanza version in the manuscripts, 'Saint Peters Complaynte' (p. 29), and with the long form of 'Saint Peters Complaint' (p. 76), see Textual Introduction, IV. IV, p. lxxxvi.

l. 25. *nothing*: (adv.) not at all; the 'Complaynte' substitutes *so little* (l. 37). The adverbial use occurs in the 'Complaint', l. 694.

l. 28. *subduëd*. This form with the diæresis is rare in Southwell's work.

l. 41. *grisely*: frightening.

Our Ladie to Christ upon the Crosse (page 112)

This is the first of the group of four poems of similar metrical structure, linked by titles and subject-matter. This version differs considerably from that printed in *Ma* as 'The virgin Mary to Christ on the Crosse' (p. 71, and notes).

Christes answere (page 113)

Title. The person addressed in these lines is undoubtedly the Virgin, although the poem is an 'answere' to the preceding poem, 'Our Ladie to Christ upon the Crosse', only in the interpretation of the compiler of the manuscript.

ll. 3, 4. *Abstract . . . Expect*: draw back from . . . wait for; these verbs of Latin derivation are not found elsewhere in Southwell's verse although *expecting*, used absolutely in the sense of 'waiting', occurs in the Letter to his Father (ed. Trotman, p. 45).

l. 4. *a hevenly vision*. The vision of the New Jerusalem, as in the Apocalypse of St. John, is recalled in the imagery of the remainder of the poem.

l. 7. *David . . . harp*. Iconographical tradition, as illustrated in the *Speculum humanæ salvationis*, associated David playing his harp with the representation of Christ stretched upon the Cross. Here David may symbolize every singer or poet inspired to religious verse, as were the harpers in the apocalyptic vision, Rev. xiv. 2.

ll. 13–16. In this apocalyptic imagery the Virgin—as the Church—is identified with the City; the river of the water of life is mentioned in Rev. xxii. 1–2, and the gems of which the City was built, xxi. 18–21.

Christ upon the Crosse to man (page 113)

No clear link can be established between this poem and the next in the manuscript, 'To the wound in Christes side' (printed as 'Man to the wound in Christs side' in *Ma*; see p. 72). In comparison with 'Man to the wound' this poem is superficial in both expression and theme. Stylistic echoes support the possibility that this is Southwell's, but if it is, it is probably early work or an unrevised draft.

l. 4. *imbrue*. The verb occurs elsewhere in phrases with reference to blood, as in the 'Complaint', l. 523 and note.

l. 7. *inur'd*: habituated (obsolete construction with *in*; see *O.E.D. v.*¹ 1b.).

. 20. *ginne*. Cf. 'Mans civill warre', l. 31 (p. 50).

The Complaint of the B. Virgin having lost her Sonne in Hierusalem
(page 114)

The first section of the poem, ll. 1–42, is found in *B* (p. 84). There are numerous but mainly insignificant textual variants, not recorded in the collational apparatus.

l. 1. The line echoes the opening lines of 'Saint Peters Complaynte' (p. 29), and of 'S. Peters complaint', the four-lined stanza version in *F* (p. 111).

ll. 7–18. This extended construction appears in the 'Complaint', ll. 487–92, 493–8, 511–16.

ll. 13–14. Cf. the imagery of 'The Nativitie of Christ', ll. 1–2 (p. 6).

ll. 19–96. The long recapitulation of *pleasures past* is carried out much more skilfully in a similar section in the 'Complaint', ll. 121–98.

l. 28. *than*: then.

l. 30. Cf. 'Sinnes heavie loade', l. 8 (p. 17).

l. 42. *B* ends with the doxology:

> Ah hallaluiah was the song
> the Angels then did sing
> All honour, might and majestie
> be given to Christ our king.

l. 49. *Angels Bread*. Cf. 'A holy Hymme', l. 61 (p. 25).

ll. 59, 98. *ne*. This negative ('not') occurs elsewhere in Southwell's verse as a form of 'nor'.

ll. 65–66. The imagery of lambs and ewes is used in the 'Complaint', ll. 565–6.

l. 71. *hardly*: with hardship.

ll. 75–76. Cf. 'Christs Childhoode', ll. 7–11 (p. 11).

l. 84. *plant*. This verb puns on the meaning of Nazareth, a flower, developed into a conceit in 'Christs returne out of Egypt' (p. 10).

l. 106. *unacquainted*: unknown; cf. the 'Complaint', l. 239.

The Annuntiation altered from that before (page 117)

The poem is a rewriting of 'The Virgins salutation' (p. 5); see Textual Introduction, IV. III, pp. lxxxiii–iv, for discussion of its authenticity and its relationship with the poem of the Sequence.

l. 12. *freëd*. This form with the diæresis is rare in Southwell's work.

INDEX OF FIRST LINES